Undergraduate Topics in Computer Science

'Undergraduate Topics in Computer Science' (UTiCS) delivers high-quality instructional content for undergraduates studying in all areas of computing and information science. From core foundational and theoretical material to final-year topics and applications, UTiCS books take a fresh, concise, and modern approach and are ideal for self-study or for a one- or two-semester course. The texts are all authored by established experts in their fields, reviewed by an international advisory board, and contain numerous examples and problems, many of which include fully worked solutions.

The UTiCS concept relies on high-quality, concise books in softback format, and generally a maximum of 275–300 pages. For undergraduate textbooks that are likely to be longer, more expository, Springer continues to offer the highly regarded Texts in Computer Science series, to which we refer potential authors.

More information about this series at http://www.springer.com/series/7592

James T. Streib

Guide to Assembly Language

A Concise Introduction

Second Edition

 Springer

James T. Streib
Department of Computer Science
Illinois College
Jacksonville, IL, USA

ISSN 1863-7310   ISSN 2197-1781   (electronic)
Undergraduate Topics in Computer Science
ISBN 978-3-030-35638-5   ISBN 978-3-030-35639-2   (eBook)
https://doi.org/10.1007/978-3-030-35639-2

This Springer imprint is published by the registered company Springer Nature Switzerland AG
The registered company address is: Gewerbestrasse 11, 6330 Cham, Switzerland

Preface

Purpose

The purpose of this text is to assist one in learning how to program in assembly language on an Intel processor using Microsoft Assembler (MASM) in a minimal amount of time. In addition, through programming the reader learns more about the computer architecture of the Intel processor and also the relationship between high-level languages and low-level languages.

Need

In the past, many departments have had two separate courses: one in assembly language programming (sometimes called computer systems) and a second course in computer organization and architecture. With today's crowded curriculums, there is sometimes just one course in the computer science curriculum in computer organization and architecture, where various aspects of both courses are included in the one course. The result might be that unfortunately there is not enough coverage concerning assembly language programming.

Importance of Assembly Language

Although the need for assembly language programmers has decreased, the need to understand assembly language has not, and the reasons why one ought to learn to program in assembly language include the following:

- Sometimes just reading about assembly language is not enough, and one must actually write assembly language code to understand it thoroughly (although the code does not have to be extremely complicated or tricky to gain this benefit).
- Although some high-level languages include low-level features, there are times when programming in assembly language can be more efficient in terms of both speed and memory.
- Programming in assembly language has the same benefits as programming in machine language, except it is easier. Further one can gain some first-hand

knowledge into the nature of computer systems, organization, and architecture from a software perspective.

- Having knowledge of low-level programming concepts helps one understand how high-level languages are implemented and various related compiler concepts.

Comparison to Computer Organization and Other Assembly Language Textbooks

Many textbooks on computer organization have only a few sections or chapters dealing with assembly language, and as a result, they might not cover the aspects of assembly language thoroughly enough. Also, instead of discussing a real assembly language, they might just use a hypothetical assembly and machine language. Although this can be helpful in understanding some of the basic concepts, the student might neither see the relevance nor appreciate many of the important concepts of a real assembly language.

On the other hand, there are a number of assembly language texts that go into significant detail which can easily fill an entire semester and almost warrant a two-semester sequence. Unfortunately, some of the more comprehensive assembly language texts might not be the best choice for learning to program in assembly language due to the same reasons that make them excellent comprehensive texts.

This current text does not attempt to fill the needs of either of these two previous varieties of texts because it falls between the scopes of these two types of texts. The purpose of this text is to provide a concise introduction to the fundamentals of assembly language programming, and as a result, it can serve well as either a stand-alone text or a companion text to the current popular computer organization texts.

Features of This Text

The primary goal of this text is to get the student programming in assembly language as quickly as possible. Some of these features that make this possible include simplified register usage, simplified input/output using C-like statements, and the use of high-level control structures. All of these features help the reader begin programming quickly and reinforce many of the concepts learned in previous computer science courses. Also, many of the control structures are implemented without the use of high-level structures to allow readers to understand how they are actually implemented. Further, many of the assembly language code segments are preceded by C program code segments to help students see the relationships between high-level and low-level languages. Other notable features at the end of each chapter include the following:

- One or more complete programs illustrating many of the concepts introduced in that chapter.
- Chapter summaries, which by themselves do not substitute for reading a chapter, but after reading a chapter they serve as a nice review of important concepts for students preparing for a quiz or exam.
- Exercises composed of a variety of questions, from short answer to programming assignments. Items marked with an ∗ have solutions in Appendix D.

Features New to the Second Edition

The second edition retains all of the features of the first edition. Of course, any known errors have been corrected and areas that could be clarified have been reworded. Features new to the second edition include the following:

- Many illustrations have had color added to them to help readers visualize important concepts.
- A new section has been added to Appendix B on floating-point number representation.
- A new chapter has been added on floating-point number processing.
- 32-bit processing has been retained throughout the text, and a new chapter has been added on 64-bit processing.
- A new section has been added to Chap. 12 on floating-point and 64-bit machine language.
- Additional exercises have been added to various chapters.

Brief Overview of the Chapters and Appendices

If this text is used in conjunction with another text in a computer organization course, then there is a potential for some duplication between the texts. For example, many texts in assembly language begin with an introduction to binary arithmetic, which of course is incredibly important in a low-level language. However, should this text be used in conjunction with a computer organization text, then many of those concepts will have already been introduced. As a result, this text begins at the outset to get students into programming quickly and introduces or reviews binary on an as-needed basis. However, should this text be used as a stand-alone text, then Appendix B introduces binary numbers, hexadecimal numbers, conversions, logic, arithmetic, and floating-point number representation, should the instructor or student wish to examine this material first. What follows is a brief overview of the chapters and the appendices:

- Chapter 1 provides an overview of assembly language and an introduction to the general-purpose registers.

- Chapter 2 introduces the reader to input/output in assembly language, specifically using the C programming language `scanf` and `printf` instructions.
- Chapter 3 explains basic arithmetic in assembly language, including addition, subtraction, multiplication, division, and operator precedence.
- Chapter 4 shows how to implement selection structures in assembly language, such as if-then, if-then-else, nested if structures, and the case (switch) structure.
- Chapter 5 continues with iteration structures, specifically the pre-test, post-test, and definite iterations loop structures, along with nested loops.
- Chapter 6 introduces the logic, shift, arithmetic shift, rotate, and stack instructions.
- Chapter 7 discusses procedures, introduces macros, and explains conditional assembly.
- Chapter 8 presents arrays, sequential searching, and the selection sort.
- Chapter 9 discusses strings, string instructions, arrays of strings, and comparisons of strings.
- Chapter 10 provides an introduction to the floating-point register stack, arithmetic, input/output, and instructions.
- Chapter 11 explains basic 64-bit input/output, storage, and processing.
- Chapter 12 introduces machine language from a discovery perspective and can serve as an introduction to some of the principles of computer organization or it might be used as a supplement to a companion computer organization text.
- Appendix A illustrates how to assemble programs using MASM.
- Appendix B provides an overview of binary and hexadecimal conversions, logic, arithmetic, and representation of floating-point numbers. The first three chapters of the text require limited use of binary and hexadecimal numbers, so one might not need to read this appendix until later in the text. However, Chap. 6 requires extensive use of binary numbers and logic. Depending on the reader's background, this appendix should be read prior to that chapter. If not covered elsewhere or it has been a while since one has studied numbering systems, this appendix can serve as a basic introduction or a good review, respectively. If one has had exposure to these topics in a previous course, concurrent course, or from another textbook in the same course, then this appendix can be skipped.
- Appendix C summarizes the assembly language instructions introduced in this text.
- Appendix D provides answers to selected exercises marked with an * that appear at the end of each chapter and at the end of Appendix B.
- The Glossary contains terms that are first introduced in *italics* in the text. The descriptions of terms in glossary should not be used in lieu of the complete descriptions in the text but rather they serve as a quick review and reminder of the basic meaning of various terms. Should a more complete description be needed, then index can guide the reader to the appropriate pages where the terms are discussed in more detail.

Scope

This text includes the necessary fundamentals of assembly language to allow it to be used as either a stand-alone text in a one-semester assembly language course or a companion text in a computer organization and architecture course. As with any text, decisions then must be made on what should be included, excluded, emphasized, and deemphasized. This text is no exception in that it does not include every idiosyncrasy of assembly language and thus it might not contain some of the favorite sub-topics of various instructors. Some of these might include 16-bit processing and Windows programming among others, but these, of course, can be supplemented at the instructor's discretion. However, what is gained is that readers should be able to write logically correct programs in a minimal amount of time, which is the original intent of this text.

The Intel architecture is used because of its wide availability, and Microsoft Assembler (MASM) is used due to a number of high-level control structures that are available in that assembler. Note that Java is a registered trademark of Oracle and/or its affiliates, Intel and Pentium are trademarks of Intel Corporation, and Visual Studio, Visual C++, and Microsoft Assembler (MASM) are registered trademarks of Microsoft Corporation.

Audience

It is assumed that the reader of this book has completed a two-semester introductory course sequence in a high-level language such as C, C++, or Java. Although a student might be able to use this text only after a one-semester course, an additional semester of programming in a high-level language is usually preferred to allow for a better understanding of the material due to increased programming skills and knowledge of data structures, specifically stacks and linked lists.

Acknowledgements

The author wishes to acknowledge both his editor Wayne Wheeler and associate editor Simon Rees for their assistance; thank his reviewers Mark E. Bollman of Albion College, James W. Chaffee of the University of Iowa, and Takako Soma of Illinois College for their suggestions; and offer personal thanks to his wife Kimberly A. Streib and son Daniel M. Streib for their patience. On a special note, this second edition is written in remembrance of Curt M. White who served as a reviewer of the first edition.

Feedback

As with any work, the possibility of errors exists. Any comments, corrections, or suggestions are welcome and should be sent to the e-mail address listed below. In addition to copies of the complete programs at the end of each chapter, any significant corrections can also be found at the Web site listed below.

Website: http://www.jtstreib.com/GuideAssemblyLanguage.html

Jacksonville, Illinois, USA   James T. Streib
September 2019   e-mail: james.streib@jtstreib.com

Contents

1   Variables, Registers, and Data Movement   1
    1.1   Introduction   1
    1.2   The First Program   2
    1.3   Variable Declaration   4
    1.4   Immediate Data   6
    1.5   Registers   7
    1.6   Data Movement   10
    1.7   Character Data   11
    1.8   Errors   13
    1.9   Complete Program: Implementing Inline Assembly in C   13
    1.10   Summary   15
    1.11   Exercises (Items Marked with an * Have Solutions
           in Appendix D)   15

2   Input/Output   17
    2.1   Introduction   17
    2.2   Hello World   17
    2.3   Integer Output   19
    2.4   Integer Input   21
    2.5   Complete Program: Using Input, Data Transfer,
           and Output   24
    2.6   Summary   25
    2.7   Exercises (Items Marked with an * Have Solutions
           in Appendix D)   25

3   Arithmetic Instructions   29
    3.1   Addition and Subtraction   29
    3.2   Multiplication and Division   32
    3.3   Implementing Unary Operators: Increment, Decrement,
           and Negation   36
    3.4   Order of Operations with Binary and Unary Operators   39
    3.5   Complete Program: Implementing I/O and Arithmetic   42

3.6	Summary	43
3.7	Exercises (Items Marked with an * Have Solutions in Appendix D)	44
4	**Selection Structures**	**47**
4.1	Introduction	47
4.2	If-Then Structure	48
4.3	If-Then-Else Structure	53
4.4	Nested If Structures	54
4.5	Case Structure	58
4.6	Characters and Logical Operations	59
4.7	Arithmetic Expressions in High-Level Directives	64
4.8	Complete Program: Using Selection Structures and I/O	67
4.9	Summary	70
4.10	Exercises (Items Marked with an * Have Solutions in Appendix D)	70
5	**Iteration Structures**	**73**
5.1	Pre-test Loop Structure	73
5.2	Post-test Loop Structures	76
5.3	Fixed-Iteration Loop Structures	78
5.4	Loops and Input/Output	81
5.5	Nested Loops	85
5.6	Complete Program: Implementing the Power Function	87
5.7	Summary	90
5.8	Exercises (Items Marked with an * Have Solutions in Appendix D)	90
6	**Logic, Shifting, Rotating, and Stacks**	**95**
6.1	Introduction	95
6.2	Logic Instructions	96
6.3	Logical Shift Instructions	100
6.4	Arithmetic Shift Instructions	105
6.5	Rotate Instructions	108
6.6	Stack Operations	111
6.7	Swapping Using Registers, the Stack, and the xchg Instruction	113
6.8	Complete Program: Simulating an OCR Machine	115
6.9	Summary	119
6.10	Exercises (Items Marked with an * Have Solutions in Appendix D)	120
7	**Procedures and Macros**	**123**
7.1	Procedures	123
7.2	Complete Program: Implementing the Power Function in a Procedure	127

7.3   Saving and Restoring Registers   130
7.4   Macros   132
7.5   Conditional Assembly   138
7.6   Swap Macro Revisited Using Conditional Assembly   141
7.7   Power Function Macro Using Conditional Assembly   145
7.8   Complete Program: Implementing a Macro Calculator   148
7.9   Summary   155
7.10   Exercises (Items Marked with an * Have Solutions
        in Appendix D)   156

8   **Arrays**   159
8.1   Array Declaration and Addressing   159
8.2   Indexing Using the Base Register   162
8.3   Searching   166
8.4   Indexing Using the `esi` and `edi` Registers   168
8.5   Lengthof and Sizeof Operators   173
8.6   Complete Program: Implementing a Queue   175
8.7   Complete Program: Implementing the Selection Sort   180
8.8   Summary   185
8.9   Exercises (Items Marked with an * Have Solutions
        in Appendix D)   185

9   **Strings**   189
9.1   Introduction   189
9.2   String Instructions: Moving Strings (`movsb`)   191
9.3   String Instructions: Scanning (`scasb`), Storing (`stosb`),
        and Loading (`lodsb`)   194
9.4   Array of Strings   196
9.5   String Instructions: Comparing Strings (`cmpsb`)   198
9.6   Complete Program: Searching an Array of Strings   204
9.7   Summary   206
9.8   Exercises (Items Marked with an * Have Solutions
        in Appendix D)   207

10   **Floating-Point Instructions**   209
10.1   Memory Storage   209
10.2   Floating-Point Register Stack   210
10.3   Pushing and Popping   210
10.4   Simple Arithmetic Expressions   213
10.5   Complex Arithmetic Expressions   215
10.6   Mixing Floating-Point and Integers   219
10.7   Input/Output   221
        10.7.1   `float` and `real4`   222
        10.7.2   `double` and `real8`   223

          10.7.3   `long double` and `real10` 225

          10.7.4   Inline Assembly 225

    10.8   Comparisons and Selection Structures 226

    10.9   Complete Program: Implementing an Iteration Structure 229

    10.10   Complete Program: Implementing an Array 232

    10.11   Summary 234

    10.12   Exercises (Items Marked with an * Have Solutions

           in Appendix D)................................. 235

11   64-Bit Processing. 237

    11.1   Four General Purpose Registers 237

    11.2   Other 64-Bit Registers............................. 240

    11.3   64-Bit Integer Output 241

    11.4   64-Bit Integer Input............................... 245

    11.5   Logic and Arithmetic Applications..................... 247

          11.5.1   Shift and Rotate 247

          11.5.2   Logic 249

          11.5.3   Arithmetic 250

    11.6   Control Structures 251

    11.7   Arrays 254

    11.8   Procedures and Macros 254

          11.8.1   Calling 64-Bit Procedures 255

          11.8.2   Using a Macro to Call `printf` 256

    11.9   Complete Program: Reversing an Array 258

    11.10   Summary 260

    11.11   Exercises (Items Marked with an * Have Solutions

           in Appendix D)................................. 261

12   Selected Machine Language Instructions 263

    12.1   Introduction 263

    12.2   `inc` and `dec` Instructions 264

    12.3   `mov` Instruction................................. 266

    12.4   `add` and `sub` Instructions 271

    12.5   `mov offset` and `lea` Instructions 272

    12.6   `jmp` Instructions 274

    12.7   Instruction Timings 275

    12.8   Floating-Point and 64-Bit Instructions 276

          12.8.1   Floating-Point Instructions.................... 277

          12.8.2   64-Bit Instructions 277

          12.8.3   Memory Addressing 280

    12.9   Complete Program: 32-Bit Assembly Listing 281

    12.10   Complete Program: Floating-Point and 64-Bit

           Assembly Listing 283

12.11   Summary 284
12.12   Exercises (Items Marked with an * Have Solutions
            in Appendix D)................................. 285

**Appendix A: Directions for MASM in Visual Studio 2019
                        Community Edition** 289

**Appendix B: Binary, Hexadecimal, Logic, Arithmetic,
                        and Data Representation** 293

Appendix C: Selected Assembly Language Instructions.............. 319

Appendix D: Answers to Selected Exercises 329

Glossary.. 335

References 339

Index 341

Variables, Registers, and Data Movement

1

1.1 Introduction

High-level languages, such as C, C++, and Java, have similarities with natural languages which help make programs easier to read and write whereas low-level languages are closer to the machine and offer a look at the machine organization and architecture. There is a one-to-many relationship between high-level languages and low-level languages, where language translators such as compilers and interpreters convert each high-level instruction into many low-level instructions. The native language of a particular machine is a low-level language known as *machine language* and is coded in ones and zeros. Further, the machine language of an Intel microprocessor is different than that of other microprocessors or mainframes, thus machine language is not transferable from one type of machine to another.

Programming in machine language can be very tedious and error prone. Instead of using ones and zeros, an *assembly language* has an advantage, because it uses *mnemonics* (abbreviations) for the instructions and variable names for memory locations, instead of ones and zeros. There is also a one-to-one correspondence between the instructions in assembly language and in machine language. Programs can be written more easily in assembly language and do not have many of the disadvantages of programming in machine language. The advantage of programming in assembly language over a high-level language is that one can gain a very detailed look at the architecture of a computer system and write very efficient programs, in terms of both increasing speed and saving memory.

Just as compilers convert a high-level language to a low-level language, an *assembler* converts assembly language to machine language. Although some newer compilers convert high-level languages (such as Java) to an intermediate language (such as bytecode) which is then interpreted to machine language, the result is that the final code is in the machine language of the machine the program is to be executed. Figure 1.1 illustrates how a language might be translated.

© Springer Nature Switzerland AG 2020
J. T. Streib, *Guide to Assembly Language*, Undergraduate Topics
in Computer Science, https://doi.org/10.1007/978-3-030-35639-2_1

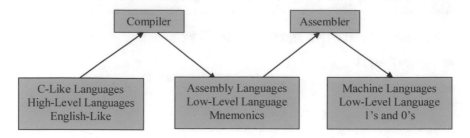

Fig. 1.1 High-level language and assembly language translation to machine language

There are a number of assemblers available to convert to Intel machine language, but the one used in this text is MASM (Microsoft Assembler). The method used for assembling and executing a program will probably be explained by one's instructor or might be demonstrated by colleagues at one's place of employment. However, if one is reading this text independently and wants to run an assembly language program on a home computer, the instructions can be found in Appendix A.

When learning any new programming language, whether high-level or low-level, it is helpful to start with a very simple program. Often when learning a high-level language, the first program is the infamous "Hello World" program, which when keyed in allows the programmer to have a correctly compiled and executable program. Unfortunately, when starting to learn a low-level language, the input/output (I/O) facilities are much more complicated and it is not necessarily the best place to start. As a result, this text will first look at some of the fundamentals of assembly language and then subsequently examine I/O to verify that the fundamentals have been learned and implemented properly.

1.2 The First Program

The first program to be implemented will be the equivalent of the following C program, which merely declares two variables, assigns a value to the first variable, and then assigns the contents of the first variable to the second variable:

```
int main(){
    int num1,num2;
    num1=5;
    num2=num1;
    return 0;
}
```

```
.686
.model flat, c
.stack 100h
.data
   num1    sdword ?      ; first number
   num2    sdword ?      ; second number
           .code
   main    proc
           mov num1,5    ; initialize num1 with 5
           mov eax,num1  ; load eax with contents of num1
           mov num2,eax  ; store eax in num2
           ret
   main    endp
           end
```

Fig. 1.2 First assembly language program

The assembly language program shown in Fig. 1.2 implements the same logic as the C program above. Although at first it might look a little intimidating, it can serve as a useful starting point in learning the basic layout and format of an assembly language program.

The first thing to understand is that some of the statements above are *directives*, while others are *instructions*. Although it will be discussed in more detail later, simply put, instructions tell the central processing unit (*CPU*) what to do, whereas directives tell the assembler what to do. Similar to directives, *operators* also tell the assembler what to do with a particular instruction.

The .686 at the beginning of the program is a directive and indicates that the program should be assembled to run on a 686 processor such as the Pentium Pro or newer processor.

The .model flat directive specifies that the program uses protected mode which indicates that 32-bit addresses will be used and thus it is possible to address 4 GB of memory. Although there exist some previous forms of addressing, this protected mode is fairly common now, is simpler to understand, and can address more memory. The c in the model directive indicates that it can link with C and C++ programs and is needed to run in the Visual C++ environment.

The .stack directive indicates the size of the stack in hexadecimal (see Appendix B) and indicates the stack should be 100 hexadecimal bytes large, or 256 bytes. The use of the stack will be discussed later in Chap. 6. The .data and .code directives will be discussed shortly, but the proc directive stands for procedure and indicates that the name of the procedure is main. Although other names can be used, the name main is similar to naming a C, C++, or Java program main and allows the assembly program to be run independently of other programs. The ret instruction serves as a return 0 statement as in C or C++. The main endp label and directive indicate the end of the procedure and the end directive indicates the end of the program for the assembler.

Label	Opcode	Operand	Comment
	.data		
num1	sdword	?	; first number
num2	sdword	?	; second number
	.code		
main	proc		
	mov	num1,5	; initialize num1 with 5
	mov	eax,num1	; load eax with contents of num1
	mov	num2,eax	; store eax in num2
	ret		

Fig. 1.3 Label, opcode, operand, and comment fields

In the past, different assembly languages have used specific columns to place the various fields of the assembly language instructions. Although the rules as to which exact columns the fields need to be placed in have become more relaxed, it is still customary to line up the fields in columns to help with the readability of the code.

In order from left to right, the four columns or fields of an instruction are the label, operation code (opcode), operand, and comment fields. The first field is typically reserved for the names of variables and possibly labels used for branching to various instructions.

The second field is typically used for operation codes (opcodes) that represent executable instructions and also assembler directives. The third field, typically only separated by a space from the second field, is used for operands of which there can be anywhere from zero to three operands. The optional last field is typically used for comments, but note that comments are not restricted to the fourth field, can start anywhere on a line, and must begin with a semicolon.

As an example, consider Fig. 1.3 illustrating a couple of lines from the previous program. Note that although the label, opcode, and comment fields typically line up, the operand field is usually separated only by a single space from the opcode field. Also as can be seen, there are two major sections to an assembly language program, the data segment and the code segment indicated by the .data and .code directives. The next section will discuss the data segment, while the following section will discuss the code segment.

1.3   Variable Declaration

The data segment in the program above declares two variables called num1 and num2 as indicated by the names listed in the label field of each of these two lines. The rules for variable names are not unlike high-level languages, with some minor differences. Similar to high-level languages, a variable name should begin with a letter and then be followed by letters or digits. They can also include the special symbols _, @, or $ anywhere in the name, but typically these three symbols should be avoided to help with readabilty. Unlike languages such as C, C++, and Java, the

Table 1.1 Valid and invalid variable names

Valid	Invalid
Auto	1num
num1	7eleven
z28	57chevy

names are not case sensitive, so the variables cat and CAT refer to the same memory location. The maximum length of a variable name is 247 characters, but typically a variable is only 1–10 characters long. Table 1.1 contains some examples of valid and invalid variable names.

When declaring a variable, the opcode field has the assembler directive sdword, which stands for signed double word, is 32 bits long, and is the same as an int variable in C. The word bit stands for binary digit, where 1 bit can hold a single binary digit, a 0 or a 1, and a group of 8 bits is called a byte. On the Intel processor, a word of memory or a signed word, sword, contains 2 bytes or 16 bits, and a double word, dword, or signed double word, sdword, contains 4 bytes or 32 bits. Should the reader not have had previous experience with bits, bytes, and binary numbers, or just needs a good review, then refer to Appendix B. Note that the 64-bit floating-point number, real8, and the 64-bit quad word, qword, are discussed in Chaps. 10 and 11, respectively.

There are other declarations possible, as shown in Table 1.2, indicating the number of bits allocated to each data type. Also included is the range of values that can be stored in each type of memory location. For now, this text will use only signed double words for positive and negative integers and bytes for characters, both for the sake of simplicity.

The third field, or operand field, for the two variables in the declaration section of the previous program each contains a question mark, which indicates that the variable would not be initialized by the assembler. It is also possible to put a number in place of the question mark, which would cause the assembler to initialize the variable at assembly time. This is similar to initializing a variable in C when one writes the following,

Table 1.2 Types, number of bits, and range of values

Type	Number of bits	Range (inclusive)
sdword	32	–2,147,483,648 to +2,147,483,647
dword	32	0 to +4,294,967,295
sword	16	–32,768 to +32,767
word	16	0 to +65,535
sbyte	8	–128 to +127
byte	8	0 to +255

```
int num3 = 5;
```

and the equivalent of the above C code in assembly language is as follows:

```
num3 sdword 5    ; num3 initialized to 5 at assembly time
```

Lastly, comments can be in the fourth field or prior to the line of code they are describing, and in each case they must be preceded by a semicolon. Both types of comments are used in assembly language, where comments located prior to a line of code tend to be more general in nature, while the ones to the right tend to be specific to the line they are on. Comments are usually not placed off to the side as much in high-level languages, due to the indenting of code in selection and iteration structures. However, since assembly language is typically not indented, there is plenty of room to the right and comments are often placed there.

1.4   Immediate Data

Moving from the data segment to the code segment, if one does not initialize a variable in the data segment, how does one assign a constant to a memory location? The instruction necessary to do this is the mov instruction, pronounced "move," but be careful not to spell it with the letter e at the end or it will cause a syntax error. A mov instruction always moves information from the operand on the right, called the source, to the operand on the left, called the destination. The mov instruction is similar to the assignment symbol, the equals sign in C, C++, and Java, where the instruction does not necessarily move data, but rather makes a copy of it. Some of the formats of the mov instruction are shown in Table 1.3 and the abbreviations stand for the following:

```
imm = immediate          mem = memory          reg = register
```

Table 1.3 Mov instructions

Instruction	Meaning
mov mem, imm	move the immediate data to memory
mov reg, mem	move the contents of memory to a register
mov mem, reg	move the contents of a register to memory
mov reg, imm	move immediate data to a register
mov reg, reg	move the contents of the source (second) register to the destination (first) register

For example, if one wants to move the integer 5 into the memory location num1, such as num1=5; in the previous listed C code, then the corresponding assembly language instruction would be as shown below and also shown in the previous assembly language code segment:

```
mov num1,5
```

The variable num1 is the previously declared memory location (abbreviated as mem in Table 1.3) and 5 is what is known as an *immediate* value (abbreviated as imm in Table 1.3). The reason the integer is known as immediate data is because it is immediately available in the assembly language instruction as a part of the instruction and it does not need to be retrieved from a variable in memory. For more information on how data is stored immediately in an instruction, see Chap. 12.

1.5   Registers

As can be seen, the initializing of a variable with an immediate value is relatively easy, so how does one transfer the contents from one memory location to another? If there is one thing that the reader should learn about computers, it is that data is typically not moved directly from one memory location to another. Although the high-level C/C++/Java instruction y=x; looks as though the contents of memory location x are being copied directly to y, in reality it has to in a sense make a detour. With the exception of a few specialized string processing instructions, the way most computers work is that the contents of one memory location in random access memory (*RAM*) need to be moved or loaded into the central processing unit (CPU) and from there moved or stored back into a memory location in RAM. This is accomplished via a fast short-term memory location in the CPU called a *register*, where in some computers registers might be called accumulators.

Initially the contents of the register and memory location y are indeterminate. The contents of memory location x are first copied into the register by an operation that is often generically called a *load* operation. Then the contents of the register are copied into the memory location y by an operation that is often generically called a *store* operation. The results of these two operations are illustrated in the green cells in Fig. 1.4. Although some computers have instructions called load and store, as will be seen shortly in the Intel processor, these load and store operations can both be accomplished with the mov instruction.

In examining any new processor architecture, one of the first things one should do is examine the register set of the processor. There are a number of registers in all processors, but the ones that are accessible to the programmer are called general purpose registers. The original Intel processors were only 16-bit machines, hence their general-purpose registers were only 16 bits long. These registers were called ax, bx, cx, and dx. When the 386 microprocessor came along in the late 1980s, it used 32-bit registers, so the original four register names

Fig. 1.4 Load and store operations

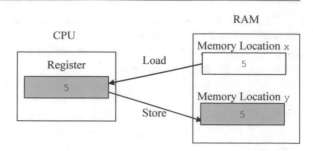

were preceded by the letter e to indicate the extended length from 16 to 32 bits. So, the four 32-bit general purpose registers in an Intel processor are called eax, ebx, ecx, and edx. Later in the early 2000s when AMD and Intel introduced their 64-bit processors, the general-purpose registers were preceded with the letter r and called rax, rbx, rcx, and rdx. However, since there are some special considerations when using the 64-bit registers, they will be discussed in Chap. 11.

Continuing, it should further be noted that the four original 16-bit registers are still accessible as the lower order, first 16 bits of the 32-bit extended registers as indicated in Fig. 1.5. Not only is the ax register the first 16 bits of the eax register, but the ax register is further subdivided into the higher order 8 bits and lower-order 8 bits, as the ah register and the al register, respectively. Although the lower 16 bits of each 32-bit register have their own name, such as ax, the upper 16 bits of the 32-bit register do not have their own name. If they do not have their own name, can they still be accessed? The answer is yes, and this will be discussed later in Chap. 6. Only a drawing of the eax, ax, ah, and al registers is given in Fig. 1.5, but the same drawing can be applied to the other registers as well, by substituting the letters b, c, and d for the letter a in the figure.

Each of the above four general purpose registers can be used for data movement, and as will be seen later they can also be used for arithmetic and logic. Further, they also have some special purposes as indicated by the letters a, b, c, and d in the names of the four registers. Although all registers might be called accumulators on some machines, only the eax register is sometimes referred to as the accumulator in the Intel processor because it is useful in various arithmetic operations. The ebx

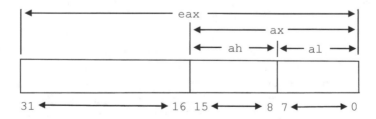

Fig. 1.5 Format of the eax, ax, ah, and al registers

register is sometimes called the base register and is useful in array processing. The ecx register can be used as a counter and is useful in special loop instructions. Lastly, the edx register is used as a data register in various arithmetic instructions. For now, the register that will be used the most is the eax register which will be demonstrated shortly.

Beyond the above four general purpose registers, there are other registers that will be used later in this text. In particular, these are ebp, esp, esi, and edi. The first two have to do with the stack and are usually accessed indirectly. The esp is a stack pointer and indicates the top of the stack and ebp is the base pointer and indicates the bottom of the stack, both of which will be discussed further in Chap. 6. The esi and edi registers indicate the source index and the destination index, respectively, and are useful with arrays and extremely useful with strings as will be seen in Chaps. 8 and 9. The cs, ds, and ss registers are 16-bit segment registers that point to the code, data, and stack segments and are set by the .code, .data, and .stack directives, respectively. Three other segment registers, es, fs, and gs, are extended segment registers that can be used for data. Beyond this basic information, the segment registers are not needed for the rest of this text.

Two more registers are the eip and eflags registers. The former is the instruction pointer and indicates which instruction is going to be executed next. Although not directly accessible, it is indirectly accessible when changing the flow of control of the program using the equivalents of selection and iteration structures discussed in Chaps. 4 and 5. Among other functions, the eflags register indicates the status of the CPU after executing various instructions and directs the flow of control of the program as will be discussed further in Chap. 4. For the sake of convenience, Table 1.4 summarizes the registers used most in this text.

Table 1.4 Summary of 32-bit registers

32-Bit registers	Name	16- and 8-bit sub-registers	Brief description and/or primary use
eax	Accumulator	ax,ah,al	Arithmetic and logic
ebx	Base	bx,bh,bl	Arrays
ecx	Counter	cx,ch,cl	Loops
edx	Data	dx,dh,dl	Arithmetic
esi	Source index	si	Strings and arrays
edi	Destination index	di	Strings and arrays
esp	Stack pointer	sp	Top of stack
ebp	Base pointer	bp	Stack base
eip	Instruction pointer	ip	Points to next instruction
eflags	Flag	flags	Status and control flags

1.6   Data Movement

Returning back to the problem of transferring information from one memory
location to another, the data needs to pass through an intermediate stop in a register.
What should be noted in Table 1.3 concerning the various formats of the `mov`
instruction is that there is no format to move from one memory location to another
memory location. In other words, there is no format for `mov mem,mem`. Again, if
there is one thing that should be learned from studying assembly language, it is that
instructions typically do not exist for memory to memory operations and such
transfers must first go through a register. So, if the instruction `num2=num1;` needs
to be implemented, `mov num2,num1` cannot be used. Instead, the contents of
`num1` must be copied to a register and then the contents of the register copied to the
memory location `num2`, as shown below:

```
; num2 = num1
mov eax,num1    ; load eax with the contents of num1
mov num2,eax    ; store the contents of eax in num2
```

Although at first this might seem a little awkward, it is a fundamental concept of
computer architecture and low-level languages. It is not unique to the Intel processor, but exists in other processors as well. Once one gets used to the idea, it just
becomes a matter of habit for the experienced assembly language programmer. Also
notice in the above that although the semicolon is at the beginning instead of at the
end in order to form a comment, the original C instruction makes a nice comment
prior to the assembly language code segment.

Similar to the previous generic drawing in Fig. 1.4, the initial contents of `eax`
and `num2` are indeterminate. When the two instructions are done executing in
Fig. 1.6, the number 5 in `num1` is copied into the `eax` register and then the number
5 is copied from the `eax` register into the variable `num2`.

In the previous code segment, notice that the comments on the side indicate load
and store instead of move. The reason for this is that on other types of CPUs, the act
of moving the contents of memory into a register or an accumulator in the CPU is
often called a load operation, whereas the reverse operation of moving the contents
of a register in the CPU into memory is called a store operation.

Fig. 1.6 `Mov` instruction

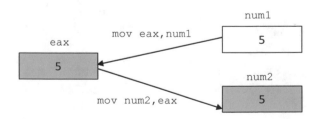

Since registers are located in the CPU itself, they can be accessed much faster than memory and it is possible to leave data in the register to gain the advantage of speed. In fact, this is one of the reasons why programmers sometimes program in assembly language. Although it might be tempting to use only registers, it should be noted that there are only four general purpose registers, where as mentioned above many of those registers in spite of being general purpose registers also have specialized uses. For example, if the ecx register was being used for loop control, the ebx register for indexing an array, and the edx register for multiplication (as will all be explained and demonstrated later), then eax would be the only register left. It might then be the case that data would have to be moved from the eax register back into memory so that the eax register could be freed up to load more data in from memory.

Furthermore, since register names are not very descriptive of their content and memory locations can be given descriptive variable names as discussed in the previous section, it is usually easier to program using variable names rather than trying to remember what is stored in which register at any particular time in a program. Although there is a performance penalty when moving data back into memory, the penalty for lost time trying to debug an assembly program as a beginning student of assembly language programming is much greater during the course of a semester. Also, since most programs written in the academic environment are used only a few times (for testing and grading), as opposed to being executed many times in the industrial environment, time is better spent writing a program that is easier to read, understand, and debug. Besides, it is usually easier to go back and modify an easy-to-read program to make it run faster and use less memory than it is to try to debug a supposedly optimized and difficult-to-read program. Once a program is written and works properly, it can always be easily modified to perform faster and use less memory in the places where it counts the most. These techniques will be introduced later, on an as-needed basis. So for now, resist the temptation to save that extra byte or nanosecond and make sure that your programs are implemented logically, correctly, and are easy to read and modify.

1.7 Character Data

Character data can also be declared. For example, to declare two variables in C/C++/Java, the first called grade1 which is not initialized and the second called grade2 initialized to the letter 'A', would be done as follows:

```
char grade1;
char grade2='A';
```

The same can be done in assembly language similar to using sdword previously, except byte is used instead. Although shown here using single quotes, note that character data can also be enclosed in double quotes:

```
grade1 byte ?
grade2 byte 'A'
```

Further, a string as an array of byte can also be declared. Although the instructions to process a string will be postponed until Chap. 9, it is sometimes necessary to output a string as a message or to serve as a prompt for input. Occasionally a string can be declared as separate letters as follows:

```
grades byte 'A','B','C'
```

But unless each letter is going to be processed separately, they are usually declared as a complete string for the sake of readability as in the following example:

```
name byte 'Abe'
```

As will be seen in Chap. 2, strings are often terminated with a binary zero taking up 1 byte to indicate the end of the string. This is often used in output statements and is declared as follows:

```
name byte 'Abe',0
```

Continuing, recall the code in Fig. 1.2 works well when moving numbers, but what if one wanted to move a character from one location to another? The same principles apply, except instead of moving 32-bit double words around, only a single byte needs to be moved because a character is only 8 bits long. For example, how would the following C code segment be implemented in assembly language?

```
char letter1,letter2;
letter1 = 'A';
letter2 = letter1;
```

As before, the variables letter1 and letter2 would need to be declared in the data section, but instead of being declared as type sdword, they would need to be declared simply as type byte. The first line of executable code would be implemented as an immediate instruction and the transfer of data between the memory locations would be done via a register, but instead of a 32-bit register, only an 8-bit register would be used. The following assembly language code segment implements the above C code:

```
            .data
letter1     byte    ?
letter2     byte    ?
            .code
            ; letter1 = 'A'
            mov letter1,'A'      ; store 'A' in letter1
            ; letter2 = letter1
            mov al,letter1       ; load al with letter1
            mov letter2,al       ; store al in letter2
```

What if one wanted to move more than a single character? Again, this can be done using special string instructions which will be introduced in Chap. 9.

1.8 Errors

As with high-level programs, there can of course be various types of errors in assembly language. The first type of error usually encountered is a syntax error which is an error in the grammar of the language. For example, if move was typed in the above code segment instead of mov, then a syntax error would occur. The second type of error is an execution or a run-time error, in which although the syntax might be correct, the instruction being executed cannot be performed by the processor. A typical error like this might be a division by zero error, where division will be discussed in Chap. 3. The last type of error is the most difficult to resolve because it does not give the programmer an error message and is known as a logic error. In the previous code segment, what would happen if the last two lines were reversed? The contents of letter1 would never be copied from the al register into letter2 because the contents of letter2 would contain the indeterminate contents of the al register. At first, one will probably make a number of syntax errors due to the newness of the language, but with the help of the assembler's error messages and with practice, the number of syntax errors will decrease. However, as with any language, it is the logic errors that can take the most time to debug, but with careful attention to the logic of the code being written and following many of the suggestions presented throughout this text, the number of logic errors can be minimized.

1.9 Complete Program: Implementing Inline Assembly in C

If one looks at the first complete C and assembly programs at the beginning of this chapter, what is noticeably absent is any form of input/output (I/O). The reason for this is that I/O in stand-alone assembly language programs can be quite complex. To help simplify the I/O in stand-alone programs, it is possible to use the I/O from the C programming language as introduced in the next chapter. Until then, in order to get a glimpse to see that the above programs do indeed work, it is possible to run 32-bit assembly instructions in a C program using Visual C++. This process is known as inline or embedded assembly and is a quick way to test program segments. However, there are some disadvantages to this method. Note that 64-bit processing introduced in Chap. 11 and also the high-level assembly directives if and while introduced in Chaps. 4 and 5, respectively, cannot be used in embedded assembly. These are some of the reasons why stand-alone assembly language programs are used in all subsequent chapters, but for quick testing of some assembly language code segments, inline assembly can be convenient.

In order to include assembly language instructions in a C program, the ___asm{
statement must be placed at the beginning of the assembly language code segment,
which is a double underscore and the word asm followed by an opening brace. After
including the needed assembly language statements, a closing brace } is included at
the end of the segment. The advantage of using inline assembly is that C input and
output can be used to see if the processing has been done correctly. Further, input
and output from the C language will be utilized in stand-alone programs since it is
easier to use and will be described in more detail in the next chapter.

To see how assembly language can be included in a C program, consider the
following program:

```
#include <stdio.h>
int main(){
    int num1,num2;
    num1 = 5;
    num2 = num1;
    printf("%s%d\n","The answer is: ",num2);
    return 0;
}
```

Although some of the code above may seem a bit cryptic to those readers who
are not familiar with C, where many of the details of the above will be discussed in
Chap. 2, it should be obvious the printf is the output of the variable num2. The
key part of the above program is the assignment statement num2=num1; and given
the mov instruction and the eax register presented in this chapter, it can easily be
converted to assembly language. The above C program can be implemented using
assembly language for the assignment statement shown below:

```
#include <stdio.h>
int main(){
    int num1,num2;
    num1 = 5;
    __asm {
       mov eax,num1
       mov num2,eax
    }
    printf("%s%d\n","The answer is: ",num2);
    return 0;
}
```

Go ahead and key in the above program using Visual C++ (see Appendix A.1)
to prove to yourself that the code works. Also, feel free to try some of the other
instructions introduced in this chapter to become more familiar with the mov
instruction and registers. For example, try converting the num1=5; statement to
assembly language and move it to the inline assembly section of the program.

1.10 Summary

- Directives tell the assembler what to do and instructions tell the processor what to do.
- A byte is 8 bits, a word is 16 bits, a double word (dword) is 32 bits, and a quad word (qword) is 64-bits.
- The four 32-bit general purpose registers are eax, ebx, ecx, and edx.
- Immediate data is data that appears in an operand.
- The mov instruction cannot move data directly from one memory location to another memory location.
- Typically, a variable name will begin with a letter and is followed by any combination of letters and numbers. Although _, @, or $ can be used anywhere in the name, in this text the use of these characters is avoided.
- To declare integers, use sdword and for characters, use byte.
- Inline or embedded assembly is good for testing small assembly language code segments, but it has limitations. Note that high-level directives, such as if statements and while structures, and also 64-bit processing cannot be used in the segment.
- As with high-level languages, error messages are given for syntax and execution (or run-time) errors, but not for logic errors.

1.11 Exercises (Items Marked with an * Have Solutions in Appendix D)

1. Which of the following are syntactically correct variable names in assembly language?

   ```
   *A. RX8          B. 325i        *C. Total$
    D. @1234        E. $1000       *F. Pi3.14
   ```

2. Implement each of the following declarations in assembly language:

   ```
   *A.    char initial;
    B.    char grade = 'B';
   *C.    char x = 'P', y = 'Q';
    D.    int amount;
   *E.    int count = 0;
    F.    int number = -396;
   ```

3. Assuming that the variables have been declared properly, indicate whether the following statements are syntactically correct or incorrect. If incorrect, indicate what is wrong with the statement:

*A.   move cat,5   B.   mov dog,cat   *C.   mov eax,ebx
 D.   mov mouse,-7   *E.   mov 1,frog   F.   mov horse,ecx
 G.   mov rat,-eax   *H.   mov edx,2

4. Assuming all the variables are declared as sdword, write assembly language
   instructions to implement each of the following C statements or segments:

   *A.   i = 1;
    B.   x = y;
   *C.   c = 2;
           b = c;
           a = b;
    D.   x = y = 1;
    E.   a = 1;
           b = 2;
           c = a;
           a = b;
           b = c;

5. Assuming all the variables are declared as byte, write assembly language
   instructions to implement each of the following C statements or segments:

   *A.   a = 'B';
    B.   b = c;
   *C.   d = 'E';
           e = d;
    D.   d = 'z';
           a = d;
           b = a;
   *E.   a = '2';
           b = '?';
           a = b;

Input/Output

2

2.1 Introduction

As mentioned in Chap. 1, input and output (I/O) in assembly language can be quite
difficult and complicated. Although the exploration of I/O at the assembly language
level is a subject worthy of study, it often times gets in the way of many of the other
important topics and reasons for studying assembly language. The result is that it is
helpful to have a simplified form of input/output. To that end, it is possible to access
the input/output capabilities that are available in the C programming language and
of the various high-level languages that MASM can interface with, C is probably
the easiest. If one has studied C before, then the following will seem fairly
straightforward. If one has not studied C previously, but rather has experience with
other languages like C++ or Java, the transition to the C language I/O should not be
too difficult. Although all the fundamentals of I/O in C that are necessary for this
text will be presented in this chapter, the reader can always refer to any number of C
programming language texts to explore some of the other options available. Note
that floating-point I/O is essentially the same and the subtleties will be discussed in
Chap. 10. Also, 64-bit I/O is different and after learning the fundamentals of 32-bit
I/O in this chapter, the differences for 64-bit I/O will be discussed in Chap. 11.

2.2 Hello World

When learning a new programming language, one of the first programs learned is
the infamous "Hello World" program. The advantage of such a program is to ensure
that the program has compiled or assembled correctly and subsequently executed
properly. This program in C often appears as follows:

© Springer Nature Switzerland AG 2020   17
J. T. Streib, *Guide to Assembly Language*, Undergraduate Topics
in Computer Science, https://doi.org/10.1007/978-3-030-35639-2_2

```
#include <stdio.h>
int main(){
    printf("Hello World!\n");
    return 0;
}
```

where printf is the method used for output, the string to be output is in double
quotes, and the \n means advance to the next line, similar to using endl in a cout
statement in C++ and similar to the ln portion of a system.out.println()
statement in Java. The corresponding program to output "Hello World" in MASM
would appear as follows:

```
        .686
        .model flat, c
        .stack 100h
printf  PROTO arg1:Ptr Byte
        .data
msg1    byte "Hello World!",0Ah,0
        .code
main    proc
        INVOKE printf, ADDR msg1
        ret
main    endp
        end
```

The PROTO directive, preceded by the label printf, indicates a prototype for the
function printf. When the assembler encounters the printf, it does not cause an
error but rather leaves space for the address of the instruction to be filled in later by the
linker prior to being loaded into memory for execution. The parameter arg1:Ptr
Byte indicates that the argument of the printf will be a pointer to a string of bytes.

In order to call the printf function, the INVOKE directive is used, which is
like calling a subprogram (see Chap. 7), but is simpler to use because it takes care
of the parameter passing. However, be very careful to note that the INVOKE
directive destroys the contents of the eax, ecx, and edx registers. Again as
mentioned in Chap. 1, it is wise to save data in memory locations instead of leaving
them in registers to avoid the possibility of long debugging sessions.

Continuing, the argument ADDR msg1 in the INVOKE above indicates the address
of the string to be output. The actual message to be output is in the .data section as
msg1 byte "Hello World", 0Ah, 0, where string data was discussed in Chap. 1.
The difference here is that the string is followed by a 0Ah, which is the hexadecimal
code for a new line, such as \n in C (see Appendix B for a discussion of hexadecimal).
The 0Ah is followed by a 0, which is the code to terminate a string used with output.

The above code is good for outputting a single string, but what if there is a need
to format and output a number of parameters? As a transition step to the ability to
output more than one argument, the original C program above could be rewritten as
follows:

```
#include <stdio.h>
int main(){
    printf("%s\n","Hello World!");
    return 0;
}
```

The advantage of the above code segment is that the formatting is separated from the data to be output. The %s indicates that there is a string in the first argument following the current formatting argument. Although in C the formatting and data are often together, their separation makes for a little cleaner code in assembly language when there is more than one item to be output. Although the cleaner code might not be readily apparent in the segment below, it paves the way for multiple arguments in subsequent examples:

```
            .686
            .model flat, c
            .stack 100h
    printf  PROTO arg1:Ptr Byte, printlist:VARARG
            .data
    msg1fmt byte "%s",0Ah,0
    msg1    byte "Hello World!",0
            .code
    main    proc
            INVOKE printf, ADDR msg1fmt, ADDR msg1
            ret
    main    endp
            end
```

First note that the PROTO statement has an additional argument printlist: VARARG, which indicates that a variable number of arguments can now follow the first argument, where the first argument will now serve as the format string. In the data declaration section, note that the %s is in a separate data declaration called msg1fmt, where %s indicates that string data will be output. Also, the string to be output is only terminated by the 0 string terminator and the 0Ah has been moved to msg1fmt. Lastly, the first ADDR in the INVOKE directive references the format string and the second one references the string to be output.

2.3 Integer Output

In addition to outputting a single string, the previous example can be expanded to output multiple strings. Further, it can be expanded to output multiple integers or a combination of strings and integers. The advantage of this is that the integer output

can be identified to the users with matching strings. For example, in the following C
program, the integer 5 is output along with an identifying string:

```c
#include <stdio.h>
int main(){
    int number;
    number = 5;
    printf("%s%d\n","The number is: ",number);
    return 0;
}
```

The first argument of the printf says that a string will be output (%s), followed by an integer (%d), followed by a line feed. The second argument of the
printf is the string and the third is the variable number. The corresponding
MASM code is as follows:

```
           .686
           .model flat, c
           .stack 100h
  printf   PROTO arg1:Ptr Byte, printlist:VARARG
           .data
  msg1fmt  byte "%s%d",0Ah,0
  msg1     byte "The number is: ",0
  number   sdword ?
           .code
  main     proc
           mov number,5
           INVOKE printf, ADDR msg1fmt, ADDR msg1, number
           ret
  main     endp
           end
```

As in the last example of the previous section, the PROTO statement remains
unchanged. Note that the msg1fmt string has the %d added to it. The variable
number has been declared as a signed double word in the data section and the
number 5 assigned to it in the code segment. Lastly, the variable number has been
added as an argument to the INVOKE directive. Both msg1fmt and msg1 need
ADDR because they are pointers to the strings, but ADDR is not needed for number
because it is a simple integer variable.

The following example further illustrates how multiple arguments work and
includes two integers in addition to a string. It also includes cleaner output by
including better vertical spacing by using \n and better horizontal spacing by using
spaces in the string as shown below:

```
#include <stdio.h>
int main(){
    int num1 = 5, num2 = 7;
    printf("\n%d%s%d\n\n",num1," is not equal to ",num2);
    return 0;
}
```

The above C program would be implemented in assembly as follows:

```
.686
.model flat, c
.stack 100h
printf    PROTO arg1:Ptr Byte, printlist:VARARG
          .data
msg1fmt   byte 0Ah,"%d%s%d",0Ah,0Ah,0
msg1      byte " is not equal to ",0
num1      sdword 5
num2      sdword 7
          .code
main      proc
          INVOKE printf, ADDR msg1fmt, num1, ADDR msg1, num2
          ret
main      endp
          end
```

Without any change to the PROTO directive in the above program, there are now three arguments after the msg1fmt string in the INVOKE directive. As mentioned previously, the reason extra arguments are allowed is due to the VARARG in the PROTO directive which allows for a variable number of arguments. Again, notice that 0Ah is used instead of \n and the careful use of spaces in the string, both to assist in the vertical and horizontal spacing. As an aside, also note that the variables num1 and num2 are initialized in the data section during assembly time rather than during execution time, corresponding to the prior C program.

2.4   Integer Input

Although having the ability to output is extremely important, it does lead to some dull programs unless one can also input data. Just as printf can be invoked to allow for output, so too can scanf be invoked for input. Instead of merely assigning an integer to the variable number, the following C program inputs a number from the user and then outputs the same number (note that when using scanf, a warning message might be issued, where one can use scanf_s instead or just ignore the warnings):

```c
#include <stdio.h>
int main(){
    int number;
    scanf("%d",&number);
    printf("\n%s%d\n\n","The number is: ",number);
    return 0;
}
```

Notice in the above code that number is preceded with an ampersand (&) in the scanf but not in the printf. Although experienced C programmers are probably familiar with this, programmers coming from other languages might not be familiar with it. The ampersand indicates the address of number is being passed to scanf to allow the value read in from the keyboard to be passed back to the variable number. Whereas with output, the value in number being passed to printf will be output and since no number will be passed back, an ampersand is not needed. The passing back of values through arguments is known as a reference parameter in languages like C++, but the equivalent is not available in Java since values can be returned from methods only via a return statement. The following assembly program implements the above C program:

```asm
            .686
            .model flat, c
            .stack 100h
printf      PROTO arg1:Ptr Byte, printlist:VARARG
scanf       PROTO arg2:Ptr Byte, inputlist:VARARG
            .data
in1fmt      byte "%d",0
msg1fmt     byte 0Ah,"%s%d",0Ah,0Ah,0
msg1        byte "The number is: ",0
number      sdword ?
            .code
main        proc
            INVOKE scanf, ADDR in1fmt, ADDR number
            INVOKE printf, ADDR msg1fmt, ADDR msg1, number
            ret
main        endp
            end
```

Although there are a number of similarities between the scanf and printf above, such as the similarity between the two prototypes, there are some important details that need to be pointed out. First, note that a %s does appear in the input format, because only an integer is being input in this example. Further, the input format is terminated only by a 0 and does not contain a 0Ah. The reason is that during input a new line is not needed because it is supplied by the user after the data has been entered and they press the "enter" or "return" key, which supplies the new line on the screen. Lastly, notice that the variable number is preceded by ADDR in the invoking of scanf, but it is not preceded by ADDR in the printf. The reason for this is that ADDR serves the same function as the ampersand (&) in C as discussed above.

Although the above code works, it is not very helpful to the user. The reason is that when either the above C or the MASM program executes, there is just a cursor blinking on the screen and no indication to the user that any input is needed or what type of input is needed. Instead, as with any language, it is a good idea to prompt the user for the type of input needed as shown in the C program below, where the prompt and output message have been changed to specify an integer instead of just a generic number:

```c
#include <stdio.h>
int main(){
    int number;
printf("\n%s","Enter an integer: ");
scanf("%d",&number);
printf("\n%s%d\n\n","The integer is: ",number);
return 0;
}
```

The corresponding assembly code is given as follows:

```
                .686
                .model flat, c
                .stack 100h
    printf      PROTO arg1:Ptr Byte, printlist:VARARG
    scanf       PROTO arg2:Ptr Byte, inputlist:VARARG
                .data
    in1fmt      byte "%d",0
    msg0fmt     byte 0Ah,"%s",0
    msg1fmt     byte 0Ah,"%s%d",0Ah,0Ah,0
    msg0        byte "Enter an integer: ",0
    msg1        byte "The integer is: ",0
    number      sdword ?
                .code
```

```
main        proc
            INVOKE printf, ADDR msg0fmt, ADDR msg0
            INVOKE scanf, ADDR in1fmt, ADDR number
            INVOKE printf, ADDR msg1fmt, ADDR msg1, number
            ret
main        endp
            end
```

Notice that the prompt in the C code does not contain a \n nor does the prompt in the MASM code contain a 0Ah, because in both cases the cursor will remain on the same line as the prompt awaiting the user to enter the integer, and then only when the user presses the "enter" key will the cursor move to the next line.

2.5   Complete Program: Using Input, Data Transfer, and Output

As one more modification to the above program to implement both the concepts learned in Chap. 1 and this chapter, consider the following program. It prompts for and inputs an integer into num1, copies it to num2, and then outputs the contents of num2:

```
#include <stdio.h>
int main(){
int num1, num2;
printf("\n%s","Enter an integer for num1: ");
scanf("%d",&num1);
num2=num1;
printf("\n%s%d\n\n","The integer in num2 is: ",num2);
return 0;
}
```

This program is then implemented in assembly language as follows:

```
            .686
            .model flat, c
            .stack 100h
printf      PROTO arg1:Ptr Byte, printlist:VARARG
scanf       PROTO arg2:Ptr Byte, inputlist:VARARG
            .data
in1fmt      byte "%d",0
msg0fmt     byte 0Ah,"%s",0
```

```
msg1fmt    byte 0Ah,"%s%d",0Ah,0Ah,0
msg0       byte "Enter an integer for num1: ",0
msg1       byte "The integer in num2 is: ",0
num1       sdword ?        ; first number
num2       sdword ?        ; second number
           .code
main       proc
           INVOKE printf, ADDR msg0fmt, ADDR msg0
           INVOKE scanf, ADDR in1fmt, ADDR num1
           mov eax,num1  ; load eax with the content of num1
           mov num2,eax  ; store the contents of eax in num2
           INVOKE printf, ADDR msg1fmt, ADDR msg1, num2
           ret
main       endp
           end
```

2.6   Summary

- Use the PROTO and INVOKE directives to implement the C functions scanf and printf.
- Be careful, the INVOKE directive destroys the contents of the eax, ecx, and edx registers.
- Use separate formatting to make the assembly language equivalents more readable.
- The 0Ah in assembly language is like a \n in C, an endl in C++, and a println in Java.
- Be sure to terminate a string for output in assembly language with a 0.
- On output, do not forget to include an ADDR for strings.
- On input, do not forget to include an ADDR for all variables, which is like an & in C.
- For floating-point and 64-bit I/O see Chaps. 10 and 11, respectively.

2.7   Exercises (Items Marked with an * Have Solutions in Appendix D)

1. Indicate whether the following statements are syntactically correct or incorrect. If incorrect, indicate what is wrong with the statement:

```
*A.    printf PROTO arg1:Ptr Byte, printlist:VARARG
 B.    msg1fmt byte "\n%s%d\n",0
*C.    INVOKE printf, ADDR msg1fmt, ADDR number
 D.    msg2fmt byte 0Ah,0Ah,"%s",0Ah,0Ah,0
 E.    msg3fmt byte "%s%d",\n,0
```

2. Assuming that the .data section is set up properly, what is wrong with the
   logic of the following code segment? How could it be rewritten to avoid the
   difficulty?

```
mov num1,5
mov eax,num1
INVOKE printf, ADDR msg1fmt, ADDR msg1, num2
mov num2,eax
```

*3. Given the following MASM program, what will be output to the screen? Be
   sure to line everything up properly. Use a lowercase letter b to represent a blank
   and the words blank line to represent a blank line:

```
                .686
                .model flat, c
                .stack 100h
printf          PROTO arg1:Ptr Byte, printlist:VARARG
                .data
msg1fmt         byte "%s%d",0
msg2fmt         byte "%s%d",0Ah,0Ah,0Ah,0
msg3fmt         byte "%s%d",0Ah,0
msg1            byte "x = ",0
msg2            byte " y = ",0
msg3            byte "z=",0
num1            sdword 1
num2            sdword 2
num3            sdword 3
                .code
main            proc
                INVOKE printf, ADDR msg1fmt, ADDR msg1, num1
                INVOKE printf, ADDR msg2fmt, ADDR msg2, num2
                INVOKE printf, ADDR msg3fmt, ADDR msg3, num3
                ret
main            endp
                end
```

4. Given the following MASM program, what will be output to the screen. Be sure to line everything up properly. Use a lowercase letter b to represent a blank and the words `blank line` to represent a blank line:

```
                .686
                .model flat, c
                .stack 100h
printf          PROTO arg1:Ptr Byte, printlist:VARARG
                .data
msg1fmt         byte 0Ah,"%s%d%s%d%s",0Ah,0
msg2fmt         byte 0Ah,"%s%d",0Ah,0Ah,0
msg11           byte "The first number is ",0
msg12           byte ", but the second number is ",0
msg13           byte ",",0
msg2            byte "while the third number is ",0
num1            sdword 5
num2            sdword 7
num3            sdword 11
                .code
main            proc
                INVOKE printf, ADDR msg1fmt, ADDR msg11, num1,
                        ADDR msg12, num2, ADDR msg13
                INVOKE printf, ADDR msg2fmt, ADDR msg2, num3
                ret
main            endp
                end
```

5. Implement the following C program in MASM. Be sure to use proper spacing on all output. If necessary, first key in the C program and then implement the MASM program to insure the MASM program works identically to the C program:

```c
#include <stdio.h>
int main(){
    int x, y, z;
    x = 1;
    y = 2;
    z = 3;
    printf(%\n%d%s%d%s%d\n\n", x, " + ", y, " = ", z);
    return 0;
}
```

6. Implement the following C program in MASM. Be sure to use proper spacing on all output. If necessary, first key in the C program and then implement the MASM program to insure the MASM program works identically to the C program:

```c
#include <stdio.h>
int main(){
    int num1, num2;
    printf("\n%s","Enter a value for num1: ");
    scanf("%d",&num1);
    printf("\n%s","Enter a value for num2: ");
    scanf("%d",&num2);
    printf("\n%s\n\n","num1     num2");
    printf("%s%d%s%d\n\n"," ",num1,"        ",num2);
    return 0;
}
```

7. Given the following input and output, write both the C and assembly code necessary to make it look exactly as below. Pay careful attention to spacing and the blank lines:

Input and Output   •

```
Enter a number: 1
Enter a larger number: 3
Enter an even larger
number: 5

1 < 3 < 5

5 > 3 > 1
```

8. Write an assembly language program to create the following input and output with the spacing shown.

```
Enter a number: 1
Enter a number: 2

Numbers
    1
    2
```

Arithmetic Instructions

3

3.1 Addition and Subtraction

After learning how to load a register, transfer data between memory locations, and perform I/O, the next step is to learn how to perform various arithmetic operations. One of the simplest ways to learn how to perform arithmetic in assembly language is to first write the equation as a high-level statement. Assuming the integer variables num1 and num2 already contain values, then how could one implement the following C statement in assembly language?

```
sum = num1 + num2;
```

Just like the discussion concerning data movement, where the contents of one memory location cannot be copied directly into another memory location without first being copied to a register, the same concept applies to arithmetic operations, where arithmetic cannot be performed between two memory locations as indicated in Table 3.1 concerning the add instruction.

Again note that an add mem,mem instruction does not appear in the list of instructions, just as there was not a mov mem,mem listed previously. Instead, one must usually move the contents of one memory location into a register, add the contents of the other memory location to the register, and then copy the contents of the register into the specified memory location. The following assembly language code segment implements the C statement from above:

```
; sum = num1 + num2
mov eax,num1    ; load eax with the contents of num1
add eax,num2    ; add the contents of num2 to eax
mov sum,eax     ; store eax in sum
```

© Springer Nature Switzerland AG 2020
J. T. Streib, *Guide to Assembly Language*, Undergraduate Topics
in Computer Science, https://doi.org/10.1007/978-3-030-35639-2_3

Table 3.1 Add instructions

Instruction	Meaning
add mem, imm	add the immediate value to memory
add reg, mem	add the contents of memory to the register
add mem, reg	add the contents of the register to memory
add reg, imm	add immediate value to the register
add reg, reg	add the contents of the source (second) register to the destination (first) register

As before, the C statement makes a nice general comment prior to the assembly language code segment. In the above segment, the contents of num1 are copied into the eax register, then the contents of num2 are added to eax, and lastly the contents of eax are copied into the variable sum. Assuming num1 initially contains a 5 and num2 contains a 7, then Fig. 3.1 shows the results after execution of the previous code segment, where eax and sum shown in green contain a 12.

Although it is possible to use any of the other three registers and accomplish the same task, it is usually better to use the accumulator, the eax register, because the arithmetic instructions that use the eax register tend to use less memory and are also a little faster, as will be seen in Chap. 12. Also, just like there are often many ways to solve a problem in high-level languages, the same is true in low-level languages. Further, just like some solutions are better solutions in high-level languages, the same is also true in low-level languages. For example, the previous assembly code segment could have been written as follows:

```
mov sum, 0        ; initialize sum to zero
mov eax, num1     ; load eax with the contents of num1
add sum, eax      ; add the contents of eax to sum
mov eax, num2     ; load eax with the contents of num2
add sum, eax      ; add eax to sum
```

Fig. 3.1 Results of an addition operation

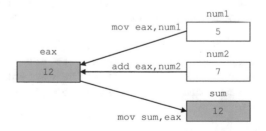

Although the above code segment works, in that sum contains the sum of both num1 and num2, it is not necessarily implementing the original C statement: sum = num1 + num2; but rather it is implementing the following C code segment:

```
sum = 0;
sum = sum + num1;
sum = sum + num2;
```

Although both of the above assembly language and C code segments work, in that the variable sum contains the sum of both num1 and num2, the second one in both languages is less efficient in terms of both memory and speed. With respect to memory, the second code segment takes up more memory because there are more instructions. Also, if there are more instructions, then the code segment will tend to take more time to execute.

As demonstrated above, one way to help write somewhat cleaner code is to not necessarily think in assembly language but rather think in a high-level language and then convert the high-level instructions into the low-level assembly language. Although at times this might introduce some inefficiencies into the low-level code with regard to register usage, the results would not usually be nearly as bad as in the last example, thus demonstrating that one can still be concerned with efficiency when programming either high or low-level languages.

Similar to the addition instruction is the subtraction instruction outlined in Table 3.2, where the same formats of instructions that apply to the addition instruction also apply to the subtraction instruction. Note again that a memory to memory instruction does not exist. As before, a simple high-level subtraction statement such as

```
difference = num2 - num1;
```

would be implemented in assembly language as follows:

```
; difference = num2 - num1
mov eax,num2             ; load num2 into eax
sub eax,num1             ; subtract num1 from eax
mov difference,eax       ; store answer in variable difference
```

Table 3.2 Sub instructions

Instruction	Meaning
sub mem,imm	subtract the immediate value from memory
sub reg,mem	subtract contents of memory from the register
sub mem,reg	subtract contents of the register from memory
sub reg,imm	subtract the immediate value from the register
sub reg,reg	subtract the contents of the source (second) register from the destination (first) register

3.2 Multiplication and Division

While addition and subtraction seem to be fairly straightforward, multiplication and division can be just a little more complicated. When adding two numbers together, it is possible that the answer will be larger than the size of the register or memory location that can hold that value which would cause an overflow error. For example, adding the numbers 999 and 999 in base 10 will result in the number 1,998, which is one digit larger than the two original numbers. The same applies to base 2, where adding the numbers 111 and 111 would result in the number 1110 (as discussed in Appendix B). However, when using 32-bit signed double words, unless the sum is greater than 2,147,483,647 as indicated Table 1.2, this should not be a problem at this time.

However, with multiplication, the situation is worse. For example, when multiplying the numbers 999 and 999 in base 10, the answer is 998,001, where there is not just one extra digit but potentially twice as many digits as is the case in this example. The same holds true for binary, where multiplying the numbers 111 and 111 results in the answer 110,001, where again there are twice as many digits.

The result is that when multiplication occurs in the computer, there needs to be room for the extra digits when two 32-bit registers are multiplied together, because the result could take up 64 bits. Although there are many variations of the multiplication instruction that can use two operands or three operands, this text will examine only the one-operand versions of the instruction which has been available since the first Intel processor (although then only in 16-bit form). Also, the one-operand instructions most closely resemble the one-operand division instructions which are the only form of division instructions available. As a result, this will help provide consistency when studying that instruction later. Although there is an unsigned version of the multiply instruction called `mul` which can work with slightly larger numbers (see Chap. 1 and Appendix B), it cannot work with negative numbers. As a result, this text will consider only the signed versions of the multiplication instruction, signified by `i` at the beginning of the instruction as `imul`. The two formats of these two versions of the `imul` instruction are shown in Table 3.3.

The way these two one-operand versions of the signed multiplication instruction work is that the `eax` register must first be loaded with the number that needs to be multiplied (the multiplicand). Then, the number to be multiplied by (the multiplier) either is placed into a register or can be located in a memory location. Note that with the one-operand `imul` instruction, there is no provision for an immediate operand and that the use of the `eax` register for the multiplicand is implied.

Table 3.3 Imul instructions

Instruction	Meaning
imul reg	multiply eax by an integer in a register
imul mem	multiply eax by an integer in a memory location

During execution of the imul instruction, the number in eax is multiplied by the number either in the specified register or in the memory location and the answer (product) is placed into what is called the edx:eax register pair. Recall from Chap. 1 that edx is the data register that is used in various arithmetic instructions, where imul is one of those arithmetic instructions. As mentioned above, it is possible that the answer from multiplication could be twice the size of the original numbers being multiplied, so what happens is that the low-order bits of the product are placed into the eax register and the high-order bits of the product are placed into the edx register. For now, there is no plan to multiply any numbers where the product is greater than 32 bits, or in other words a positive 2,147,483,647 or negative 2,147,483,648 and if larger numbers are needed, 64-bit numbers can be used as discussed in Chap. 11. Regardless, it is still important to realize that the edx register will be filled with any high-order bits, which in our case will usually be zeros or ones depending on whether the product is positive or negative, respectively. As a result, this would destroy any values that might have been placed in the edx register previously. Given the above, one can implement the following C instruction

```
product = num1 * num2;
```

as follows in assembly language:

```
; product = num1 * num2
mov eax,num1          ; load eax with the contents of num1
imul num2             ; multiply eax by mum2
mov product,eax       ; store eax in product
```

Again, at the end of the above segment the contents of the edx register will have been destroyed. Assuming num1 contained a positive 2 and num2 contained a positive 5, the results in the edx:eax register pair would be that the 0 located in the 31st bit (leftmost bit) of the eax register would be copied or propagated throughout all 32 bits of the edx register. If num1 instead contained a negative 2 and num2 still contained a positive 5, then the results in the edx:eax register pair would have been that the 1 located in the 31st bit of the eax register would have been copied or propagated throughout all 32 bits of the edx register as shown in Fig. 3.2. (See Appendix B for a discussion of positive and negative numbers.) This

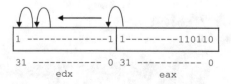

Fig. 3.2 The edx:eax registers after execution of the imul instruction

is yet another good reason not to keep values in registers, but rather to store values in memory.

Given the above description of the `imul` instruction, how would one implement the following C statement?

```
product = num1 * 2;
```

Although it is possible to use immediate values with the two- and three-operand versions of the `imul` instruction, it is also possible to easily solve this problem using only the one-operand version. The immediate value can first be moved into an empty register and then that register can be used in the `imul` instruction. Again, this mimics the `idiv` instruction to be discussed immediately after the following code segment:

```
; product = num1 * 2
mov eax, num1           ; load eax with the contents of num1
mov ebx,2               ; load ebx with the value 2
imul ebx                ; multiply eax by ebx
mov product, eax        ; store eax in product
```

Just as there is an instruction for the multiplication for unsigned numbers (`mul`), there is also a division instruction for unsigned numbers (`div`). Although it can divide somewhat larger numbers, it cannot divide negative numbers, so this text will consider only the signed division instruction called `idiv`. As mentioned previously, the `idiv` instruction follows the same format as for the previously introduced one-operand `imul` instruction. The only two formats of the `idiv` instruction are shown in Table 3.4.

The division statement works much like the multiplication statement, except in reverse. Just like the product of multiplication can be larger than the multiplier and multiplicand, so it is that the answer (quotient) and remainder can be smaller than the original number to be divided (the dividend). The result is that where the product for multiplication is in the `edx:eax` pair, with division the dividend must be initially placed in the `edx:eax` pair prior to using the `idiv` instruction. After execution of the `idiv` instruction, the quotient is in the `eax` register and the remainder is in the `edx` register.

But how does one take a number, whether immediate data or in memory, and put it in the `edx:eax` pair? Without any special instructions, one already has the ability to do this. For example, what if one wanted to implement the following C statement?

```
answer = number / amount;
```

Table 3.4 `Idiv` instructions

Instruction	Meaning
idiv mem	divide the edx:eax register pair by memory
idiv reg	divide the edx:eax register pair by a register

Table 3.5 Convert instructions

Opcode	Meaning	Description
cbw	Convert byte to word	Extends the sign from al to ax
cwd	Convert word to double	Extends sign from ax to eax
cdq	Convert double to quad word	Extends sign from eax to edx:eax pair

First, the contents of number would be moved into the eax register. Then assuming that the contents of number are positive, a 0 could be moved into the edx register. But what if the contents of number were negative? Then instead of moving a 0 into edx, a -1 could be moved into the edx register. This would cause each of the bits in the edx register to be set to a binary 1, thus setting the sign bit to 1. However, this solution would require the use of a selection structure which has not been discussed yet and would be a clumsy solution at best. Luckily the designers of the Intel processor thought of this problem and have special instructions to propagate or extend the sign bit from a smaller register to a larger register. These instructions are shown in Table 3.5.

It is the latter instruction in Table 3.5 that is of interest here. The cdq instruction allows the sign bit, whether a 0 or a 1, to be propagated throughout the edx register and thus avoids the initial messy solution proposed above. For example, if the eax register originally contains a -2, then the sign bit (a 1 in bit position 31) of eax is copied into each bit position of the edx register as illustrated in Fig. 3.3. The solution to the previous C code is as follows:

```
; answer = number / amount
mov eax,number    ; load eax with number
cdq               ; propagate sign bit into the edx register
idiv amount       ; divide edx:eax by amount
mov answer,eax    ; store eax in answer
```

Assuming that the contents of number is a 5, and the contents of amount is a 2, then the contents of the edx:eax pair would be as follows after the execution of the above code segment, where the remainder of a 1 is in the edx register and the quotient of a 2 is in the eax register shown in binary in Fig. 3.4:

Although the two- and three-operand formats for the imul instruction allow for an immediate operand, the idiv does not have this luxury and the single operand can only be a memory location or a register. So how would one implement an

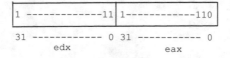

Fig. 3.3 Propagating the sign bit from eax through edx

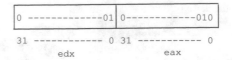

Fig. 3.4 Contents of edx:eax after execution of the idiv instruction

immediate value as in answer = number/2? As a hint, look at the proposed
solution using an immediate value in the discussion concerning multiplication.
Further, how would one implement the % operator in the C programming language,
as in answer = number % amount? If one remembers what the % operator does
(the mod or remainder function) and reviews how the idiv instruction works, the
answers to the above two questions should be obvious and both of these problems
are left as exercises for the reader at the end of the chapter.

3.3 Implementing Unary Operators: Increment, Decrement, and Negation

In high-level languages, the arithmetic operations presented in the previous two
sections are known as binary operators, not because they perform arithmetic on
binary numbers but rather because they have two operands as in x + y. However
other high-level language operators have only one operand, such as the negative
sign −y, and these are known as unary operators.

Although it is possible to implement all of the arithmetic necessary to implement
unary operators with the instructions presented previously, there are some extra
arithmetic instructions that tend to take up a little less memory, might be a little
faster, and also make life a little easier for the assembly language programmer. In
addition to introducing these instructions, some of the concepts concerning the
order of operations are introduced in this section.

For example, if one needed to increment a variable x by 1 and decrement a
variable y by 1, such as

```
x = x + 1;
y = y - 1;
```

or one could alternatively use the increment and decrement operators

```
x++;        or    ++x;
y--;        or    --y;
```

Table 3.6 Inc and dec
instructions

Instruction	Instruction
inc reg	dec reg
inc mem	dec mem

where in a stand-alone statement it does not matter whether the ++ or — goes before or after the variable. The above can be implemented by merely using the add and sub instructions:

```
add x,1
sub y,1
```

Although the above works, the designers of the Intel processor built in two instructions that specifically increment and decrement by only 1. The format of each of these instructions is shown in Table 3.6.

As mentioned at the beginning of this section, these instructions take up less memory than do add or sub instructions. In fact, on older 16-bit processors if one needed to add or subtract the number 2 to or from a register, it was faster to use two inc or dec instructions than it was to use a single add or sub instruction to add or subtract the number 2. Although this is not true with newer 32-bit processors, a single inc or dec instruction is still more memory efficient than using an add or a sub instruction to increment or decrement by 1 (see Chap. 12). The result is the following:

```
inc x
dec y
```

As shown previously, it does not matter in C/C++/Java whether the increment or decrement operators in a stand-alone statement are used in prefix or postfix notation. However, as may have been learned in a previous computer science course, it is quite different when they are used in conjunction with other operators in an arithmetic expression. Although these combinations should probably be avoided by the novice programmer, they do arise on occasion and one should understand how they work in a high-level language and how to implement them in a low-level language. As either a review or an introduction, how do the following two instructions differ?

```
x = y++;        x = ++y;
```

In the first case on the left, the value of y is first assigned to x and then the value of y is incremented. In the second case, the value of y is first incremented and then it is assigned to x. Assuming in both cases that y initially contains the number 2, the results of both are illustrated respectively on the left and right in Fig. 3.5.

Fig. 3.5 Results of x = y++ and x = ++y

Clearly there is a difference between the two, and the above two statements can alternatively be implemented as

```
x = y;                  y = y + 1;
y = y + 1;              x = y;
```

and thus can be implemented correspondingly in assembly language as

```
mov eax,y               inc y
mov x,eax               mov eax,y
inc y                   mov x,eax
```

What if one needed to negate a number, or in other words find the two's complement of a number (see Appendix B), and store it in another memory location? For example,

```
x = -y;
```

As shown before with increment and decrement, one could accomplish negation using the instructions that have already been introduced:

```
mov eax,0
sub eax,y
mov x,eax
```

Again as before, there is another instruction that is shorter and faster for negation called neg and has the format shown in Table 3.7.

Using the neg instruction, the code segment above can then be rewritten as

```
mov eax,y
neg eax
mov x,eax
```

Table 3.7 Neg instructions

Instruction	Meaning
neg reg	two's complement of the contents of the register
neg mem	two's complement of the contents of a memory location

Notice that the variable y is not negated, since the negation symbol does not alter the contents of the variable it precedes. Rather, the value of y is first moved to a register and then negated prior to being moved to the variable x. Although it takes the same number of instructions as the previous assembly language code segment, the neg instruction takes up less memory than does the corresponding sub instruction.

Although there was some possible confusion of using the increment and decrement instructions in an expression, the negation instruction is less complicated. One must remember that the unary minus symbol for negation has precedence over the other binary operators of +, -, *, and /. Given the following statement on the left, the negation of y occurs prior to the addition, and if one wants to negate after the addition, parentheses must be used as shown on the right:

```
x = -y + z;        x = -(y + z);
```

The above two statements are implemented correspondingly below in assembly language:

```
mov eax,y          mov eax,y
neg eax            add eax,z
add eax,z          neg eax
mov x,eax          mov x,eax
```

3.4 Order of Operations with Binary and Unary Operators

Although the previous section delved into some issues concerning order of operation, it did so only with respect to the unary operators. This section discusses order of operation in more depth with all arithmetic operators, including the binary operators, and in conjunction with the unary operators. To help understand the order of operation and sharpen one's skills using assembly language arithmetic instructions, this section examines how slightly more complicated arithmetic statements might be implemented. Again, it helps to first write it out as a high-level instruction:

```
answer = num1 - 3 + num2;
```

Remembering the order of operations from C, C++, and Java, since addition and subtraction have the same level of precedence, the order of operation is from left to right. In this case, the subtraction should be done first and the addition done second. Although some compilers and skilled assembly language programmers might change the order of various arithmetic operations to help optimize the efficiency of the machine code, this text will adhere to the pre-defined rules for the sake of consistency and help reinforce the rules regarding the order of operation.

First, the contents of the variable num1 should be loaded into the eax register, then the number 3 needs to be subtracted from to the eax register, where the number 3 is not in a memory location but rather is implemented as an immediate value. Next the value in num2 needs to be added to the eax register and lastly, the contents of the eax register need to be copied into the variable answer, as shown below:

```
; answer = num1 - 3 + num2
mov eax,num1        ; load eax with the contents of num1
sub eax,3           ; subtract 3 from eax
add eax,num2        ; add num2 to eax
mov answer,eax      ; store the result in answer
```

As before, there is usually more than one way to solve a problem in assembly language, such as the following code segment suggests:

```
; *** caution: poorly implemented code ***
sub num1,3          ; subtract 3 from num1
mov eax,num1        ; load num1 into eax
add eax,num2        ; add num2 to eax
mov answer,eax      ; store the result in answer
```

At first the code immediately above seems to be just as good as the code given previously. It has the same number of instructions and it places the correct number into the memory location answer. However, it should be noticed that it references memory one additional time, which might cause it to be just a little bit slower than the first code segment.

However, there is something else wrong with the code segment that does not concern speed or memory, but rather with the implementation of the original C/C++/Java code segment. Note that in the original high-level instruction answer = num1 - 3 + num2; the only variable altered is the variable answer that appears on the left of the assignment symbol (=). The variables num1 and num2 would not be altered by this statement. However, in the second assembly language implementation, the immediate value 3 is added to the variable num1, thus altering its contents. The above assembly language code segment does not implement the C statement answer = num1 - 3 + num2; but rather implements the following C code segment:

```
num1 = num1 - 3;
answer = num1 + num2;
```

If the value in the variable num1 was not going to be used again, this might not be a problem. However, if one is not sure at the time the code segment is written whether that value is going to be used again or not, then as a general rule it is probably better not to alter the contents of the variable in the first place. Again, it is best to write out the original arithmetic operation in a high-level language (or pseudo-code), use it as a general comment, and then carefully implement the assembly language to insure that it does indeed implement the high-level statement correctly.

To illustrate further the rules concerning order of operation, consider the following C statement:

```
answer = num1 + 3 * num2;
```

First, it must be remembered that multiplication has a higher precedence over addition so that the value 3 must be loaded into the eax register first and then multiplied by the value in num2. Then the value in num1 must be added to eax and lastly the value in eax should be stored in answer as follows:

```
; answer = num1 + 3 * num2
mov eax,3          ; load eax with the number 3
imul num2          ; multiply eax by num2
add eax,num1       ; add the contents of num1 to eax
mov answer,eax     ; store the contents of eax in answer
```

Again, be sure to remember that any value in the edx register is altered by the imul instruction. As another example, consider the following C statement:

```
result = num3 / (num4 - 2);
```

Although division has a higher precedence over subtraction, remember that the expression in parentheses should be evaluated first so that the subtraction must be performed prior to the division. Then the value in num3 must be divided by the results of the subtraction and lastly the value in eax should be stored in result:

```
; result = num3 / (num4 - 2);
mov ebx,num4      ; load ebx with num4
sub ebx,2         ; subtract 2 from ebx
mov eax,num3      ; load eax with the contents of num3
cdq               ; propagate the sign bit into the edx register
idiv ebx          ; divide edx:eax by num4 - 2
mov result,eax ;  store the contents of eax in result
```

Note that the ebx register was used to store the temporary results of the subtraction so that the difference could be used later in the division instruction. Combining the unary instructions from the previous section and the binary instructions from the current section, consider the following C statement:

```
v = -w + x * y - z++;
```

The order of operation should be that the value in w should be negated first, followed by the multiplication of x and y, then the addition of the negated value of w, then the subtraction of z, then the results assigned to v, and finally the value of z should be incremented since it is a postfix ++, as shown in the assembly code below:

```
; v = -w + x * y - z++
mov ebx,w
neg ebx
mov eax,x
imul y
add eax,ebx
sub eax,z
mov v,eax
inc z
```

Again note that the value in w is not actually negated, and the value in z is only incremented after the assignment to v. The best way to become more familiar with operator precedence is to attempt some problems on one's own. For further practice, there are a number of problems in Sect. 3.7.

3.5 Complete Program: Implementing I/O and Arithmetic

Combining all the material from Chaps. 1, 2, and 3, one can now write a complete program to prompt for and input various numbers, perform a wide variety of calculations, and output answers as needed. Derived from the last program in Chap. 2, the following program is still relatively simple, but it can serve as a model for even more complicated programs to test various arithmetic equations as needed and help implement some of the programs in the exercises at the end of this chapter.

For example, how would one write a program to calculate the number of amperes given the number of volts and ohms? The solution uses Ohm's law and is often written as $E = IR$, where E is the electromotive force (volts), I is the impedance (amperes), and R is the resistance (ohms). Obviously the equation will not work as written, but it is nothing that a little algebra cannot fix, hence $I = E/R$. Granted the answer will be off a little since the program is written using only integers; however it will serve the purpose of illustrating a complete program. As in the past, it is helpful to see the solution in C first as follows:

```
#include <stdio.h>
int main(){
    int volts, ohms, amperes;
    printf("\n%s", "Enter the number of volts: ");
    scanf("%d", &volts);
    printf("%s", "Enter the number of ohms: ");
    scanf("%d", &ohms);
    amperes = volts / ohms;
    printf("\n%s%d\n\n","The number of amperes is: ",amperes);
    return 0;
}
```

The corresponding assembly code is given below:

```
            .686
            .model flat, c
            .stack 100h
printf      PROTO arg1:Ptr Byte, printlist:VARARG
scanf       PROTO arg2:Ptr Sdword, inputlist:VARARG
            .data
in1fmt      byte "%d",0
msg1fmt     byte 0Ah,"%s",0
msg2fmt     byte "%s",0
msg3fmt     byte 0Ah,"%s%d",0Ah,0Ah,0
msg1        byte "Enter the number of volts: ",0
msg2        byte "Enter the number of ohms: ",0
msg3        byte "The number of amperes is: ",0
volts       sdword ?      ; number of volts
ohms        sdword ?      ; number of ohms
amperes     sdword ?      ; number of amperes
            .code
main        proc
            INVOKE printf, ADDR msg1fmt, ADDR msg1
            INVOKE scanf, ADDR in1fmt, ADDR volts
            INVOKE printf, ADDR msg2fmt, ADDR msg2
            INVOKE scanf, ADDR in1fmt, ADDR ohms
            ; amperes = volts/ohms
            mov eax,volts    ; load volts into eax
            cdq              ; extend the sign bit
            idiv ohms        ; divide eax by ohms
            mov amperes,eax  ; store eax in amperes
            INVOKE printf, ADDR msg3fmt, ADDR msg3, amperes
            ret
main        enp
            end
```

3.6   Summary

- Be careful not to alter any variables that appear only to the right of an assignment symbol, unless ++ or −− is used.
- Remember that the contents of the edx register contain the high-order bits after multiplication.
- Do not forget to use the cdq instruction prior to division.

• Follow the order of operations when implementing arithmetic statements:

  – Parentheses first with the most nested first.
  – Unary minus sign has precedence over multiplication and division.
  – Multiplication and division prior to addition and subtraction.
  – In a tie, go left to right.

• Be careful with increment and decrement (++ and —) operators:

  – When stand-alone, no difference between prefix and postfix.
  – In an assignment statement, prefix is performed first prior to an assignment
    and postfix is performed after an assignment.

3.7   Exercises (Items Marked with an * Have Solutions in Appendix D)

1. Indicate whether the following statements are syntactically correct or incorrect.
   If incorrect, indicate what is wrong with the statement:

   *A.   `inc eax,1`   B.   `add ebx,ecx`   *C.   `add dog,cat`
    B.   `idiv 3`   *E.   `sub 2,number`   F.   `imul eax`

2. Convert the following C arithmetic statements to the equivalent Intel assembly
   language statements (hint: as discussed in the text, do not forget to move any
   immediate values into a register first for the `imul` and `idiv` instructions, if
   necessary):

   *A.   `product = 3 * number;`
    B.   `result = number % amount;`
   *C.   `answer = number / 2;`
    D.   `difference = 4 - number;`

3. Using order of operations from C, convert the following arithmetic statements
   into the equivalent assembly language statements. Be sure not to destroy the
   contents of any of the variables that appear only to the right of the assignment
   symbol, unless ++ or −− is used.

```
*A.   x = x * y + z * 2;
 B.   a = b - c / 3;
*C.   total = num1 / num2 - (num3 * num4);
 D.   r = -s + t++;
 E.   m = n * ((i - j) * k);
 F.   q = a - b + c / d * e;
```

4. Using the order of operations from C, convert the following arithmetic statements into the equivalent assembly language code segment. Be careful to
   implement the unary minus sign, increment, and decrement operators carefully:

```
*A.   --i;
 B.   j = ++k - m;
*C.   z = -(x + y);
 D.   a = ++b - c++;
 E.   x = -y + z--;
```

5. Write a complete assembly language program to implement the following C
   program:

```
#include <stdio.h>
int main(){
    int number;
    printf("\n%s","Enter an integer: ");
    scanf("%d",&number);
    number=7-number*3;
    printf("\n%s%d\n\n","The integer is: ",number);
    return 0;
}
```

6. Given Ohm's law from the complete program at the end of this chapter and
   Watt's law as $W = IE$, where W stands for the number of watts, write a complete
   assembly language program to prompt for and input the number amperes and
   ohms, and then calculate both the number of volts and number of watts. The
   form of the input and output can be found below, and as always be careful with
   the vertical and horizontal spacings:

Input and Output

```
Enter the number of amperes: 5
Enter the number of ohms: 4

The number of volts is: 20
The number of watts is: 100
```

7. Write a complete assembly language program to prompt for and input the temperature in degrees Fahrenheit, calculate the degrees in Celsius, and then output the degrees in Celsius. The equation to be used is $C = (F - 32)/9 * 5$, where C stands for Celsius and F stands for Fahrenheit. Note that the answer will be off slightly due to using integers and be very careful to use the proper order of operations. The form of the input and output can be found below. Be sure to use proper vertical and horizontal spacings:

Input and Output

```
Enter the degrees in Fahrenheit: 100
The degrees in Celsius is: 35
```

Selection Structures

4

4.1 Introduction

As one should have learned in Computer Science I, there are two basic types of control structures available regardless of the language used. These two types of control structures are selection structures and iteration structures, also commonly known as ifs and loops.

At a lower level, all control structures can be created using if and branch statements. There are two types of branch statements known as conditional and unconditional branches, where the former branches only under certain conditions (such as if equal to 0) and the latter branches unconditionally, regardless of the conditions. The unconditional branch or goto is often avoided in high-level languages, but in low-level languages the unconditional branch or goto statement can hardly be avoided, since it is the use of the goto statement that allows all the other high-level control structures to be created via a compiler or an interpreter. As a result, most assembly languages often use the equivalent of a goto statement in their programs.

MASM, however, is relatively unique in that it allows the programmer to use the equivalent of high-level control structures with 32-bit integers and 8-bit characters. Although this somewhat negates the reason why one might use an assembly language, it does provide a nice segue from high-level languages to low-level languages and provides an opportunity to see how high-level language control structures can be implemented in a low-level language. After examining the high-level control structures in a low-level language, the corresponding low-level implementation of the structure will also be examined.

Note that although floating-point numbers can be used within the body of high-level control structures, they cannot be used to control the high-level structures. Also, high-level control structures cannot be used in 64-bit mode. However, after reading this and the next chapter, both of the above can be implemented using low-level structures and further discussion can be found in Chaps. 10 and 11, respectively.

© Springer Nature Switzerland AG 2020
J. T. Streib, *Guide to Assembly Language*, Undergraduate Topics
in Computer Science, https://doi.org/10.1007/978-3-030-35639-2_4

Continuing, of the selection structures, the most common are the if-then and if-then-else structures. These structures can also be nested to form the if-then-else-if and if-then-if structures, where the former is probably the more commonly used of the two. Lastly, there is what is known as the case structure, also known as the switch statement in C, C++, and Java. Although a high-level version of this is not available in MASM, it can be constructed fairly simply out of conditional and unconditional branches. The longest of the following sections is the first one on the if-then structure, because once all of the details are covered there, the others are essentially variations on theme.

4.2   If-Then Structure

The common if-then structure has the following form in C, where if there is only one statement in the then section, the use of the opening and closing braces { } is optional. However, should more than one statement be used in the then section of the if structure, the use of the braces is required as shown on the right:

```
if (number == 0)      if (amount != 1) {
    number--;             count++;
                          amount = amount + 2;
                      }
```

Assuming number is declared as an sdword, the corresponding MASM code for each of the above is shown below:

```
.if number == 0       .if amount != 1
dec number            inc count
.endif                add amount,2
                      .endif
```

First, notice that there is a decimal point prior to the words if and endif which indicates that these words are not actual executable instructions but rather directives that tell the assembler to insert the necessary code to implement the directives, not unlike the .data and .code directives encountered previously in Chap. 1. Also note that there are no parentheses around the relationals as in C, but rather they are optional in MASM, where any of the relationals available in C are available in MASM as well. Also, the use of the directive .endif is required, whether there are many instructions in the then section or just one instruction. By now the implementation of the arithmetic statements introduced in Chap. 3 should be starting to become familiar, and given an understanding of if statements in languages such as C, the above should look fairly straightforward.

However, there are some additional capabilities in MASM, as well as some limitations. With respect to additional capabilities, instead of just comparing a variable to a literal as shown above, a register can be compared to a literal and two registers can be compared. However a limitation in these two later instances is that the assembler assumes by default for the purpose of comparison that the values are unsigned, which can lead to some logic errors. In these two cases, be sure to compare only non-negative numbers or should negative numbers need to be compared, be sure one of the two values being compared is declared in a variable as an sdword. With respect to another limitation, what if one wants to compare two memory locations as follows in C?

```
if (count > number)
    flag = -1;
```

As might be suspected, given the mov instruction in Chap. 1, two memory locations cannot be compared in the .if directive. The reason why the memory to memory comparison cannot be performed is due to the compare instruction (cmp) generated by the .if directive. Like the mov instruction, the cmp instruction cannot have both operands reference memory locations. As will be seen in the discussion of the cmp instruction, the contents of one of the two variables need to be copied into a register and then a comparison between the register and the other variable can be performed as illustrated below:

```
mov eax,count
.if eax > number
mov flag,-1
.endif
```

Although the above is a mild inconvenience, the use of MASM directives makes the implementation of the if-then structure fairly easy. But if MASM did not have high-level directives, how could the if-then structure be implemented? One might say that since MASM has high-level directives, why should this be a concern? However, not all low-level languages have high-level structures nor for example, can high-level directives be used in 64-bit mode. So, knowledge of how high-level structures are implemented can be very useful. It is also helpful in understanding how high-level control structures, whether in a high-level or a low-level language, are ultimately implemented in a low-level language.

As discussed in Chap. 1, a programmer has direct access to the four general purpose registers. Although there are other registers that a programmer cannot directly access, they can often be accessed indirectly. One of the most important of these registers is the eflags register that controls various aspects of the CPU and contains the status of the CPU at any particular time. As various instructions execute, they set various 1-bit and 2-bit flags within the eflags register. Instead of having to use logic instructions to access the individual bits as is done in many other processors, each flag is given an individual two-letter abbreviation and some of these flags can be accessed in high-level control structures using a high-level operator as will be discussed later in this chapter. As seen in Table 4.1, the direction flag does not contain a high-level operator because it is a control flag and there are specific instructions to manipulate it as will be seen in Chap. 9. In addition to the

Table 4.1 Commonly used flags

Flag	Abbreviation	High-level operator	Bit position	Indication when set to 1
Carry	CF	CARRY?	0	A carry out of an unsigned integer
Parity	PF	PARITY?	2	An even number of set bits
Zero	ZF	ZERO?	6	The result of an operation is zero
Sign	SF	SIGN?	7	The result is negative
Direction	DF		10	Process strings from high to low
Overflow	OF	OVERFLOW?	11	Overflow of a signed integer

direction flag, Table 4.1 indicates some of the more common flags used by assembly language programmers.

Two of the most important flags for the discussion here indicate whether the result of the last instruction executed was zero, negative, or positive. If the result was zero, the zero flag (ZF) would be set to 1 and the sign flag (SF) would be set to 0. At first the setting of the zero flag to 1 might seem counter-intuitive, but if 1 is thought of as representing true, it makes more sense. Continuing, if the result was negative, then SF would be set to 1 and ZF would be set to 0. Lastly, if the result was positive, then both ZF and SF would be set to 0, as can be seen in Table 4.2.

One convenient way to alter these flags is by using the cmp instruction which compares the two operands and sets the flags accordingly. The comparison is accomplished by the CPU performing an implied subtraction between the two operands and then setting the corresponding flags accordingly, where an implied subtraction means that neither of the operands is altered in the operation. For example, if the first and second operands are equal, then a subtraction would result in a value of 0, or should the first operand be greater than the second, then the result of the subtraction would be positive. The format of the cmp instruction is given in Table 4.3.

Table 4.2 ZF and SF flags

Result	ZF	SF
Zero	1	0
Negative	0	1
Positive	0	0

Table 4.3 Cmp instruction

Instruction	Meaning
cmp reg,imm	compare a register to an immediate value
cmp imm,reg	compare an immediate value to a register
cmp reg,mem	compare a register to memory
cmp mem,reg	compare memory to a register
cmp mem,imm	compare memory to an immediate value
cmp imm,mem	compare an immediate value to memory
cmp reg,reg	compare a register to a register

Table 4.4 Je and jne instructions

Instruction	Meaning
je	Jump equal
jne	Jump not equal

Table 4.5 Signed conditional jump instructions

Instruction	Meaning	Instruction	Meaning
jg	Jump greater than	jnle	Jump not less than or equal to
jge	Jump greater than or equal to	jnl	Jump not less than
jl	Jump less than	jnge	Jump not greater than or equal to
jle	Jump less than or equal to	jng	Jump not greater than

As can be seen in Table 4.3 and as mentioned previously, one can compare a register to an immediate value, a register to memory, an immediate value to memory, or compare two registers, but one cannot compare two memory locations. Once two operands have been compared, the corresponding flags will be set and then one can branch or jump based on the flags, where two of the conditional jump instructions are as shown in Table 4.4.

The je and jne instructions can be used with either signed or unsigned data. The conditional jump instructions for signed numeric data are listed in Table 4.5.

Notice in Table 4.5 that the instructions on the same line in the columns on the right are equivalent to the instructions on the left. Although the instructions on the right are equivalent, the use of the word "not" can sometimes be confusing and as a result, these instructions are not used as much as their counterparts on the left. To help illustrate how the above instructions can be used to implement if-then structures, consider a previously introduced example:

```
.if number == 0
dec number
.endif
```

The decrementing of number occurs when it is equal to 0; otherwise number remains unchanged. As mentioned previously, in order to implement the .if directive, one needs to use the cmp instruction along with one of the conditional jump instructions listed above. However, there is one small complication: When the condition in an if statement is true in a high-level implementation, the code immediately below the if in the then section is executed; otherwise the flow of control branches to the code following the then section. Unfortunately, the jump statements mentioned above branch when the result is true and do not fall through to the code immediately below, but rather jump or branch around the code.

There are a couple of ways to resolve this problem, but the easiest is to just reverse the relationship. The result is that the code above could be implemented as shown below, where first the comparison is done between number and 0. If the two are not equal, a jump not equal (jne) occurs to the endif01 label, but should the two be equal, the flow of control falls through to the decrement statement immediately below, which was the original intent:

```
                ; if number == 0
    if01:       cmp number,0        ; compare number and zero
                jne endif01         ; jump not equal to endif01
    then01:     dec number          ; decrement number by one
    endif01:    nop                 ; end if, no operation
```

A few other remarks are necessary concerning the above code segment. First, since the jump is opposite of the equivalent high-level statement, a good high-level comment prior to the assembly code is always helpful. Second, the label endif01 is used instead of just endif to help distinguish it from other subsequently numbered endifs that can appear in the program. Also, the label if01 is used instead of just if1, because if1 is used for a process known as conditional assembly as discussed in Chap. 7. The nop statement takes up 1 byte of memory, means "no operation," and is a statement that does nothing. At first this might sound unusual, but it is sometimes useful to place a label on a nop instruction. In the case above, the nop could be omitted and the opcode area left blank. However, for beginning assembly language programmers, it is often a good idea to include it to make it easier to add statements before or after the nop. The if01: and the then01: labels are optional, since there are no jumps to them, but they help to indicate the beginning and middle of the if-then structure and including them is highly recommended. Lastly, notice that the labels end in a colon, as with the if01: label, where should the colon is omitted, a syntax error will occur.

If one expanded the .if directive of the previous code segment to see what the underlying code would look like, one would see very similar results using cmp and jne instructions. This can be accomplished by following the directions Appendix A.4, reassembling the program, and then opening the .lst fie.

The first thing one would notice is the use of @C0001 as a label generated by the assembler. For each label generated by the assembler the number is incremented so that the next label would be @C0002. The use of the @ symbol at the beginning of the label is to make it less likely that there would be a duplicate label error with a label created by a programmer. This is one of the reasons why it was suggested in Chap. 1 that programmers should avoid the use of the @ symbol when creating label names. The other thing one should notice is that a nop statement is not included at the bottom of the code segment. As mentioned previously, although nop statements are optional, they will be included in the programmer-generated code in this text to help readability and they can always be removed later if memory and speed were a concern:

```
    .           cmp number,000h
                jne @C0001
                dec number
    @C0001:
```

For further practice, how would the following previously introduced segment be implemented without using the .if directive?

```
mov eax,count
.if eax > number
mov flag,-1
.endif
```

At first, it might be tempting to implement it with a jump less than (jl) instruction, but be careful. What is the opposite of greater than? It is not less than, but rather it is less than or equal to, which is one of the more common mistakes that are made by beginning assembly language programmers when trying to write low-level implementations. This would also be a difficult logic error to debug, because until there was an instance where the two operands are equal, the code would work correctly. The following is the correct implementation:

```
                ; if count > number
if02:           mov eax,count
                cmp eax,number
                jle endif02
then02:         mov flag,-1
endif02:        nop
```

4.3   If-Then-Else Structure

Given the above, it is relatively easy to extend the implementation of if-then structure to the if-then-else structure. For example, the following C code on the left would be implemented using the .else directive as shown on the right:

```
if x >= y          ; if x >= y
    x--;           mov eax,x
else               .if eax >= y
    y--;           dec x
                   .else
                   dec y
                   .endif
```

Further, it can be implemented without the use of directives by using compares, jumps, and labels. The first part of the implementation is just like a simple if-then, but instead of branching to the endif03 label, control is transferred to an else03 label as follows:

```
                    ;if x >= y
if03:               mov eax,x
                    cmp eax,y
                    jl else03
then03:             dec x
                    jmp endif03
else03:             dec y
endif03:            nop
```

The most important thing about the above implementation is that one must not forget to include the unconditional jump (jmp) at the end of the then section, otherwise the flow of control will fall through into the else section, which would not correctly implement the if-then-else structure. An unconditional jump means that it will jump regardless of the conditions, or in other words, it will jump no matter how the flags in the eflags register are set. Also, since the unconditional jump instruction can branch to anywhere in the program, extra care must be taken to insure that it branches only to the end of the if-then-else structure, otherwise the program will be unstructured and difficult to subsequently modify.

4.4   Nested If Structures

Just as one can nest if structures in a high-level language, the same can be done in a low-level language. This is especially easy with the use of high-level directives in MASM. For example, the following C code segment on the left can be implemented in MASM as shown on the right:

```
if (x < 50)               .if x < 50
     y++;                 inc y
else                      .else
   if (x <= 100)            .if x <=100
      y=0;                 mov y,0
   else                    .else
      y--;                 dec y
                          .endif
                          .endif
```

It should be noted that since there are two .if directives, then there also need to be two corresponding .endif directives. Should an .endif be omitted, a syntax error will occur, although there is an exception to this as will be shown later with the .elseif directive. The C code above can also be implemented without the use of the directives as shown in Fig. 4.1, where the entire nested if is contained within the else of the outer if.

Fig. 4.1 Nested
if-then-else-if structure

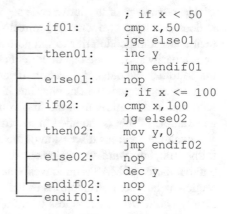

```
                                    ; if x < 50
        if01:          cmp x,50
                       jge else01
        then01:        inc y
                       jmp endif01
        else01:        nop
                                    ; if x <= 100
        if02:          cmp x,100
                       jg else02
        then02:        mov y,0
                       jmp endif02
        else02:        nop
                       dec y
        endif02:       nop
        endif01:       nop
```

   Note that each if-then-else has a complete set of labels so that there are two `if`,
`then`, `else`, and `endif` labels. Sometimes it is helpful to draw what are known
as scoping lines as shown in Fig. 4.1 to help insure that there is the correct number
of labels in the appropriate locations. It is possible to have the first `jge` jump
directly to the `if02` instead of the `else01` and also terminate both ifs with a
single `endif` label which would make the code a little shorter. As mentioned
before, it is usually better to include both the jump to `else01` label and the two
`endif` labels. This allows statements to be added both before and after the nested
if structure in the outer else section and makes it easy to modify the code at a later
date. An example of this is included in the complete program in Sect. 4.8.

   It might be argued further that the additional labels and `nop` instructions take up
extra memory, but as mentioned previously, the `nop` instructions could be removed
from the labels and memory would be saved. One could further ask, what about the
labels? In response, it should be pointed out that although labels need to be
accounted for by the assembler in what is known as a symbol table during the
assembly process, the labels do not take up any extra memory in the corresponding
machine language and it does not hurt to leave them in the program.

   Although C, C++, and Java do not have what is known as an `elseif` statement,
MASM does have an `.elseif` directive. This can simplify the previous assembly
code that contains the MASM directives and the code could be rewritten as follows:

```
.if (x < 50)
inc y
.elseif (x <=100)
mov y,0
.else
dec y
.endif
```

The advantage of the above code segment is that it is a little less cluttered in that it does not have two .endif directives. The disadvantage is that it does not facilitate adding code prior to the nested if structure in the outer else section, nor does it easily allow code that does not belong in the inner else section to be added at the bottom of the outer else section. If code is not going to be modified in the future, then the above code works fine, but if there is a good chance that code will be modified in the future, then the first example is probably the better choice. Again, an example of this is included in the complete program in Sect. 4.8.

Given the previous discussion of the nested if-then-else-if structure, it should be fairly straightforward to implement the nested if-then-if structure both with and without the use of MASM directives, where the nested if structure could be in the then section of the outer if structure instead of the else section. Instead of having the first if simply check whether x is less than 50, it should check for the equivalent of two possibilities. The first if structure would now check whether x is less than or equal to 100 and then subsequently check with another if structure whether x is less than 50:

```
if (x <= 100)          .if x <= 100
    if (x < 50)        .if x < 50
        y++;           inc y
    else                .else
        y = 0;         mov y,0
else                   .endif
    y--;               .else
                       dec y
                       .endif
```

Note that in the assembly code to the right it is necessary to include the .endif to terminate the nested if within the then portion of the outer if structure. The above assembly code can also be implemented without the use of high-level directives using only compare and jump statements as shown in Fig. 4.2.

Fig. 4.2 If-then-if structure
with double jump

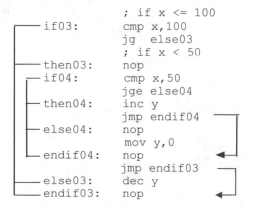

```
                          ; if x <= 100
        if03:             cmp  x,100
                          jg   else03
                          ; if x < 50
        then03:           nop
        if04:             cmp  x,50
                          jge  else04
        then04:           inc  y
                          jmp  endif04
        else04:           nop
                          mov  y,0
        endif04:          nop
                          jmp  endif03
        else03:           dec  y
        endif03:          nop
```

As always, one needs to be careful with the conditional jump statements to be sure that they are actually implementing the opposite relation to help avoid logic errors. Likewise, one needs to be sure not to forget to include the unconditional jump statements in the necessary locations and jump to the appropriate places. Again, the use of scoping lines makes it easier to insure that appropriate labels have not been forgotten.

As before, the code segment could be modified to avoid the possibility of a double jump from the end of the then04 section to the endif04 label and again from just after the endif04 label to the endif03 label as illustrated by the arrows on the right in Fig. 4.2. However, again that would make the code less modifiable should code need to be added at the end of the outer if structure's then section. For example, what if one wanted to add an instruction such as mov x, 0 after the endif04 label in the original code in Fig. 4.2? The answer is that x would be set to 0 whenever x is 100 or less. However, what would happen if the jump to endif04 were modified to jump directly to endif03 label as illustrated in Fig. 4.3?

The result would be that x would not be set to 0 when x is less than 50 as was originally intended. As the code in Fig. 4.3 illustrates, it is usually best not to modify the code to avoid what appear to be unnecessary jumps. For the beginning assembly language programmer, doing so can result in rather messy logic errors that are difficult to debug and probably should not be done unless execution efficiency is of critical importance.

With respect to nested if statements, given the choice between if-then-else-if and if-then-if structures, the if-then-else-if is probably the more common of the two since it more closely mimics the way one normally states a problem in natural languages. However, on occasion, some logic can be implemented more simply as a

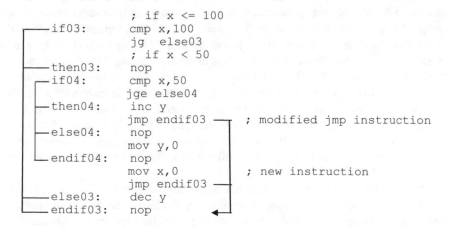

Fig. 4.3 If-then-if structure with inadvisable jump

nested if-then-if structure or it is possible that previously written code might have been implemented using this structure, so it does not hurt to have knowledge of the if-then-if structure as part of one's repertoire.

4.5 Case Structure

As mentioned previously, a case structure directive (known as the `switch` statement in C) does not exist in MASM. When a case structure is unavailable, a nested if structure can always be used instead. However, should there be too many nested `if` statements in a program, the resulting code can be difficult to read and maintain, thus the reason why many languages include a case structure. Even though MASM does not have a case structure directive, one can be created using a combination of conditional and unconditional jumps. Consider the following C `switch` statement:

```
switch (w) {
  case 1: x++;
             break;
  case 2:
  case 3: y++;
             break;
 default: z++;
}
```

The above switch structure can be implemented as a series of `cmp` and `je` instructions. When the variable in question is equal to the various constants, control is transferred to the corresponding particular case. The default case can be implemented simply as an unconditional jump. Just as a `break` statement is usually entered at the end of each particular case in C, an unconditional jump needs to be included in assembly language as well to cause the flow of control to be transferred to the end of the case structure. Also, just as the last `case` or `default` does not need a `break` statement in C, neither does assembly language need an unconditional jump, because the flow of control will merely fall through to the next statement. Unlike the `break` statement in C, where control is only transferred to the end of the `switch` statement, the `jmp` instruction can transfer control to anywhere in the program, so care should be taken by the programmer to only transfer control to the end of the `switch` statement. Otherwise unstructured code can be created that can become very difficult to modify or debug, especially in assembly language.

The assembly language code segment below implements the C code segment above, and continues to use unique numbers in the labels, so as not to cause a syntax error should more than one switch structure be used in a program. For example, the label `case12` indicates that it is the second case in the first switch structure. Other labeling schemes can be used at the discretion of the instructor or the programmer:

```
switch01:        cmp w,1
                 je case11;
                 cmp w,2
                 je case12
                 cmp w,3
                 je case12
                 jmp default01
case11:          inc x
                 jmp endswitch01
case12:          inc y
                 jmp endswitch01
default01:       inc z
endswitch01:     nop
```

Granted, a `switch` statement in a C program can sometimes provide cleaner code compared to a series of nested `if` statements. However, given all the jump statements in the low-level implementation in an assembly program, it is a matter of taste as to whether the above implementation is better than a series of nested `.if` directives. Should the `if` statements be implemented without the directives, the above case structure would probably be easier to read and modify, but with the availability of the `.if` directive, the above case structure might be more complicated. Regardless, knowledge of how a case structure is implemented is useful, especially if one uses a low-level language that does not have any high-level control structures.

4.6 Characters and Logical Operations

Just as it is possible to compare individual characters in high-level languages like C, it is also possible to do the same in assembly language using high-level directives. Assuming that the variable `initial` is declared as type `char` in the C code on the left below, it can be implemented in assembly language as shown on the right, assuming that `initial` is declared as a `byte`:

```
if (initial < 'e')        .if initial < 'e'
    count++;              inc count
                          .endif
```

Table 4.6 Unsigned conditional jump instructions

Instruction	Meaning	Instruction	Meaning
ja	Jump above	jnbe	Jump not below or equal to
jae	Jump above or equal to	jnb	Jump not below
jb	Jump below	jnae	Jump not above or equal to
jbe	Jump below or equal to	jna	Jump not above

It is also possible to implement the above without using high-level directives by using a compare and appropriate jump instruction. It might be possible to use the previously introduced signed conditional jumps for character data (see Table 4.5), since many characters (such as the letters of the alphabet) contain a 0 in the sign bit and do not risk the possibility of being considered as smaller values. For example, the character 'a', which is a binary 01000001, is less than the character 'b', which is a binary 01000010. However, what if one is comparing one of the extended ASCII characters that use the sign bit such as 'ä' which is a binary 10000100 (see Appendix B) to an 'a' which is a binary 01000001? The result is that the 'ä' would be considered smaller than the 'a', which is not true. This would result in a logic error and might be difficult to debug. Given the old adage "use the right tool for the job," it is good programming practice to use instructions that were designed for the particular circumstances under consideration. In addition, it again provides some self-documenting code to use unsigned jump instruction to indicate that it is unsigned data that is being compared. The corresponding unsigned jump instructions are given in Table 4.6.

Note that je and jne are not included in Table 4.6. As mentioned previously, they can be used with either signed or unsigned data, because when two things are equal, it does not matter whether they are signed or unsigned. As before, the instructions in the right column of Table 4.6 are equivalent to the instructions in the left column. Again, the use of a "not" in an instruction can be confusing, so the instructions on the left are generally preferred over the instructions on the right.

Given the above and similar to past examples, the assembly code at the beginning of this section can be implemented without high-level directives as

```
                    if initial < 'e'
    if01:           cmp initial,'e'
                    jae endif01
                    inc count
    endif01:        nop
```

Turning to high-level logical operators, how might they be implemented in assembly language? The simplest of these is the "not" operator (!). Returning to the use of integers for the sake of convenience, the following C code segment on

the left can be easily implemented in assembly language using high-level directives
as shown on the right:

```
if (!(x == 1))            .if !(x == 1)
    y++;                  inc y
                          .endif
```

Given the code above, how can this be implemented without using high-level
directives? Although the "not" operator is the simplest of the logical operators, it
sometimes can cause the largest number of errors in logic. The simplest way to
avoid any problems is try to avoid the use of the "not" in the first place. However,
there are times that the use of the "not" cannot be avoided, so the easiest way is to
try to simplify the code as much as possible to minimize many of the potential
pitfalls. In this case the solution is simple, because the previous code !(x==1)
could be implemented as x!=1. It can then easily be rewritten at the assembly level
without using high-level directives:

```
                    ; if !(x == 1)
    if02:           cmp x,1
                    je endif02
    then02:         inc y
    endif02:        nop
```

What about an expression that contains the logical "or" operator (||)? Given the
C code on the left below, it could be implemented as one might suspect in assembly
language to the right:

```
if(x==1 || y==2)          .if x==1 || y==2
    z++;                  inc z
                          .endif
```

Again, how would this be implemented without the use of MASM directives? In
order to implement the logical "or" operator, two compare instructions would need
to be used. At first, one might be tempted to reverse the jump statement immediately after the first compare as was discussed previously. However, if one thinks
about it for a few minutes, is there any need to check the second conditional if the
first cmp is true? It should be obvious that there is no need to fall through and check
the second conditional, since in a logical "or" statement, only one of the relationals
needs to be true. The result is that the first jump needs to branch around the second
compare and go straight to the then section. As should be recalled from Introduction
to Computer Science, this is known as "short circuit," where if the first part of the
logical "or" is true, the second part need not be tested. In the second compare, the
jump is the same as in a simple if-then structure discussed previously in Sect. 4.2,
where the conditional jump is reversed.

```
                    ; if x==1 or y==2
if03:               cmp x,1
                    je then03
                    cmp y,2
                    jne endif03
then03:             inc z
endif03:            nop
```

How then would the logical "and" operator (&&) in C be implemented? Remember that with a logical "and", both conditionals must be true. Given the C code on the left and the assembly language using high-level directives on the right, how would they be implemented in assembly language without using high-level directives?

```
if (x==1 && y==2)        .if x==1 && y==2
   z++;                  inc z
                         .endif
```

Using analysis similar to that demonstrated in the previous example, the correct use of jump statements can be determined. In this case, one cannot jump around the second condition because with an "and" operation, both conditions must be true before the whole expression can be considered to be true. However, if the first one is false, then there is no need to compare the second relational and the jump can be to the end of the if structure:

```
                    ; if x==1 and y==2
if04:               cmp x,1
                    jne endif04
                    cmp y,2
                    jne endif04
then04:             inc z
endif04:            nop
```

In more complicated examples, the rules of precedence for logical operators should be remembered. First, similar to the unary arithmetic minus sign, the logical unary "not" operation (!) has the highest precedence. Next, the "and" operator (&&) has higher precedence over the "or" operator (||). A helpful way to remember this is to know that an "and" operation is sometimes called logical multiplication and an "or" operation is sometimes called logical addition, where similar to arithmetic, logical multiplication has a higher precedence over logical addition. As with arithmetic, parentheses can always be used to override these rules of precedence where the most nested parentheses are evaluated first. Lastly in the case of a tie between operations, the order is from left to right. Given this information, how would the following logical expressions in the C and assembly language code segments be implemented in assembly language without using high-level directives?

```
if (w==1 || x==2 && y==3)    .if w==1 || x==2 && y==3
    z++;                         inc z
                                 .endif
```

Remember that the && has precedence over the ||, so the && should be handled first. One might think at this point in time that it really does not matter whether the w==1 is handled first or the (x ==2 && y==3) is handled first. Although this might be true under some circumstances, it might not be what the writer of the original C code intended. For example, what if w is undefined when x==2 && y==3 is true? Then obviously the w==1 should not be checked first and there might be a logic error. The result is that it is usually best to do a direct translation of the code as written to avoid any possible unforeseen circumstances which might cause subsequent errors:

```
            ; if w == 1 || x==2 && y == 3
if05:       cmp x,2
            jne or05
            cmp y,3
            je then05
or05:       cmp w,1
            jne endif05
then05:     inc z
endif05:    nop
```

Notice that if x does not equal 2, then the && will be false, but that does not mean that the entire logical expression is false. So if the && operation is false, then the w==1 must be checked indicated by the code at the or05 label. If x==2 is true, it is necessary to check to see if the y==3 is true and if so, then the rest of the || can be short circuited. However, if it is false, then the && expression is false, and as before, the w==1 needs to be checked.

What would happen if parentheses were added around the w == 1 || x == 2 in the segments above? How could it be implemented in assembly language without using high-level directives? Again using the techniques presented in this section, the problem can carefully be solved and this is left as an exercise at the end of the chapter.

In previous classes, the reader may or may not have heard of De Morgan's rules. These rules allow the distribution of a "not" over an "and" or an "or", provided the "and" is changed to an "or" and conversely an "or" is changed to an "and" as shown in Table 4.7.

For example given the following C program on the left and assembly language program on the right, it might be difficult to implement the equivalent code in assembly language without using high-level directives:

Table 4.7 De Morgan's rules	not (x and y)	=	not x or not y
	not (x or y)	=	not x and not y

```
if (!(x==1 || y==1))          .if !(x==1 || y==1)
    z++;                       inc z
                              .endif
```

This is where De Morgan's rules come in handy, where each of the above can be rewritten as follows:

```
if (!(x==1) && !(y==1))       .if !(x==1) && !(y==1)
    z++;                      inc z
                              .endif
```

Note that each of the "not" operators (!) has been distributed over the two checks for equality and that the "or" operator (||) has been changed to an "and" operator (&&). To help further convert the above code to assembly language without directives, the !(x==1) and the !(y==1) above have been changed to x! = 1 and y! = 1 below, respectively:

```
if (x!=1 && y!=1)        .if x!=1 && y!=1
    z++;                 inc z
                         .endif
```

Now the code can be converted easily to assembly language without using high-level directives, where the relations are reversed and only when both variables are not equal to 1 does the flow of control fall through to the then06 label of the if structure as shown below:

```
if06:         cmp x,1
              je endif06
              cmp y,1
              je endif06
then06:       inc z
endif06:      nop
```

4.7 Arithmetic Expressions in High-Level Directives

When programming in C and C++ it is possible to not use a relational in an if statement, whereas in Java this is not possible. As might already be known, the reason for this is that in C and C++, the result of an expression is not true or false, as it is in Java, but rather the result is non-zero or zero. This means that if the result is zero, it is treated as though it is false and the then portion of the `if` is not executed, but if the result is anything but zero (positive or negative), then the result is considered to be true and the subsequent then portion of the `if` is executed. Given this, a statement such as the following is possible:

```
if (x-1)
    y++;
```

Notice that there is no equality symbol (==) in the expression. When x is equal to 1, then x-1 would be equal to 0 which is considered to be false and the then portion of the if statement is *not* executed. In any other case the result is non-zero which is considered as true and the then portion of the if would be executed. For example, if x is equal to 0, the result would be that x-1 is equal to -1 which is considered true and the then portion would be executed. Of course the above code could have been written as `if (x != 1)` and this code is much more straightforward. Although this is the preferred method of this text, one might run into code written using only arithmetic statements, so it does not hurt to understand how it might be implemented.

At first, one might be tempted to write the above code segment in assembly language using directives as follows:

```
; *** Caution: Incorrectly implemented code ***
.if x-1
inc y
.endif
```

However, the above code does not implement the same thing as the C code shown previously. Instead, if one looks at the code generated by the assembler in the .lst file, one would see something similar to the following:

```
            cmp x-001h,000h
            je @C0001
            inc y
@C0001:
```

Although it appears that a 1 is being subtracted from the variable x in the compare statement, in fact it is not being subtracted from the contents of the variable x at all, but rather a 1 is being subtracted from the address of the variable x for the purpose of the comparison. As will be discussed in Chap. 8, it is possible to access other variables by way of a positive or a negative offset using an addition or a subtraction symbol. For example, assume the following variables are declared:

```
w       byte 0
x       sdword 0
y       sdword 0
```

In the original C code segment, when x is 0, the intent was that x-1 would result in -1, which is non-zero, and y would be incremented. However, in the generated assembly language code segment, x-1 refers to the byte above x, which is the variable w that contains a 0. Since w is equal to 0, the flow of control branches around the then section and does not increment y. This was not the original intent and it might be a difficult logic error to uncover. The result is that unless accessing an element of an array or a string, arithmetic statements should generally not be used in high-level directives. Further, when writing questionable code, it does not hurt to examine the .lst file to insure that the instructions generated are correct.

Although all of the past examples that have been written without high-level directives in assembly language have been implemented utilizing a cmp instruction, it is not always necessary to do so and a statement like if(x-1) above is a good example. As discussed in Sect. 4.1, the cmp instruction sets various flags in the eflags register and the same is true for arithmetic expressions. After a subtraction, an addition, an increment, or a decrement, the zero flag (ZF) and the sign flag (SF) are set accordingly. Should x be equal to 1, then x-1 is 0 and the zero flag would be set to 1. Further, if the result is positive or negative, the zero flag would be set to 0 and the sign flag would be set to 0 or 1, respectively.

There are two methods that can be used to solve this problem. The first uses high-level directives and the second uses conditional jump instructions. Recall from earlier in this chapter (Table 4.1) that there were high-level operators that returned the value of various flags. One of these was ZERO? that returns a 1 should the zero flag be set, and a 0 otherwise. Using this operator, the following code can be written:

```
mov eax, x
dec eax
.if(!ZERO?)
inc y
.endif
```

Note that the value in x is first moved into a register and then decremented. Since an assignment symbol (=) does not appear in the expression of the previous C code segment, the value of x was not and should not be altered. Should x be equal to a 0, then x-1 would be equal to -1. The result is that the zero flag would not be set, !ZERO? would be true, and y would be incremented.

In the second way to solve this problem, a new conditional jump instruction is needed. Listed in Table 4.8 are branch instructions that jump based on the contents of various flags in the eflags register. Note that the instructions on the left branch when the corresponding flag is set (true) and the instructions on the right branch when the corresponding flag is not set (false). The instructions that are of most interest here are the ones that are concerned with the zero flag and the sign flag.

Table 4.8 Jump instructions based on `eflags` register

Instruction	Description	Flag	Instruction	Description	Flag
jc	Jump if carry	CF = 1	jnc	Jump if not carry	CF = 0
jp	Jump if parity (even)	PF = 1	jnp	Jump if not parity	PF = 0
jz	Jump if zero	ZF = 1	jnz	Jump if not zero	ZF = 0
js	Jump if sign (neg)	SF = 1	jns	Jump if not sign	SF = 0
jo	Jump if overflow	OF = 1	jno	Jump if not overflow	OF = 0

Given the information in Table 4.8, the previous C code segment can be written in assembly language as follows:

```
if07:       mov eax,x
            dec eax
            jz endif07
then07:     inc y
endif07:    nop
```

Unlike using relationals, there is no reversing of the logic since when the result is not zero, the code falls through to the then section, otherwise when the result is zero, the jump is to the `endif07` label. As before, note that the value in x is first moved into a register and then decremented so that the value in x is not altered. Again, the preferred method of this text is the use of relationals, but when necessary, if statements can be implemented without them.

4.8 Complete Program: Using Selection Structures and I/O

It is now possible to start creating some more interesting programs using both selection structures and I/O. For example, suppose that one wanted to input a value representing an alternating current (AC) voltage, indicate whether the voltage was either too high, too low, or at an acceptable level, and then output an appropriate message according to Table 4.9.

Table 4.10 contains three samples of the prompt and messages needed in order from left to right. First, notice that there is a blank line after the prompt and input, but prior to the output. Also notice that the "Warning!" message appears on a separate line. In order to write the program, it should be obvious that a nested if-then-else-if structure would be the best choice. The question should then be which test should be done first. A good choice might be to go in the order as they

Table 4.9 Voltages and messages

Voltage	Message
109 and below	Warning! Voltage too low
110–120, inclusive	Voltage is acceptable
121 and above	Warning! Voltage too high

Table 4.10 Sample input/output

Sample I/O	Sample I/O	Sample I/O
Enter an AC voltage: 109	Enter an AC voltage: 110	Enter an AC voltage: 121
Warning! Voltage too low	Voltage is acceptable	Warning! Voltage too high

are presented in the table, starting with the low voltages. In terms of logic, this is the simplest order to implement. However, given that there is a separate output line for the "Warning!" message, it might be best to group these two together to make the I/O simpler. Although this would mean the use of logical operators, the I/O is sufficiently more complicated at this level and starting with the acceptable voltages first appears to be the better solution.

To help understand the logic and I/O better, it is probably best to show the solution in a C program first and then convert it to assembly language as has been done in the past:

```c
#include <stdio.h>
int main () {
   int voltage;
   printf("%s", "Enter an AC Voltage: ");
   scanf("%d", &voltage);
   if (voltage >= 110 && voltage <= 120)
      printf("\n%s\n", "Voltage is Acceptable");
   else {
      printf("\n%s\n","Warning!");
      if voltage < 110)
         printf("%s\n","Voltage too Low");
      else
         printf("%s\n","Voltage too High");
   }
   printf("\n");
   return 0;
}
```

Notice that there are two occurrences of \n in both the acceptable message and the warning message, where the one before the %s causes the blank line after the prompt and input. Also note that only two ifs are needed because if the voltage is not in the first two ranges, it must be in the third. Lastly, notice that the "Warning!" message appears prior to the nested if, thus avoiding having to output it in two different locations within the nested if statement. This is a very good example to illustrate why an elseif statement in any language is not always as effective. In this particular situation in assembly language, the .elseif directive would not allow the "Warning!" message to be placed between an .else and an .if directive and would result in code that would be more difficult to maintain. The code below illustrates the benefit of using separate directives. Of course the code below could be implemented without using directives and this is left as an exercise:

```
                    .686
                    .model flat,c
                    .stack 100h
scanf               PROTO arg2:Ptr Byte, inputlist:VARARG
printf              PROTO arg1:Ptr Byte, printlist:VARARG

                    .data
in1fmt              byte "%d",0
msg1fmt             byte "%s",0
msg2fmt             byte 0Ah,"%s",0Ah,0
msg4fmt             byte "%s",0Ah,0
msg6fmt             byte 0Ah,0
msg1                byte "Enter an AC voltage: ",0
msg2                byte "Voltage is Acceptable",0
msg3                byte "Warning!",0
msg4                byte "Voltage too Low",0
msg5                byte "Voltage too High",0
voltage             sdword ?

                    .code
main                proc
                    INVOKE printf, ADDR msg1fmt, ADDR msg1
                    INVOKE scanf, ADDR in1fmt, ADDR voltage
                    .if voltage >=110 && voltage <= 120
                    INVOKE printf, ADDR msg2fmt, ADDR msg2
                    .else
                    INVOKE printf, ADDR msg2fmt, ADDR msg3
                    .if voltage < 110
                    INVOKE printf, ADDR msg4fmt, ADDR msg4
                    .else
                    INVOKE printf, ADDR msg4fmt, ADDR msg5
                    .endif
                    .endif
                    INVOKE printf, ADDR msg6fmt
                    ret
main                endp
                    end
```

4.9   Summary

- If possible, avoid instructions that contain "nots" (for example, `jg` is preferred to `jnle`).
- When implementing if statements without high-level directives, the conditional jump often needs to be reversed to implement the if statement correctly.
- Nested if-then-else-if structures are usually preferred over if-then-if structures.
- MASM does not have a high-level case structure (`switch` statement), but one can be constructed using compare and jump statements.
- The complexity of creating a case structure without high-level directives needs to be compared to the simplicity of using nested high-level `.if` directives.
- When used properly, the `.elseif` directive can be helpful but can make it slightly more difficult to modify code segments in various situations.
- When not using high-level directives, use good label names to help readability.
- When comparing characters, use unsigned jumps instead of signed jumps (for example, use `ja` instead of `jg`).
- Remember that a logical "and" operation (`&&`) has precedence over a logical "or" operation (`| |`).
- Unless accessing an element of an array or a string, avoid using arithmetic expressions in high-level directives. Instead write the corresponding code using relationals.

4.10   Exercises (Items Marked with an * Have Solutions in Appendix D)

1. Indicate whether the following statements are syntactically correct or incorrect in MASM. If incorrect, indicate what is wrong with the statement:

   *A.   `.if (number = 0)`
                `add number,2`
                `.endif`

   B.   `.if count >= 0 then`
                `sub count,2`
                `.else`
                `add count,3`
                `.endif`

   *C.   `.if x-1`
                `dec x`
                `.endif`

   D.   `if01:`   `cmp x,y`
                        `jle endif01`
                        `then01: inc x`
           `endif01:`   `nop`

2. Using MASM directives, write an assembly language code segment to implement the following:

```
if ( a > b )
   a = a - 1;
else
   if ( b >= c )
       b = b - 2;
   else
      if ( c > d)
         c = c + d;
      else
         d = d / 2;
```

3. Convert the following C selection structures to the corresponding assembly language code segments. Do *not* use MASM directives, but rather only compares, jumps, and appropriate labels (hint: Problem B, use De Morgan's rules):

*A.   `if (w == 1 && x == 2)`
          `y-;`

B.   `if (!(num > 0 && num <= 3))`
          `count=count-2;`

*C.   `if ( ( w == 1 || x == 2 ) && y == 3)`
          `z++;`

D.   `if (a == 1 || b == 2 && c > 3 || d <= 4)`
          `e--;`

4. Given the example of the if-then-else-if structure in Problem 2 above, re-implement it using a nested if-then-if structure:

   A. Use MASM directives.
   B. Do not use MASM directives, but rather compares, jumps, and appropriate labels.

5. Implement the following C switch statement, which does not have a default statement, using compares, jumps, and appropriate labels. If number does not contain a 0 through 3, then the value of count should not change:

```
switch number {
   case 0:
   case 1: count = count +2;
           break;
   case 2:
   case 3: count = count - 2;
}
```

6. Implement the program in Sect. 4.8 in assembly language without using high-level directives with only compares, jumps, and appropriate labels.

Iteration Structures

5

As should be recalled from previous courses, there are many different types of iteration structures available to a programmer in a high-level programming language. Just as there are many structures in a high-level language, there are corresponding structures in assembly language, such as the pre-test, post-test, and fixed-iteration loop structures. Depending on the circumstances, one should use the best structure for the task at hand.

5.1 Pre-test Loop Structure

Probably the most versatile loop is the count-controlled pre-test while loop, where any number of tasks can be performed in the body of the loop. The basic structure of this loop can be found below in the C code segment:

```
i=1;
while(i<=3) {
    // body of loop
    i++;
}
```

The three parts of any loop are "initialization," "test," and "change." In the segment above, i is known as the loop control variable (LCV), where it is initialized to 1, it is then tested, and loops when i is less than or equal to 3, and it changes when it is incremented by 1. As with the if-then structure, MASM has directives that simplify the implementation of the while loop structure. The directives are the .while and .endw directives as shown below:

© Springer Nature Switzerland AG 2020
J. T. Streib, *Guide to Assembly Language*, Undergraduate Topics
in Computer Science, https://doi.org/10.1007/978-3-030-35639-2_5

```
mov i,1
.while i<=3
; body of loop
inc i
.endw
```

The `.while` directive has the same limitations as the `.if` directive, where a comparison cannot be made between two memory locations. Also, unless addressing elements of an array or a string, the use of arithmetic expressions should be avoided. Further, regardless of the number of statements in the body of the loop, the structure must end with the `.endw` directive. Lastly, a register could be used in place of the variable i to help increase speed, but as will be seen shortly, there is another loop that could be used if speed is a concern.

As with the if structure, the while structure can be implemented using a compare statement and the appropriate jump statements. As before, one must be sure to use the opposite jump from the relational. Also as with the if-then-else structure, one must be careful to include an extra unconditional jump, but in this case the jump is back to the beginning of the loop:

```
               mov i,1
               ; while i<=3
while01:       cmp i,3
               jg endw01
               ; body of loop
               inc i
               jmp while01
endw01:        nop
```

Keeping the label scheme used with the if structure, numbers are used to avoid multiple label names with the same name when more than one loop is used in a program. As mentioned above, notice the inclusion of the unconditional `jmp while01` at the bottom of the loop, because without it, the loop would execute the body of the loop only once.

As an example of how the while loop could be used, some very small microprocessors do not have a multiplication or a division instruction as part of their instruction sct. These processors are not designed to solve mathematical problems, but rather to control devices. Further, these types of processors have very little memory and are known as embedded systems. Although a processor might not have a multiplication instruction, it would have a way to perform iteration. If multiplication does need to be performed, one way is to implement it is as repetitive addition. For the sake of convenience, assume that multiplication can only be between non-negative numbers, similar to the `mul` instruction in the Intel processor:

```
ans=0;
i=1;
while(i <= y) {
    ans=ans+x;
    i++;
}
```

In the C code above, should y be 0, then the loop will never be executed and the ans will be equal to 0. However, if x is 0, then it is possible that the loop will iterate y times and redundantly add x to ans. How could this problem be solved? An if statement could be added as shown below:

```
ans=0;
if(x!=0) {
    i=1;
    while(i<=y) {
        ans=ans+x;
        i++;
    }
}
```

The above C code can be implemented in assembly language below illustrating the use of the .while directive and further illustrating the use of the .if directive:

```
mov ans,0          ; initialize ans to 0
.if x != 0
mov i,1            ; initialize i to 1
mov eax,y          ; load eax with y for while
.while i<=eax
mov eax,ans        ; load eax with ans
add eax,x          ; add eax to ans
mov ans,eax        ; store eax in ans
mov eax,y          ; reload eax with y for while
inc i              ; increment i by 1
.endw
.endif
```

Note in the .while directive, as with the .if directives in the previous chapter, one of the variables is moved into the eax register to be compared in the .while directive. Using eax might seem incorrect at first, since it is being used for addition in the body of the loop, but since ans is loaded into and subsequently stored back into ans, using eax is acceptable. Note that toward the bottom of the body of the loop, the value of y is copied back into eax for the subsequent times through the loop. Although another register could have been used, this method minimizes the number of registers used and on completion of the segment, all the values of the respective memory locations contain the same values as in the previous C code.

Alternatively, instead of using i as a loop control variable, a register could be used as shown below. Since ecx is known as the counter register, this would be a good choice and would cause the loop to execute quicker at the expense of using one more register to implement the code. If the variable i needs to contain the corresponding final value as it would in the previous C code, then the value in ecx can simply be moved into the variable i at the end of the segment as illustrated below. Provided one does not branch out of the middle of the loop, which would result in unstructured code and should be avoided, the code below would work and should be acceptable:

```
mov ans,0          ; initialize ans to 0
.if x!= 0
mov ecx,1          ; initialize ecx to 1
.while ecx<=y
mov eax,ans        ; load eax with ans
add eax,x          ; add x to ans
mov ans,eax        ; store eax in ans
inc ecx            ; increment ecx by one
.endw
mov i,ecx          ; store ecx in i
.endif
```

Although embedded processors might not have high-level directives, the solution to the problem is still the same and the above can be implemented with compares and jumps in their respective assembly languages. The result would be similar to implementing the code without directives in MASM, which is left as an exercise at the end of the chapter.

5.2 Post-test Loop Structures

The C programming language has a post-test loop structure called the do-while. The unique feature of post-test loops is that the body of the loop is executed at least one time, unlike the pre-test loop where the body of the loop might not be executed at all. It is because of this difference that the pre-test loop is sometimes used more often than the post-test loop, but the latter is helpful in various circumstances in some languages, such as filtering interactive input or reading files. In MASM, the post-test loop structure is implemented using the .repeat and .until directives. Given the following C do-while loop on the left, the corresponding assembly language appears on the right:

```
i=1;                          mov i,1
do {                          .repeat
    // body of loop           ; body of loop
    i++;                      inc i
} while (i<=3);               .until i>3
```

Note that instead of i<=3, the .until has i>3. This is not a mistake. Whereas the do-while continues to loop while i is less than or equal to 3 and falls through when i is equal to 4, the repeat-until loops until i is greater than 3, where it also falls through to the next instruction when i is equal to 4. This is similar to other languages such as Pascal and VBA (Visual Basic for Applications), where the latter has both do-while and repeat-until instructions. One just has to be careful to use the exact opposite relational and must not forget to consider the case where the values are equal, which could result in a subsequent logic error. The implementation of this loop without MASM high-level directives using compares, jumps, and labels is shown below. As before, the relation of the jump is reversed from the one in the .until directive above:

```
                 mov i,1
repeat01:        nop
                 ; body of loop
                 inc i
                 cmp i,3
                 jle repeat01
endrpt01:        nop
```

Implementing the multiplication of the previous section using .repeat - .until directives requires a little rethinking, since the body of a post-test loop structure is executed at least once. If the value of y is equal to 0, then the loop will execute once and the answer will be incorrect. As a result, there needs to be an if statement prior to either do-while in the C code on the left or the .repeat - .until directives in the assembly code on the right. The requirement that there often needs to be an if statement prior to a post-test loop is one of the reasons why these types of loops are not usually the first choice when solving many problems:

```
ans=0;                        mov ans,0
if (y!=0) {                   .if y!=0
    i=1;                      mov ecx,1
    do {                      .repeat
        ans=ans+x;            mov eax,ans
        i++;                  add eax,x
    } while (i<=y);           mov ans,eax
}                             inc ecx
                              .until ecx>y
                              mov i,ecx
                              .endif
```

However, if the value of x is checked to see if it is equal to 0 as done in the while loop in the previous section, then this is not much of an imposition, where the values of both x and y could be checked in the if statement using an "and" operation. As with the previous section, notice that the above code is implemented using the ecx register. The advantages and disadvantages of using ecx as a loop control variable will be made more apparent in the next section where it is not an option, but rather a requirement. Given that an if statement is often needed prior to the .repeat, the .while loop will tend to be used more often in this text.

5.3 Fixed-Iteration Loop Structures

As found in many high-level languages, there usually exists a fixed-iteration loop structure often called a for loop structure. Its primary advantage is that it is used when a loop needs to iterate only a fixed number of times. An example of such a loop is the for loop in C, where the braces are optional when there is only one statement:

```
for(i=1;i<=3;i++) {
    // body of loop
}
```

Typically most machine architectures have a specialized instruction to accomplish this task and it can often execute a little faster than the loops discussed in the previous two sections. In MASM, the directives that can be used for this task are the .repeat and .untilcxz directives. If one recalls when the general purpose registers were first introduced in Chap. 1, it was mentioned that the ecx register was sometimes used as a counter register. As with some other instructions, the .repeat and .untilcxz directives use the ecx register as a counter. Unlike using the separate compare and jump instructions in the previous two loop structures, the .untilcxz directive performs two tasks: it decrements the ecx register by 1 and then jumps to the .repeat directive when ecx is not equal to 0. In other words, it loops until the ecx register equals 0 (cxz). Unfortunately, unlike the for statement which is typically implemented as a pre-test loop, the .repeat and .untilcxz directives are implemented as a postfix loop structure, which means the body of the loop is executed at least once. However, if one is careful with the .repeat and .untilcxz directives, they can prove to be very useful. An understanding of how it works can be helpful later in Chap. 9 when learning how to manipulate strings. The above for loop can be implemented as follows:

```
mov ecx,3
.repeat
; body of the loop
.untilcxz
```

•

First, the ecx register is loaded with the number of times the body of the loop should be executed. Then, each time the .untilcxz directive is executed, the value of the ecx register is decremented by 1 and then compared to 0. If the value is not equal to 0, the loop repeats. When the value is 0, the flow of control is passed onto the instruction immediately following the .untilcxz directive.

One temptation that the beginning assembly language programmer has is to decrement the ecx register within the body of the loop. Just like with a for loop in many high-level languages, where the loop control variable should not be altered in the body of the loop, neither should the ecx variable be altered in the body of the .repeat - .untilcxz loop.

As with the other structures before, the .repeat and .untilcxz directives can be implemented using only assembly language instructions. In this case, it is the loop instruction which implements the .repeat and .untilcxz directives:

```
              mov ecx,3
for01:        nop
              ; body of the loop
              loop for01
endfor01:     nop
```

The loop instruction works the same as the .repeat and .untilcxz directives, where the ecx register is loaded with the number of times to iterate and the loop instruction then decrements the ecx register by 1, branches to the label indicated in the operand field when ecx is not equal to 0, and falls through otherwise.

With both the .repeat and .untilcxz directives and the loop instruction, one has to be careful that the ecx register does not contain a 0 or a negative number. If one takes a moment and thinks of how the loop instruction works, the potential problem should be apparent. If ecx is initially 0, then what is the first thing the loop instruction does? It decrements the ecx register by 1, thus causing ecx to be a negative one. Since it is not 0, it branches back to the beginning of the loop and the process continues. Would this be an infinite loop? No, because the loop instruction would continue to decrement ecx until it hits −2,147,483,648 and on the subsequent decrement, the negative number would turn to a positive 2,147,483,647 (see Appendix B). Eventually it would decrement that number back to 0. Although it would not be an infinite loop, it would loop over four billion times.

If the value is merely being assigned to ecx prior to the loop, this might not be as much of a problem. However, if, for example, the value of ecx is being input from a user, then the value ecx should be checked. An instruction that can help with this problem is the jecxz instruction that will jump to a label after the loop should the value of ecx be equal to 0. This is especially useful when using the loop instruction where labels are already being used. Although this works to prevent a situation where ecx might contain a 0, it does not check for negative values which can cause just as much havoc as a value of 0. If necessary, an if structure can be used to check for a non-positive value and the .if directive would work well when using the .repeat - .untilcxz directives. An example of each can be seen below, where the value of ecx is not assigned and it can be assumed to already have a value that needs to be checked:

```
                ; check for zero          ; check for non-positive
                jecxz endfor01            .if ecx >0
for01:          nop                       .repeat
                ; body of the loop        ; body of the loop
                loop    for01             .untilcxz
endfor01:       nop                       .endif
```

Another problem with this loop is that the .repeat directive can only be 128 bytes prior to the .untilcxz directive, or the label referenced in a loop instruction can also only be 128 bytes prior to the loop instruction. As will be discussed in Chap. 10, the instructions used in this text vary from 1 byte (such as the inc eax instruction) to 6 bytes (such as a mov ebx, amount instruction). Given that the loop instruction is 2 bytes long, there could be 126 one-byte instructions and in the worst case only 11 six-byte instructions could be in the body of a .repeat - .untilcxz loop. If the number of bytes is exceeded, the assembler will generate an error message indicating how many bytes the loop has exceeded this limit. Although this seems rather restrictive, in practice this does not occur too often, and if it does, a .while loop can always be used instead.

In spite of some of the above restrictions, the .repeat-untilcxz directives and loop instructions are very useful and can be used in a variety of situations. For example, the previous multiplication problem can be solved with this loop as well:

```
ans = 0;                          mov ans,0
if (y != 0)                       .if y != 0
    for(i=1; i<=y;i++)            mov ecx,y
        ans = ans + x;            .repeat
                                  mov eax,ans
                                  add eax, x
                                  mov ans,eax
                                  .untilcxz
                                  .endif
```

Note that in the assembly code on the right, the final value of the ecx register is not moved into i. The reason is that unlike the previous two loops, where i or ecx started at 1 and ended up being one more than the variable y, here the ecx register starts at the variable y and counts down to zero. It is possible that the final value of i could be mathematically calculated to be equal to the correct value whether through normal termination or branching outside from somewhere within the loop. However, in many languages the final value of the loop control variable in a fixed-iteration loop structure is said to be indeterminate, and the result here is consistent with those languages.

5.4 Loops and Input/Output

If a code segment needs to be written to input, process, and output a fixed number of items, then a fixed-iteration loop is probably the best choice. Although a simple example, assume that the segment needs to input and sum exactly 10 integers and then output the sum:

```
sum=0;
for(i=1; i<=10;  i++) {
    printf("%s","Enter an integer: ");
    scanf("%d",&num);
    sum=sum+num;
}
printf("\n%s%d\n\n","The sum is ",sum);
return 0;
```

Assuming all the formats and variables are declared correctly, the partial equivalent in assembly is shown below. Note that the value of ecx is stored in a memory location called temp at the top of the loop and then the value of ecx is restored at the bottom of the loop. Recall from Chap. 2 that the INVOKE directive can destroy the eax, ecx, and edx registers. Since the .repeat-untilcxz directive uses the ecx register, care must be taken to save and restore its value. In the next chapter, the stack will be discussed and will be a convenient way to accomplish the same task:

```
            .data
msg1        byte "Enter an integer: ",0
msg2        byte "The sum is ",0

            .code
            mov sum,0
            mov ecx,10
            .repeat
            mov temp,ecx
            INVOKE printf, ADDR msg1fmt, ADDR msg1
            INVOKE scanf, ADDR in1fmt, ADDR num
            mov eax,sum
            add eax,num
            mov sum,eax
            mov ecx,temp
            .untilcxz
            INVOKE printf, ADDR msg2fmt, ADDR msg2, sum
```

Should more or fewer than 10 numbers need to be input and summed, the above code segments would be rather restrictive. In order to allow more versatility, a prompt and input for the number of integers could be added prior to the loop. Also, to help avoid the problems of entering a 0 or a negative number, the loop could be changed from a .repeat - .untilcxz to a .while - .endw. Again, assuming the formats and data declarations are correct, the partial program is as follows:

```
            .data
msg0        byte "Enter the number of integers to input: ",0
msg1        byte "Enter an integer: ",0
msg2        byte "The sum is ",0

            .code
            mov sum,0
            INVOKE printf, ADDR msg1fmt, ADDR msg0
            INVOKE scanf, ADDR in1fmt, ADDR count
            mov ecx,1
            .while ecx<=count
            mov temp,ecx
            INVOKE printf, ADDR msg1fmt, ADDR msg1
            INVOKE scanf, ADDR in1fmt, ADDR num
            mov eax,sum
            add eax,num
            mov sum,eax
            mov ecx,temp
            inc ecx
            .endw
            INVOKE printf, ADDR msg2fmt, ADDR msg2, sum
```

However, what if one did not want to enter the number or integers to be input and summed? A convenient way to solve this problem is to use what is known as a sentinel-controlled loop, or what is sometimes called an end-of-data loop (EOD). As commonly presented in a first semester computer science text, it contains two input statements, where the first one appears prior to the loop and is sometimes referred to as a priming read and the second one appears as the last statement in the body of the loop. The appearance of two input statements sometimes confuses the beginning programmer, but remembering the three parts of any loop, "initialization," "test," and "change," this priming read can be thought of as the initialization portion of the loop. Next, the test does not check a loop control variable (LCV), but rather the test is of the value input. Of course this is not to say that a counter cannot be added to the loop, where the counter may or may not be part of the control of the loop. Lastly, the second input statement appears as the last statement in the body of the loop, which serves as the change in the loop:

```
sum = 0;
printf("%s","Enter an integer or a negative integer to stop: ");
scanf("%d",&num);
while (num >0) {
    sum=sum+num;
    printf("%s","Enter an integer or a negative integer to stop: ");
    scanf("%d",&num);
}
printf("\n%s%d\n\n","The sum is ",sum);
```

Again assuming that all the formats and variables are declared properly, the partial assembly language equivalent is as follows:

```
      .data
msg1  byte "Enter an integer or a negative integer to stop: ",0
msg2  byte "The sum is ",0
      .code
      mov sum,0
      INVOKE printf, ADDR msg1fmt, ADDR msg1
      INVOKE scanf, ADDR in1fmt, ADDR num
      .while num >=0
      mov eax,sum
      add eax,num
      mov sum,eax
      INVOKE printf, ADDR msg1fmt, ADDR msg1
      INVOKE scanf, ADDR in1fmt, ADDR num
      .endw
      INVOKE printf, ADDR msg2fmt, ADDR msg2, sum
```

It is possible to implement a sentinel-controlled loop using only one input statement, but this is not considered good programming practice. This is usually not a problem in many high-level languages because of the lack or discouraged use of a goto statement. If it is not a good method, then why present it here? The reason is that some older programs may have been written with this style of loop and should the code need to be debugged or modified, then knowledge of this type of loop might be helpful. At the same time, by understanding the loop, the disadvantages of such a structure can be understood and its use in the future limited.

This style of loop is written by having only one input statement in the body of the loop and then comparing the value to see if it is equal to the sentinel value, and if so branching out of the middle of the loop. The actual loop is often written to possibly loop an infinite number of times so that the only way out of the loop is the comparison from somewhere in the middle of the loop. Another and possibly more common way that these loops are written is that the loop itself is controlled by a loop control variable, which is then the default number of times to loop. Should the sentinel value be encountered prior to the default number of times, the branch is then taken to some point outside the loop. Using the equivalent of a goto statement, this can be anywhere else in the program, creating a very hard to follow program known as spaghetti code. In C, this effect can be minimized by using the break statement, which restricts the branch to the end of the current structure, not unlike with the switch statement discussed previously. The following C code segment loops infinitely until the sentinel value is detected by the if statement and the break is executed:

```
sum = 0;
while (1) {
   printf("%s","Enter an integer or a negative integer to stop: ");
   scanf("%d",&num);
   if (num <0)
      break;
   sum=sum+num;
}
printf("\n%s%d\n\n", "The sum is ",sum);
```

Since the above code does not exit from either the beginning or the end of the loop but rather from the middle, some purists would say that the code is unstructured, while others would say that since the break statement limits the branch to the end of the while statement, it is an acceptable branch. In the purist's defense, it is possible that the if might not appear as the first statement immediately after the scanf and it might be tempting for a programmer to add code prior to the if statement. This can possibly introduce a potential logic error that when the loop terminates, some processing has occurred that should not have prior to the input of a sentinel value. Although it might be counter-argued that was the intended reason for placing code prior to the if statement anyway, it does introduce the possibility of misplaced code and subsequent unintended logic errors, especially by beginning programmers.

Unlike the break statement in C which only branches to the end of the loop structure, in assembly the jump instructions can branch anywhere in the program. So, the endl: label in the code segment below does not necessarily need to be located at the end of the loop but placed anywhere in the program, even pages away from the loop itself which is not recommended. The above C code can be implemented as shown in the partial assembly language code segment below:

```
       .data
msg1   byte "Enter an integer or a negative integer to stop: ",0
msg2   byte "The sum is ",0

       .code
       mov sum,0
       .while 1
       INVOKE printf, ADDR msg1fmt, ADDR msg1
       INVOKE scanf, ADDR in1fmt, ADDR num
       cmp num,0
       jl endl

            mov eax,sum
            add eax,num
            mov sum,eax
            .endw
       endl:  nop
            INVOKE printf, ADDR msg2fmt, ADDR msg2, sum
```

As mentioned above, the result of this approach of using the single input is some-what controversial and will not be used in this text. However, if the instructor of the class says it is okay to use this method or if it is used extensively at work, then hopefully the reader has learned the potential dangers of this method and will thus use it sparingly and carefully.

5.5   Nested Loops

As one might recall from a first or a second computer science course, nested loops are helpful when accessing a two-dimensional array or with various sorting algorithms, such as the selection, bubble, or insertion sorts. In this section, the equivalent of nested while and for loop structures will be introduced and the actual application of nested loops will be deferred until Chap. 8.

As might be suspected, the implementation of a nested while loop is not much more difficult than the implementation of a nested if statement. The most important thing that should be remembered is to be sure to use different loop control variables for each of the loops as shown in the C code segment below to the left and the assembly code using high-level directives to the right:

```
i = 1;                             mov i,1
while(i<=2) {                      .while i <= 2
   j=1;                            mov j,1
   while(j<=3) {                   .while j <= 3
      // body of nested loop       ; body of nested loop
      j++;                         inc j
   }                               .endw
   i++;                            inc i
}                                  .endw
```

Of course, the code gets a little more complicated without the benefit of high-level directives. One must pay particularly close attention to the conditional jumps to make sure that the relational is reversed properly and also that the unconditional jumps branch to the appropriate location as shown below:

```
                       mov i,1
  while02:             cmp i,2
                       jg endwhile02
                       mov j,1
  while03:             cmp j,3
                       jg endwhile03
                       ; body of nested loop
                       inc j
                       jmp while03
  endwhile03:          nop
                       inc i
                       jmp while02
  endwhile02:          nop
```

Often when dealing with two-dimensional arrays and sorting algorithms, when there are a fixed number of times to loop in both the outer and inner loops, a fixed-iteration loop structure is understandably used for convenience and speed as shown below:

```
for (i = 1; i <= 2; i++)
   for (j = 1; j <= 3; j++) {
      // body of nested loop
   }
```

As learned previously, the above can be implemented using the .repeat and .untilcxz directives in assembly language. However, care must be taken when writing the code or it can be implemented incorrectly as shown below:

```
; *** Caution: Incorrectly implemented code ***
mov ecx,2
.repeat
mov ecx,3
.repeat
; body of nested loop
.untilcxz
.untilcxz
```

What is wrong with the above code? Although it is syntactically correct, there is a logic error. Unlike the while loops above that can use two different variables, or alternatively could use two different registers, the .repeat and .untilcxz directives can work with only one register. The result is that the value of ecx is 0 upon completion of the nested loop, which causes the outer loop to never terminate. Could another register be used with the .repeat - .untilcxz directives? Unfortunately no, because as should be recalled, the underlying loop instruction that implements the .untilcxz directive works only with the ecx register. The question then is how can the above problem be solved? One way is to store the value of ecx in a memory location prior to the inner loop and then restore the value of ecx when the inner loop is complete as follows, where it can be assumed that tempecx is declared as a temporary memory location:

```
; *** Note: Correctly implemented code ***
mov ecx,2
.repeat
mov tempecx,ecx
mov ecx,3
.repeat
; body of nested loop
.untilcxz
mov ecx,tempecx
.untilcxz
```

There is of course another way to save and restore the value of ecx. Again, a stack is a convenient way to save and restore registers, and this will be discussed in the next chapter. Could the above be implemented without using the .repeat and .untilcxz directives? Of course, by using the loop instruction and that is left as an exercise at the end of this chapter.

5.6 Complete Program: Implementing the Power Function

The selection structures of the previous chapter and the iteration structures of this chapter can obviously be combined. As an example of a complete program, consider the implementation of the power function (x^n), where an iterative definition of the power function is as follows:

x^n = If $x < 0$ or $n < 0$, then negative message
    Else if $x = 0$ and $n = 0$, then undefined message
        Else if $n = 0$, then 1
            Otherwise $1 * x * x * \ldots * x$ (n times)

For the purposes of this program, it will not calculate the case where either x or n is negative and should both x and n be 0, the result is undefined. In each case, an appropriate error message is output. The following C program implements the above definition:

```c
#include <stdio.h>
int main() {
    int x,n,i,ans;
    printf("%s","Enter x: ");
    scanf("%d",&x);
    printf("%s","Enter n: ");
    scanf("%d",&n);
    if(x<0 || n<0)
        printf("\n%s\n\n","Error: Negative x and/or y");
    else
      if(x==0 && n==0)
        printf("\n%s\n\n","Error: Undefined answer");
      else {
          i=1;
          ans=1;
          while(i<=n) {
              ans=ans*x;
              i++;
          }
          printf("\n%s%d\n\n","The answer is: ",ans);
      }
    return 0;
}
```

The above can be implemented in assembly language using directives and as follows:

```
                .686
                .model flat,c
                .stack 100h
scanf           PROTO arg2:Ptr Byte, inputlist:VARARG
printf          PROTO arg1:Ptr Byte, printlist:VARARG

                .data
in1fmt          byte "%d",0
msg1fmt         byte "%s",0
msg3fmt         byte "%s%d",0Ah,0Ah,0
errfmt          byte "%s",0Ah,0Ah,0
errmsg1         byte 0Ah,"Error: Negative x and/or y",0
errmsg2         byte 0Ah,"Error: Undefined answer",0
```

```
msg1            byte "Enter x: ",0
msg2            byte "Enter n: ",0
msg3            byte 0Ah,"The answer is: ",0
x               sdword ?
n               sdword ?
ans             sdword ?
i               sdword ?


                .code
main            proc
                INVOKE printf, ADDR msg1fmt, ADDR msg1
                INVOKE scanf, ADDR in1fmt, ADDR x
                INVOKE printf, ADDR msg1fmt, ADDR msg2
                INVOKE scanf, ADDR in1fmt, ADDR n
                .if x<0 || n<0
                INVOKE printf, ADDR errfmt, ADDR errmsg1
                .else
                .if x==0 && n==0
                INVOKE printf, ADDR errfmt, ADDR errmsg2
                .else
                mov ecx,1
                mov ans,1
                .while ecx <= n
                mov eax,ans
                imul x
                mov ans,eax
                inc ecx


                .endw
                mov i,ecx
                INVOKE printf, ADDR msg3fmt, ADDR msg3, ans
                .endif
                .endif
                ret
main            endp
                end
```

The implementation of the above MASM code is fairly straightforward and follows the corresponding C program. Note that ecx is used for loop control, but the value of i is updated upon completion of the loop to reflect the logic of the corresponding C code.

5.7 Summary

- The .while - .end directives implement a pre-test loop structure.
- The .repeat - .until and .repeat - .untilcxz directives are both post-test loop structures.
- The .repeat - .untilcxz directives are a fixed-iteration loop structure.
- The loop instruction underlies the .repeat - .untilcxz directives.
- As with the .if directive, the .while - .end and .repeat - .until directives cannot compare memory to memory due to the underlying cmp instruction.
- Be extra careful to initialize ecx to a positive number (not zero or negative) when using the loop instruction or the .repeat - .untilcxz directives. The jecxz instruction or an .if directive, respectively, can be helpful in avoiding this problem.
- When using either the loop instruction or the .repeat - .untilcxz directives, it is a good idea to not alter the contents of the ecx register in the body of the loop.
- When nesting .repeat – .untilcxz directives or loop instructions, be careful to save and restore the ecx register just before and after the inner loop.
- The beginning of the .repeat – .until directives or loop instruction cannot be more than 128 bytes away.

5.8 Exercises (Items Marked with an * Have Solutions in Appendix D)

1. Given the following assembly language statements, indicate whether they are syntactically correct or incorrect. If incorrect, indicate what is wrong with the statement:

*A.
```
.for i=1;i<=3;i++
;body of loop
.endfor
```

B.
```
mov i,1
while i <= x
;body of loop
inc i
.endw
```

*C.
```
mov i,0
.repeat
; body of loop
add i,2
.until i>10
```

D.
```
mov edx,3
.repeat
;body of loop
.untiledx
```

E.
```
mov ebx,2
.do
;body of loop
.while ebx>0
```

2. Implement the last code segment in Sect. 5.1 without using directives and using only conditional and unconditional jumps.

3. Given the following while loops implemented using conditional and unconditional jumps, indicate how many times the body of each loop will be executed:

*A.
```
                    mov i,2
    while04:        cmp i,8
                    jge endwhile04
                    ; body of loop
                    add i,2
                    jmp while04
    endwhile04:     nop
```

B.
```
                    mov k,0
    repeat05:       nop
                    ; body of loop
                    add k,3
                    cmp k,3
                    jl repeat05
    endrepeat05:    nop
```

```
C.                      mov j,1
        while06:        cmp j,0
                        jg endwhile06
                        ; body of loop
                        inc j
                        jmp while06
        endwhile06:     nop
```

4. Implement the .repeat and .until directive at the end of Sect. 5.2 using only compare and jump instructions, along with the appropriate label names.
5. Implement unsigned divide (similar to the div instruction) using repetitive subtraction, with your choice (or your instructor's choice) of any of the following (start with the dividend in eax and the divisor in ebx, then place the quotient in eax and the remainder in edx. Note: Do not worry about division by zero or negative numbers):

```
*A.    .while
 B.    .repeat - .until
 C.    .repeat - .untilcxz
```

6. Implement the following C segment using the .repeat - .untilcxz directives. What if the value of n is 0 or negative? Does your code segment still work properly? How can this problem be rectified?

```
sum = 0;
for (i=1; i<=n; i++)
    sum = sum + i;
```

7. Implement the following do-while loop first using the .repeat - .until directives and then using only compares, and conditional and unconditional jumps:

```
i=10;
sum=0;
do {
    sum=sum+i;
    i=i-2;
} while i>0;
```

8. Implement the last code segment in Sect. 5.5 using the `loop` instruction instead of `.repeat` and `.untilcxz` directives.

9. Given the factorial function (n!) defined iteratively as follows:

    If $n = 0$ or $n = 1$, then 1
    If $n = 2$, then 1 * 2 = 2
    If $n = 3$, then 1 * 2 * 3 = 6
    If $n = 4$, then 1 * 2 * 3 * 4 = 24
    etc.

    Implement the above function iteratively with your choice (or your instructor's choice) of any of the following:

    A.   `.while`
    B.   `.repeat - .until`
    C.   `.repeat  - .untilcxz`

10. Given the Fibonacci sequence defined iteratively as follows:

    if $n = 0$, then 0
    if $n = 1$, then 1
    if $n = 2$, then 0 + 1 = 1
    if $n = 3$, then 1 + 1 = 2
    if $n = 4$, then 1 + 2 = 3
    etc.

    Implement the above function iteratively with your choice (or your instructor's choice) of any of the following:

    A.   `.while`
    B.   `.repeat - .until`
    C.   `.repeat  - .untilcxz`

Logic, Shifting, Rotating, and Stacks

6

6.1 Introduction

As introduced in most first semester computer science courses and previously discussed in Chap. 4, various relationals in an if statement can be connected via the use of logical operators such as "and" (&&), "or" (| |), and "not" (!), where these operators in assembly language work with comparisons between variables, registers, and literals. However, sometimes it is necessary to not just compare the contents of variables or registers but check the individual bits within a memory location or a register. These types of operations are known as *bit-wise* operations. An example of this is when interfacing with an external device, when often only a single bit is needed to be checked or set on the external device.

As may or may not have been learned in a previous course, one of the reasons why the C-like languages are very popular is that they have some capabilities to manipulate individual bits. Instead of having to learn a particular low-level language for a particular processor, basic bit-wise operations can be done in a high-level language that is transferable from processor to processor, provided there is a C or C++ compiler for that particular processor. Of course, assembly language has these same capabilities by using logic, shifting, and rotating instructions for manipulating the contents of registers and memory locations, as well as built-in instructions for manipulating a stack.

Although previous exposure to both bit-wise manipulations (such as in a course in C or C++) and binary arithmetic (such as in a course in computer organization) is helpful, it is not a requirement for this text since this material is contained in Appendix B. Should one not have the above previous experience, then Appendix B is recommended reading prior to starting this chapter.

© Springer Nature Switzerland AG 2020
J. T. Streib, *Guide to Assembly Language*, Undergraduate Topics
in Computer Science, https://doi.org/10.1007/978-3-030-35639-2_6

6.2 Logic Instructions

There are many times in low-level programming that individual bits need to be set, cleared, tested, or toggled in a register or a memory location. In order to do so, the use of the logic operations "or", "and", and "exclusive-or" can be very useful. As also shown in Appendix B, Table 6.1 can be helpful in summarizing which logic operation is used under which circumstances.

So how are the above logic operations to set, clear, test, and toggle bits implemented in assembly language? As before, it is helpful to start with similar code in a language like C. As mentioned previously, one of the advantages of the C-like languages is their ability to perform some logic operations. To help introduce this topic, what happens if the second ampersand (&) is accidentally left off when performing an "and" (&&) operation in an if statement? Depending on the compiler or the level of the warning messages set in the compiler, either a warning would be issued or there might be some unintended results. The reason for this is that using only one of the symbols causes a bit-wise logic operation to be performed which might not be what was originally intended. However, this is precisely how logic operations are performed in a programming language like C.

For example, to test if a particular bit is a 1, a single ampersand logical "and" operator (&) would be used instead of the double ampersand logical "and" operator (&&). In the code segment below, the variable flag contains various bits that are set as a result of some previous operation. The variable maskit is what is known as a *mask* that has a particular bit set to 1 that will be used to test and others at 0 to filter or clear all the other bits that do not need to be tested in this instance:

```
if(flag & maskit)
  count++;
```

The above is not trying to determine whether both flag and maskit are true, but rather assuming that flag equals 01101110 in binary and maskit equals 00000100 in binary, the above is a bit-wise & operation between flag and maskit, where the result is equal to 00000100 as shown below:

Table 6.1 Logic operations

Operation	Logic
Set	Or
Clear	And
Test	And
Toggle	Xor

```
    01101110
    00000100
 &  ───────
    00000100
```

Since anything that is not zero is assumed to be true, the then section of the `if` statement is performed. On the other hand, should flag equal 01101010 in binary, then the result of the bit-wise & operator would be 00000000, where zero is interpreted to be false, and the then portion would not be executed. As one might suspect, given the high-level directives in MASM, the above is very easy to implement as shown below:

```
mov eax, flag
.if eax & maskit
inc count
.endif
```

In the above code segment, why do the contents of `maskit` need to be moved to a register prior to the `.if` directive? As indicated in the past two chapters, many assembly languages do not have the benefit of having high-level directives, so it is necessary to use the logic instructions that are part of the instruction set. In the case of the Intel processor, these are and, or, xor, and not as shown in Table 6.2.

Further, just like the compare and arithmetic instructions, these logic instructions cannot have two operands that are memory locations. Given the above, the previous code can be implemented without directives as follows:

```
if01:      mov eax, flag
           and eax, maskit
           jz endif01
then01:    inc count
endif01:   nop
```

Table 6.2 Logic instructions

And instructions	Or instructions	Xor instructions	Not instructions
and reg,reg	or reg,reg	xor reg,reg	not reg
and reg,imm	or reg,imm	xor reg,imm	not mem
and reg,mem	or reg,mem	xor reg,mem	
and mem,reg	or mem,reg	xor mem,reg	
and mem,imm	or mem,imm	xor mem,imm	

Note the use of the `jz` instruction instead of `jne`, where the `jz` instruction was introduced in Chap. 4. The reason for this is that variables such as flag and `maskit` are typically unsigned numbers and are not compared to determine if one is greater or less than the other. As before, care must be taken to reverse the jump to allow the if-then logic to work correctly.

Is there a way to use both the logic instructions and the high-level directives? Yes, the logic instruction can be used followed by the `.if` directive as shown below. The advantage of this format is that one can gain familiarity with the use of the actual logic instructions and still have relatively clean code using high-level directives:

```
mov eax,flag
and eax, maskit
.if !ZERO?
inc count
.endif
```

As with the `cmp` and other arithmetic instructions, the result of the and operation sets various bits in the `eflags` register. These individual bits can be accessed via the logical operators introduced in Chap. 4. In particular, the `ZERO?` operator is of interest here which returns true should the zero flag be set. Thus in the above code segment, if the result of the and operation is 1, indicating a bit is set, then `ZERO?` would be false and `!ZERO?` would be true allowing the increment of the variable count.

It should be noted that instead of using a variable such as `maskit`, an immediate value in any of the above examples could be used, thus avoiding the need to move the mask into a register prior to the and instruction. The disadvantage of this method is that if the mask has to be used many times, the chance of making an error in one of the instances is greater. However, if the mask is going to be used only once, then the literal method is acceptable. Of course, do not forget to use the letter b after the literal to indicate a binary number, otherwise a decimal number will be assumed and a logic error would probably occur. Although it is possible to use decimal numbers with logic operations, they are rarely used in these situations because the exact bit pattern cannot be seen by other programmers. If the number is larger than 8 bits, then a hexadecimal number followed by an h can be used. Further, it is always a good idea to show all the bit positions used to help any reader of the code understand how many bits are being compared. Below are three different ways of using an immediate value as a mask:

```
.if flag & 00000010b            and flag,00000010b    and flag,00000010b
inc count          if02:        jz endif02            .if !ZERO?
.endif             then02:      inc count             inc count
                   endif02:     nop                   .endif
```

Lastly, it should be noticed that in the process of testing an individual bit, the other bits are cleared to zero. In this sense the and instruction is useful in not only testing bits but clearing bits as well. But what if when testing bits, one does not want to clear the other bits? Although on some processors this is not a possibility, this can be accomplished in MASM with the test instruction which is illustrated at the end of the next section.

Although probably not seen much in a first-year computer science sequence, a particular bit can be set in a memory location in the C programming language using the bit-wise or (|) operator:

```
flag = flag | maskit;
```

The same can be accomplished in assembly language using the or instruction. As in previous chapters, notice the high-level comment prior to the code segment below:

```
; flag = flag | maskit
mov eax,flag
or eax,maskit
mov flag,eax
```

As application of the bit-wise or, consider the changing of an uppercase character to a lowercase character. In looking at the ASCII table in Section B.8, notice that the bit pattern for an uppercase character always has bit 5 (sixth from the right) equal to 0, whereas the bit pattern for lowercase characters always has bit 5 equal to 1. For example, the letter "S" is equal to 53 in hexadecimal or 01010011 in binary and the letter "s" is equal to 73 in hexadecimal or 01110011 in binary. In order to convert an uppercase character to a lowercase character, an or instruction using a mask of 00100000 in binary could be used to set bit 5. Assuming the variable letter is declared as a byte and already contains a letter, the following instruction would work:

```
or letter,00100000b
```

To convert a lower-case letter "s" to an upper-case letter "S", bit 5 is cleared to zero. This is accomplished using an and operation as follows:

```
and letter,11011111b
```

Although C does not have a logical exclusive-or operation that could be used between two relationals in an if or a while statement, it does have a bit-wise exclusive-or operation (^). As mentioned above, the "xor" operation can be used for toggling a bit. For example, if one wanted to toggle bit 1 from a 0 to a 1 or from a 1 to a 0, the following instruction would accomplish that task:

```
flag = flag ^ maskit;
```

which can be written in assembly language using the `xor` instruction as

```
; flag = flag ^ maskit
mov eax,flag
xor eax,maskit
mov flag,eax
```

On occasion, when examining code previously written by someone else, one might see something similar to the following instruction:

```
xor eax,eax
```

At first, it may seem a bit strange to see a logic operation with the same register for both operands. If this was done with any of the other logic instructions, it would not accomplish anything. For example, with the `or` operation, 0 or 0 is 0 and 1 or 1 is 1. However, it is in this second case that there is a difference with the `xor` instruction where 1 `xor` 1 is 0. In other words, all the bit positions with a 0 remain a 0 and all the bits with a 1 become a 0, thus clearing all the bit positions in the register to 0. Logic instructions are some of the fastest instructions in most processor architectures and using `xor eax,eax` is usually faster than using `mov eax,0`. This is one of those tricks used by experienced assembly language programmers to speed up the execution of a program, but unless it is used in a critical location such as within a loop or nested loops, the speed gained is negligible compared to the loss of readability for inexperienced assembly language programmers.

6.3 Logical Shift Instructions

Sometimes if there are more than one bit to test, set, or toggle in a register or a memory location, it is easier to move the bit patterns instead of having multiple if statements. This can be accomplished by using a shift or a rotate instruction. The C programming language has the ability to shift bits to the left or the right in a memory location by using the $<<$ or $>>$ operators, respectively. For example, if the memory location `num` contained a 2 and the following instruction was executed, the contents of `num` would then be a 16:

```
num = num << 3;
```

Assuming only 8 bits for the sake of convenience, the 2 in `num` would be represented as a 00000010 in binary. Then shifting the bits three places to the left would cause `num` to contain a 00010000, which is a 16 in base 10. Once the bit in question is in the correct location, the previous logical operators could be applied to the memory location.

However, a question arises as to whether to move the bits in the mask or move the bits in either the register or the memory location to be tested. Which should be moved is largely up to the application, the preference of the instructor, or the preference of the programmer. There are, however, some guidelines that can help one make a choice. If only part of the register or the memory location needs to be checked and it is moved, then the original contents of the register or the memory location will be altered. Of course, if it is no longer needed, then this is not a concern, but if the original contents are needed again in the future or if there is a chance that they might be needed, it might be better to move the mask instead.

However, if the mask is relatively complicated, where more than a single bit is set, then it might be better to move the register or the memory location. Also, by shifting the data, the mask can be kept as immediate data and the actual code might be a little cleaner. One technique is to save the original contents in a temporary location, shift the data, and then the original data in the temporary location can always be restored back into the original location later. (An alternative to using a temporary memory location is to use a stack, which will be discussed later in this chapter.) A second option is to move the original to a temporary memory location or register and then shift the temporary location, which would preserve the original contents from alteration. A third technique to be discussed later is to rotate the bits back to the original location so that subsequent logic can access the data in its original format. All three of these methods have their advantages under various circumstances, but for the time being the first alternative will be used to illustrate how data must be saved and restored.

Two very helpful instructions are the logical shift instructions, which shift the contents of a register or a memory location to either the left or the right of a specified number of bits. The instructions are known as logical instructions, because they do not assume the presence of a sign bit. These two instructions are listed in Table 6.3.

Note that on older 8086/8088 processors, the only immediate number in an operand that could be used was 1 so that any other number would first need to be loaded into the cl register. Although any number can now be used on newer processors, on occasion, some programmers who originally programmed these older processors might carry on that tradition. These instructions move each bit the

Table 6.3 Shift instructions

Shift left instructions	Shift right instructions
shl reg,cl	shr reg,cl
shl reg,imm	shr reg,imm
shl mem,cl	shr mem,cl
shl mem,imm	shr mem,imm

CF   7 ------------0

Fig. 6.1 Initial contents of al register

number of positions indicated to the left or the right, accordingly. Assuming an 8-bit register is being used, the shl instruction moves the contents of the leftmost bit (bit 7) into the carry flag (CF), moves the contents of the other 7 bits to the left one bit, and then moves a 0 into the rightmost bit (bit 0). For example, assume that the al register contained the bit pattern in Fig. 6.1 and that the content of the carry flag on the left was unknown, as indicated by the question mark.

After the execution of the instruction shl al,1, the 0 in bit position 7 on the left would be moved into the carry flag, the contents of bit position 6 would be moved into bit position 7, the contents of bit position 5 would be moved into bit position 6, and so on, where finally the contents of bit position 0 would be filled with a 0 as shown in Fig. 6.2.

What happens to the previous contents of the carry flag? Some might say it disappears into thin air or some "old timers" might say that its contents are moved to the *bit bucket*. With respect to the latter, the old timers might sometimes further inform beginning assembly language programmers that when the bit bucket gets full, it needs to be emptied. However, be aware there is no such thing as a bit bucket nor does it need to be emptied. It is just an expression to mean that bit is no longer accessible and more importantly it is merely a way to have a little fun at the expense of beginning assembly language programmers!

The shifting of bits in the reverse direction is also possible, where if a shr al,1 were executed on the original contents of al in Fig. 6.1, the contents of al would appear as shown in Fig. 6.3. The contents of the carry flag would go into the bit bucket (see how convenient the terminology is?), the contents of bit position 0 would move into the carry flag, the contents of bit position 1 would move into bit position 0, and so on, where a 0 would be placed into bit position 7.

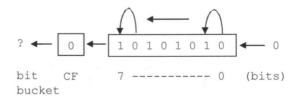

bit   CF   7 ----------- 0   (bits)
bucket

Fig. 6.2 Results in al register after shl instruction

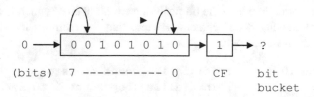

Fig. 6.3 Results in al register after shr instruction

The carry flag is now drawn on the right side of the al register just for the sake of convenience. For the most part, one usually does not worry about the carry flag when doing logical shifting. In a number of other processors, the end bit usually goes directly to the bit bucket.

Given the original contents of the al register in Fig. 6.1, what would happen if instead of a shl al,1 the instruction shl al,8 was executed? If each bit was shifted to the left eight times, bit 0 would end up in the carry flag, the other 7 bits would be in the bit bucket, and all 8 bits of the register would be filled with zeros. This same concept could be expanded to 32 bits and on rare occasions, one might see code such as this to clear a 32-bit register such as eax to zero. However, shift instructions are traditionally some of the slower instructions on most processors and this method can be slower than using either the mov instruction or the xor instruction mentioned in the last section. If however each of the bits in a register needed to be processed one at a time and the register also needed to be cleared to zeros, then clearing a register to zero is a nice by-product of using the shl instruction in a loop as discussed below.

As an example of processing each bit individually and using only a byte instead of a double word to save space, assume that each bit in the al register represents a device that is connected to the processor. Further, if a bit is a 1 or a 0, it would indicate whether the device is turned on or off, respectively. For this task, also assume that the original data needs to be retained. Given these assumptions, how could one determine how many devices are turned on?

In order to solve this problem, there are a number of questions that need to be answered. First, a loop is obviously needed, but which loop should be used? Since there are a fixed number of bits in a byte, the equivalent of a for loop structure appears to be the best choice, which in MASM is the .repeat-.untilcxz loop. Another question is should the mask be shifted or should the register be shifted? As mentioned previously, it often depends on whether the original data needs to retained and since it was mentioned above that it needs to be retained, it might be simpler to shift the mask. However, as also mentioned previously, shifting the data means that the mask can be kept as immediate data. This makes the actual code a little simpler even though the original data will need to be saved and restored in a temporary memory location. Lastly, should the shl or the shr instruction be used? Often it really does not make a difference, unless one is only processing the bits on one side of the register or the other. By default it is probably best to process the bits in the order in which the bit positions are numbered, which is from right to left. In the following code segment, assume that the memory location temp is declared as an unsigned byte:

```
mov count,0          ; initialize count to zero
mov ecx,8            ; initialize loop counter to zero
mov temp,al          ; save al in temp
.repeat
mov ah,al            ; mov data in al to ah for testing
and ah,00000001b     ; test bit position zero
.if !ZERO?           ; is the bit set?
inc count            ; yes, count it
.endif
shr al,1             ; shift al right one bit position
.untilcxz
mov al,temp          ; restore al from temp
```

Note that the first thing prior to the loop is that the data in al is saved in memory location temp declared as a byte and the last thing after the loop is that the data in temp is restored to the al register. Further, notice that there appears to be an extra move instruction at the top of the body of the loop. The reason for this is that since there are bits set to 0 in the mask and as a result the and instruction will destroy other bits in the al register, the data needs to be moved to another register. Since the upper 8 bits of the ax register are not being used, the ah register is a good choice. At the bottom of the body of the loop, the al register is shifted one bit to the right and then back at the top of the loop the al register is again moved into the ah register so that the next bit can be tested.

However, would it not be nice to have a method of checking a particular bit without having to destroy the other bits around it? Luckily, the designers of the Intel processor have designed just such an instruction. It is called the test instruction, and instead of performing an actual and operation, it performs what is known as an implied and operation. This means it performs the and operation and sets the eflags register, but it does not actually alter the corresponding register or memory location. Although in the example above the contents of the al register will still be altered due to the shift instruction, the contents will not be destroyed each time through the loop by the test instruction and the above code can be rewritten without the extra mov instruction as shown below:

```
mov count,0        ; initialize count to zero
mov ecx,8          ; initialize loop counter to zero
mov temp,al        ; save al in temp
.repeat
test al,00000001b  ; test bit position zero
.if !ZERO?         ; is the bit set?
inc count          ; yes, count it
.endif
shr al,1           ; shift al right one bit position
.untilcxz
mov al,temp        ; restore al from temp
```

6.4 Arithmetic Shift Instructions

Besides the logical shift instructions, there are also the arithmetic shift instructions called sal and sar, which stand for shift arithmetic left and shift arithmetic right, respectively. The arithmetic shifts have the same operand formats as their logical counterparts as shown in Table 6.4.

Unlike the logical instructions, the arithmetic shifts assume that the leftmost bit in a register or memory location is a sign bit. With the sal instruction, this does not make any difference and it performs the same as the shl instruction because when shifting to the left, the leftmost bit is moved into the carry flag whether the leftmost bit is or is not a sign bit. Using the original data from Fig. 6.1, the result of the shl in Fig. 6.2 is the same as the sal in Fig. 6.4.

Although the sal instruction works the same as the shl instruction, this is not the case with the sar instruction. With the sar, the leftmost bit is copied to the bit to the right as with the slr, but instead of bringing in a 0 into the leftmost position, the leftmost position is copied into itself, thus preserving the sign bit as shown in Fig. 6.5.

Table 6.4 Arithmetic shift instructions

Shift arithmetic left	Shift arithmetic right
sal reg,cl	sar reg, cl
sal reg,imm	sar reg, imm
sal mem,cl	sar mem, cl
sal mem,imm	sar mem, imm

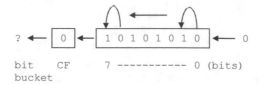

```
? ◄──   0  ◄─  1 0 1 0 1 0 1 0  ◄── 0

bit     CF      7 ----------- 0 (bits)
bucket
```

Fig. 6.4 Results in al register after sal instruction

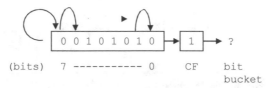

```
         0 0 1 0 1 0 1 0 ─┤ 1 ├─► ?

(bits)   7 ----------- 0     CF    bit
                                   bucket
```

Fig. 6.5 Results in al register after sar instruction

The result is that the arithmetic shifts can be used for performing arithmetic. Again for the sake of simplicity in the following examples, 8-bit registers and memory locations will be used instead of 32-bit ones. Assume that the memory location number contains a 5 as 00000101 in binary. If this number was shifted to the left one bit, the result would be 00001010, which is the number 10 and is twice the number 5. Likewise, shifting number to another bit position results in 00010100, which is the number 20. In other words, for every bit position shifted to the left, the number in the register is effectively multiplied by a power of two. Likewise, shifting the number 00010100 two bits to the right results in the number 00000101 and is the equivalent of dividing by 4.

However, what about negative numbers? For example, when shifting a −4, 11111100 one bit to the right using a shr instruction, the result would be a 01111110, which is a positive 125 and is clearly incorrect. This is the reason for the arithmetic sar instruction, which would cause the sign bit to be copied not only to the right but also back into the leftmost bit position. This would result in a 11111110, a −2 which is correct. If the original number was a −5, 11111011, then a sar al,1 would result in a 11111101, which is a −2 demonstrating that it is the equivalent of integer division, where the remainder would be in the carry flag.

When multiplying, choosing either the sal or the shl instruction is not really a problem, because to multiply 11111100 by 2 the result would be 11111000 in binary, which is a −8. The reason why one would use a sal instead of a shl in this instance is to indicate to others that the purpose of the shift is the arithmetic operation of multiplication. Although a good comment is always in order, this is in a sense an example of self-documenting code.

However, should a number be shifted too many times to the left, a negative number would eventually become a positive number. Although the numbers used in the examples in this text will be smaller, as with the arithmetic instruction counterparts from Chap. 3, one should always be careful with the possibility of overflow and underflow.

So given the above and for further practice, how would the following C statement be implemented using a shift instruction?

```
product = num1 * 8;
```

Assuming 32-bit words and using the sal instruction, it could be implemented as follows:

```
; product = num1 * 8;
mov eax,num1            ; load eax with num1
sal eax,3              ; multiply by 8
mov product,eax        ; store eax in product
```

Notice that num1 above is not shifted, but rather it is first moved to the eax register and then it is shifted. As in Chap. 2, num1 appears to the right of the assignment symbol in the original high-level code implementation and it should not be altered. Another common mistake made by beginners is putting the multiplier in the second operand of the shift instruction instead of the number of positions to be shifted. For example, if the number 8 was accidentally used as the second operand in the shift instruction in the above example, it would cause num1 to be multiplied by the number 256 which is clearly incorrect. As another example to help reinforce these concepts, how would one implement the following using shift instructions?

```
answer = amount / 4;
```

With positive numbers the choice of slr or sar does not really make a difference. For example, if amount in the above example contained a 32 (00100000 in binary), then after shifting to the right 2 times to divide by 4, the result would be 8 (00001000 in binary). Since the sign bit is 0, it would not make a difference whether a 0 was shifted into bit position 7 by a slr instruction or it was copied onto itself by a sar instruction.

However, it cannot always be known whether the number in a memory location such as amount is positive or negative. Unlike above with multiplication, the choice of which shift to use, logical or arithmetic, is of critical importance with division when dealing with negative numbers or the possibility of negative numbers. Consider the following implementation:

```
; *** Caution: Possible incorrect code ***
; answer = amount / 4
mov eax,amount
shr eax,2           ; divide by 4
mov answer,eax
```

Again assuming 8-bit words for convenience, if in the above code segment, amount contains a −8, or 11111000 in binary, then shifting the eax register to the right two positions would result in a 00111110 in binary, or 62 in decimal, which is clearly not correct. However, if the above code segment is rewritten with the appropriate instruction as follows:

```
; *** Note: Correctly implemented code ***
; answer = amount / 4
mov eax,amount
sar eax,2           ; divide by 4
mov answer,eax
```

Then when 11111000 in binary is shifted to the right arithmetically, the result is that eax contains 11111110 in binary, because in addition to being moved the right, the sign bit is copied back into bit 7 and answer is a −2 as it should be.

The result is that when using shift instructions to perform multiplication and division, it is best to use the arithmetic versions to not only help alert other programmers that the shift is being done for the purposes of arithmetic but also avoid a potential logic error in the event that the quotient in the division operation is a negative number. If the code using shifts is not as clear as using imul and idiv, why would one want to use this method? The answer is that it can be faster and more convenient than are its multiplication and division counterparts, especially when multiplying and dividing by multiples of two, respectively.

6.5   Rotate Instructions

There are many cases with shifting where the unused bits are not needed and their disappearance into the bit bucket is not a problem, especially with multiplication and division. However, there are other cases where it might be convenient to keep the unused bits. The instructions that help in these cases are known as rotate instructions. The rotate instructions are similar to the logical shift instructions in that the end bit goes into the carry flag, and the previous contents of the carry flag go into the proverbial bit bucket. However, instead of zeros being inserted at the other end as with the logical shift instructions, with the rotate instructions the bits from the one end are carried around and inserted into the other end as will be shown shortly.

The format of the two rotate instructions can be found in Table 6.5, where `rol` means rotate left and `ror` means rotate right. Although there are two other rotate instructions, `rcl` and `rcr` that rotate out of the carry flag, they will not be considered here.

Using the same initial drawing from Fig. 6.1 used previously with the shift instructions and as repeated in Fig. 6.6, a `rol al,1` instruction would have the results shown in Fig. 6.7.

Similarly, rotating the drawing in Fig. 6.6 to the right using `ror al,1` would work as shown in Fig. 6.8.

Table 6.5 Rotate instructions

Rotate left instructions	Rotate right instructions
rol reg,cl	ror reg,cl
rol reg,imm	ror reg,imm
rol mem,cl	ror mem,cl
rol mem,imm	ror mem,imm

```
   ?          0 1 0 1 0 1 0 1

  CF          7------------ 0
```

Fig. 6.6 Initial contents of `al` Register

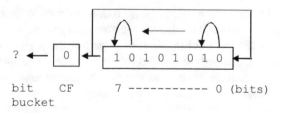

```
?  ←  0  ←  1 0 1 0 1 0 1 0  ←

bit    CF    7 ---------- 0 (bits)
bucket
```

Fig. 6.7 Results in `al` register after `rol` instruction

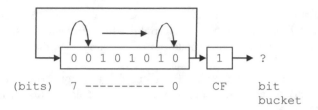

(bits)   7 ----------- 0   CF   bit
                                          bucket

Fig. 6.8 Results in al register after ror instruction

The advantage of the rotate instructions is that if the bits are rotated the exact number of times as there are bits in a register or a memory location, the register or the memory location is returned back to its original state. The advantage of this is that there is no need to save or restore the register or the memory location prior to testing it and the same would apply if one were to rotate the mask instead of the data.

The example of testing the 8 bits shown previously is now redone below using a rotate instruction instead of a shift instruction:

```
mov count,0            ; initialize count to zero
mov ecx,8              ; initialize loop counter to zero
.repeat
test al,00000001b      ; test bit position zero
.if !ZERO?             ; is the bit set?
inc count              ; yes, count it
.endif
rol al,1               ; shift al left one bit position
.untilcxz
```

Again, the advantage here of using a rotate instruction instead of a shift instruction is that the contents of the al register need not be saved and restored. The only danger is that sometimes when only part of the register or the memory location needs to be processed, one might forget to rotate the rest of the register or the memory location back to its original location, or inadvertently rotate the wrong number of times, which could lead to a logic error later in the program. When in doubt, one can always save and restore the register or the memory location, whether either a shift or a rotate instruction is used.

6.6 Stack Operations

If one took the second semester computer science course that is usually required in a computer science major or minor, there is a good chance that one has been exposed to the data structure called the *stack* and the related methods or functions, push and pop. A stack is a *LIFO* (last in first out) structure, where the last item pushed onto the stack is the first one popped off the stack. As should be recalled, there are number of useful applications for stacks. Some of those applications include reversing data, matching, number conversions, evaluation of expressions, and implementing recursion. Given the usefulness of a stack, most processors include built-in stack instructions and this is true with the Intel processor as well.

In order to use the stack instructions, one must be sure to reserve memory space for the stack itself. As introduced in Chap. 1, this is accomplished by using the .stack directive which indicates how much memory should be reserved, where typically 100 hexadecimal bytes, or in other words 256 decimal bytes, is usually sufficient as shown below:

```
.stack 100h
```

Although there are other variations of the push and pop instruction, only the two simplest versions are introduced at the present time. As would be expected, the instructions push and pop are used to put data on top of the stack and remove data from the top of the stack, respectively. Note that 16, 32, or 64-bit registers and memory locations work with the push and pop instructions. However, if the al register needs to be pushed on the stack, then either the entire ax, eax, or rax register would need to be used. The format of these instructions can be found in Table 6.6, where obviously it is possible to push an immediate value onto a stack, but it is not possible to pop a value off the stack and put it into an immediate value.

The use of push and pop instructions is typically a good way to save and restore values. On some processors the use of a stack can be faster than using a temporary memory location. However, on the Intel processor it tends to be a little slower when saving and restoring a memory location but is about the same speed when saving and restoring a register. If there is not much of a difference and in some cases using the stack might be a little slower, what is the advantage of using the stack to save and restore values over a temporary memory location? The benefit of using the

Table 6.6 Push and pop instructions

Push instructions	Pop instructions
push reg	pop reg
push mem	pop mem
push imm	

stack is primarily convenience. Since memory for the stack has already been allocated using the `.stack` directive, extra temporary memory locations do not need to be declared. Further, the stack is always available and the names of various temporary memory locations do not need to be remembered.

As indicated in the last section, it is often useful to use a stack to hold the original contents of a register or a memory location prior to manipulation of the bit pattern. Instead of moving the original bit pattern into a memory location, it can be pushed onto the stack prior to the loop and then restored to its original pattern after the loop as shown below. Although this might not be necessary when using a rotate instruction as mentioned in the last section, sometimes one might accidentally not rotate the register or the memory location the correct number of times. So saving or restoring the original pattern is inexpensive insurance and the `push` and `pop` instructions make this easy. For example, the following uses the shift instruction to demonstrate the use of the `push` and `pop` instructions. As mentioned previously, note that although only the `al` register needs to be pushed on and popped off the stack, the `eax` register is used here, where the `ax` register would have worked as well:

```
push eax
mov count,0          ; initialize count to zero
mov ecx,8            ; initialize loop counter to zero
.repeat
test al,00000001b    ; test bit position zero
.if !ZERO?           ; is the bit set?
inc count            ; yes, count it
.endif
shr al,1             ; shift al right one bit position
.untilcxz
pop eax
```

If for some reason more than one register needs to be saved and restored, the order of the pushes and pops must be taken into consideration. For example, what if following arithmetic statement needs to be evaluated?

```
w = x / y - z;
```

Fig. 6.9 Saving and restoring multiple registers

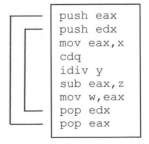

Assuming that the previous contents of the registers used to evaluate the expression should not be altered, they would need to be saved and restored. Using the stack, Fig. 6.9 illustrates how this could be accomplished.

It should be noted that both the eax and edx registers are pushed onto the stack. Although it is obvious that the eax register is used by the sub and mov instructions, do not forget that the cdq instruction extends the sign bit through the edx register and that the idiv instruction leaves the remainder in the edx register. As a result, both registers need to be pushed onto the stack. As can be seen, the first register popped off the stack is the edx register. Recall that a stack is a LIFO structure, where the last item pushed onto the stack is the edx register, so it is the first item that needs to be popped off the stack.

A possible problem when using the stack extensively is that one might forget which items were pushed onto the stack and in what order. This can result in some difficulty in debugging logic errors. To help avoid these errors, one possibility is to avoid overusing the stack. Further, when using the stack it is a good idea to keep the associated pushes and pops relatively close to one another so that the connections between the two can easily be seen. It can be quite confusing to see a push in a middle of a code segment only to find the corresponding pop many pages further away in the code. Yet another technique that can help is to use scoping lines to help match push instructions with the corresponding pop instructions to insure that the item being popped off the stack is the correct one. Scoping lines can be drawn on a program listing by hand to help with creating or debugging code and are illustrated in the code segment in Fig. 6.9.

6.7 Swapping Using Registers, the Stack, and the xchg Instruction

As another example of using the stack, assume that two values need to be swapped, such as is done in a number of sorting algorithms. The typical high-level code is as follows:

```
temp  = num1;
num1  = num2;
num2  = temp;
```

This could be implemented on a line-by-line basis in assembly language using registers, but that would require two instructions for each line of code as follows:

```
mov eax,num1
mov temp,eax
mov eax,num2
mov num1,eax
mov eax,temp
mov num2,eax
```

Clearly, the above seems inefficient. Instead, a register such as edx could be used instead of the temporary memory location temp. The edx register is chosen as the temporary register to make sure that the ecx register is free to be used for loop control and ebx is free to be used as an index register, both of which will be discussed further in Chap. 8. However, the middle high-level instruction would still need to use another register such as eax to enable the transfer between the two memory locations:

```
mov edx,num1
mov eax,num2
mov num1,eax
mov num2,edx
```

The above use of the registers can be rearranged as follows to help in readability:

```
mov eax,num1
mov edx,num2
mov num1,edx
mov num2,eax
```

Instead of using registers and mov instructions, another possibility is to use the stack. Not only is a stack a nice way to save and restore values, it can also be useful in swapping two values. An advantage over the mov instructions is that the stack does not need to use any of the general purpose registers which free them up for other uses. The following code segment swaps the values in num1 and num2:

```
push num1
push num2
pop num1
pop num2
```

Is the order of the pop instructions above correct? Yes, since the purpose of the above code is not to save and restore the contents of num1 and num2 but rather to swap their contents. In other words, since the last value pushed onto the stack is the contents of num2, it is the first value popped off the stack. Instead of being popped back into num2, it is popped into num1. The same happens with the value originally in num1, thus swapping the two values.

Table 6.7 Exchange instructions

Xchg instructions
xchg reg,reg
xchg reg,mem
xchg mem,reg

Yet another method of swapping two values is to use the exchange (xchg) instruction. When swapping two registers, it is faster than the two methods previously presented. The format of this instruction is given in Table 6.7.

Of course the one instruction that would directly allow the swapping of two memory locations is noticeably absent. Like many previous instructions, memory to memory exchanges are not possible. However, the above does allow an exchange between two memory locations to occur in only three instructions, instead of the four needed in the previous three examples:

```
mov eax,num1
xchg eax,num2
mov num1,eax
```

This is accomplished by moving one of the two values into a register, swapping the register with the other memory location, and then moving the contents of the register back into the original memory location. Assuming that num1 originally contains a 5 and num2 originally contains a 7, the three diagrams in Fig. 6.10 illustrate the three instructions in the above code segment.

With respect to register usage when swapping to memory locations, the stack does not use any general purpose registers, the xchg instruction uses one register and mov instructions require two registers. With respect to speed, using mov instructions is the fastest, the xchg instruction is just a little slower, and using the stack is the slowest. The result is that the xchg instruction is a nice compromise between the other two methods in terms of both register usage and speed. Also, given the convenience of the xchg instruction, it will usually be the method of choice in subsequent examples.

6.8 Complete Program: Simulating an OCR Machine

As alluded to in many of the preceding sections, computers use individual bits in a register or a memory location to indicate the status or to control various parts of the CPU or peripheral devices. One such machine might be an optical character

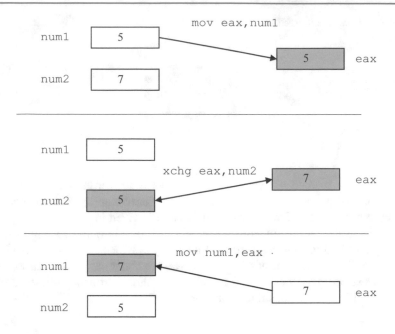

Fig. 6.10 Swapping using the xchg instruction

recognition (OCR) device that reads typed or handwritten characters from a piece of paper. On larger machines, they use a transport device that can handle more than a single piece of paper at one time, similar to a copying machine, where a memory location might be used to indicate the status of the paper in the transport. For the following simulation, the memory location used will be called the document status byte (DSB). There are a variety of problems that can happen with any sheet of paper in a transport as indicated in Table 6.8.

Table 6.8 Simulated error messages

Bit	Message	Meaning
0	Short document	The document just read is shorter than anticipated
1	Long document	The document just read is shorter than anticipated
2	Close feed	Current document is too close to the preceding document
3	Multiple feed	Two documents were detected at the same time
4	Excessive skew	The document is skewed (crooked) in the transport
5	Document misfeed	The document fails to feed into the transport
6	Document jam	The document jammed in the transport
7	Unspecified error	An unknown/unspecified error occurred

As can be seen, the bit number indicates the corresponding location of the error bit in the DSB, remembering that the low-order bit in a byte is located on the right. It is also possible that more than one of the above conditions could occur at the same time. For example, if two documents are overlapped, it might cause both a multiple feed and a long document error condition.

To help create appropriate input to test the program, it would be inconvenient to input the bit patterns in decimal (base 10). Instead it would be easier to input in binary or hexadecimal, where fortunately C has the ability to input hexadecimal numbers. This is accomplished by using the letter x instead of the letter d in the format string as shown below. Further, in writing this program, one might be tempted to use nested if statements in order to make the code more readable and efficient. However, recall from above that it is possible to have more than one error condition and the use of nested if statements would rule out this possibility. It might be possible to use the equivalent of the switch statement but leave the break statements out of the code to allow more than one case to be tested. However, not using break statements in a switch statement might be considered by some to be unstructured. Further, given that there is no high-level directive equivalent of the case structure, it would have to be implemented using only low-level code. As has been seen previously, sometimes the code can get rather ugly using a lot of jump statements. Instead the approach taken here is the use of non-nested high-level if directives:

```
                .686
                .model flat,c
                .stack 100h
scanf           PROTO arg2:Ptr Byte, inputlist:VARARG
printf          PROTO arg1:Ptr Byte, printlist:VARARG
                .data
msg1fmt         byte "%s",0
in1fmt          byte "%x",0
msg2fmt         byte "%s%x",0Ah,0Ah,0
msg1            byte 0Ah,"Enter a hexadecimal number: ",0
msg2            byte "The hexadecimal number is: ",0
msgshort        byte "SHORT DOCUMENT",0Ah,0
msglong         byte "LONG DOCUMENT",0Ah,0
msgclose        byte "CLOSE FEED",0Ah,0
msgmult         byte "MULTIPLE FEED",0Ah,0
msgskew         byte "EXCESSIVE SKEW",0Ah,0
msgfeed         byte "DOCUMENT MISFEED",0Ah,0
msgjam          byte "DOCUMENT JAM",0Ah,0
msgerror        byte  "UNSPECIFIED ERROR",0Ah,0
dsb             dword ?
                .code
main            proc
```

```
        INVOKE printf, ADDR msg1fmt,ADDR msg1
        INVOKE scanf, ADDR in1fmt,ADDR dsb
        INVOKE printf, ADDR msg2fmt, ADDR msg2, dsb
        .while dsb<=0ffh
        test dsb,00000001b
        .if !ZERO?                      ; if bit 0 = 1 then
        INVOKE printf, ADDR msg1fmt,ADDR msgshort
        .endif
        test dsb,00000010b
        .if !ZERO?                      ; if bit 1 = 1 then
        INVOKE printf, ADDR msg1fmt,ADDR msglong
        .endif
        test dsb,00000100b
        .if !ZERO?                      ; if bit 2 = 1 then
        INVOKE printf, ADDR msg1fmt,ADDR msgclose
        .endif
        test dsb,00001000b
        .if !ZERO?                      ; if bit 3 = 1 then

        INVOKE printf, ADDR msg1fmt,ADDR msgmult
        .endif
        test dsb,00010000b
        .if !ZERO?                      ; if bit 4 = 1 then
        INVOKE printf, ADDR msg1fmt,ADDR msgskew
        .endif
        test dsb,00100000b
        .if !ZERO?                      ; if bit 5 = 1 then
        INVOKE printf, ADDR msg1fmt,ADDR msgfeed
        .endif
        test dsb,01000000b
        .if !ZERO?                      ; if bit 6 = 1 then
        INVOKE printf, ADDR msg1fmt,ADDR msgjam
        .endif
        test dsb,10000000b
        .if !ZERO?                      ; if bit 7 = 1 then
        INVOKE printf, ADDR msg1fmt,ADDR msgerror
        .endif
        INVOKE printf, ADDR msg1fmt,ADDR msg1
        INVOKE scanf, ADDR in1fmt,ADDR dsb
        INVOKE printf, ADDR msg2fmt,ADDR msg2, dsb
        .endw
        ret
main    endp
        end
```

As can be seen in the while loop, any bit combination that is less than or equal to 0FFh, or 11111111b is allowed, where the h and b stand for hexadecimal and binary, respectively. Note that when a hex number begins with a letter, it has to be preceded with a 0 so that the assembler does not confuse it with a variable name. Once a number of 100h or greater is entered, the loop stops, as can be seen in the sample input/output below.

Sample Input/Output

```
Enter a hexadecimal number: 1
The hexadecimal number is: 1

SHORT DOCUMENT

Enter a hexadecimal number: 2
The hexadecimal number is: 2

LONG DOCUMENT

Enter a hexadecimal number: 3
The hexadecimal number is: 3

SHORT DOCUMENT
LONG DOCUMENT

Enter a hexadecimal number: ff
The hexadecimal number is: ff

SHORT DOCUMENT
LONG DOCUMENT
CLOSE FEED
MULTIPLE FEED
EXCESSIVE SKEW
DOCUMENT MISFEED
DOCUMENT JAM
UNSPECIFIED ERROR

Enter a hexadecimal number: 100
The hexadecimal number is: 100

Press any key to continue . . .
```

6.9   Summary

- The inclusive-or includes the case when both operands are true and the result is true, whereas the exclusive-or excludes this case and the result is false when both operands are true.

- To set, clear or test, and toggle bits, use the or, and, and xor instructions, respectively.
- If data is needed later, be sure to save the data when using the shl and shr instructions.
- As a by-product of other tasks, a register or a memory location can be cleared to zero using the shl and shr instructions. However, the shift instructions can be slower than the mov or xor instructions and the latter two are usually a better choice.
- To multiply or divide by powers of two, use sal and sar, respectively, to communicate to others that arithmetic is being performed and to insure that negative numbers are handled properly with division.
- If a bit pattern is rotated exactly the same number of bits that are in a register or a memory location, then the bit pattern does not need to be saved and restored.
- When saving and restoring data using push and pop instructions, be sure to remember that the last one pushed on the stack should be the first one popped off the stack (LIFO).
- The use of scoping lines when using push and pop instructions can be helpful when creating or debugging code.
- Data in memory can be swapped using only mov instructions which use more registers and are faster compared to using the push and pop instructions which do not use any general purpose registers. Using the xchg instruction along with the appropriate mov instructions is a good compromise in terms of register usage and speed.

6.10   Exercises (Items Marked with an * Have Solutions in Appendix D)

1. Given the following assembly language statements, indicate whether they are syntactically correct or incorrect. If incorrect, indicate what is wrong with the statement:

   *A. or eax,ebx   B. xor al,ah   *C. rotate al,1
    D. shr ax,2   *E. sar eax,3   F. xchg dog,cat
    G. ror exc,1   H. lol dx,8   I. shift 2,ax

2. Given the following C arithmetic instructions, implement them using arithmetic shift instructions, where possible:

   A. answer = num - total / 32;
   *B. result = (amount + number) * 4;
   C. x = y * 8 + z / 2;
   D. a = a / 16 - b * 6;

3. Write a code segment that takes the contents of eax, ebx, ecx, and edx, and puts them in the reverse order of edx, ecx, ebx, and eax using only the push and pop instructions. In other words, eax should contain the contents of edx and vice versa, etc.

4. Assume that a status register in a processor indicates the current state of a photocopying machine according to the following table. For each bit, output an appropriate message indicating the status of the machine. Note that although there can be more than one bit set at one time, only one error message can be generated, where bit 0 has the highest priority, followed by bit 1, etc. At the discretion of the instructor, implement using high-level directives, without high-level directives, or a combination as shown in the text.

Bit Message

0   Paper jam
1   Paper misfeed
2   Paper tray empty
3   Toner low
4   Toner empty

5. Similar to the program in Sect. 6.8, write a program to simulate a security alarm system according to the following table, where it is possible that any of the first three high-priority items could happen at the same time. Although the last three items can also occur at the same time, the program should check and output messages for them only when none of the higher priority first three items have occurred.

Bit Message

0   Fire alarm
1   Carbon monoxide
2   Power outage
3   Gate unlocked
4   Door open
5   Window open

Procedures and Macros

7

This chapter will first show the reader how procedures are implemented in assembly language. The implementation of macros is introduced next which is probably a new topic to most readers. Both procedures and macros are tools that allow programmers to save time by not having to rekey the same code over and over again, but there are important differences between the two mechanisms. The chapter then continues with the introduction of conditional assembly which can be a difficult concept for new assembly language programmers. Lastly, this chapter shows the beginning of the implementation of what might be called a macro calculator which simulates a one register (accumulator) computer.

7.1 Procedures

Most readers are probably familiar with procedures from a previous programming class. Depending on what language was used in that class, procedures may have also been called subprocedures, subprograms, subroutines, functions, or methods. The most generic of these terms is subprograms, which encompass all the others. Functions and many methods can or should return only a single value, whereas procedures, subprocedures, and subroutines are designed to return anywhere from zero to many values. In assembly language, subprograms are called procedures and belong to this last group. Although there are ways to make it possible to utilize parameters, the simplest way to communicate between a program and a procedure is to use either global variables or registers.

The instruction used to invoke a procedure is the `call` instruction. The `call` instruction has one operand that specifies the name of the procedure to be invoked. Upon return from the procedure, execution will continue with the instruction after the `call` instruction. An example is given below, where `pname` is a placeholder for the procedure name:

© Springer Nature Switzerland AG 2020
J. T. Streib, *Guide to Assembly Language*, Undergraduate Topics
in Computer Science, https://doi.org/10.1007/978-3-030-35639-2_7

```
call pname
```

Although the actual procedure can be placed in a number of locations in the program, probably the most convenient place is after the endp statement in the main program and prior to the end statement. The first line of the procedure contains the name of the procedure in the label field, represented by the word pname, followed by the proc directive in the opcode field. Next comes the body of the procedure, followed by the return instruction ret, followed by the endp directive, which has the name of the procedure in the label field as shown below:

```
pname proc
      ; body of the procedure
      ret
pname endp
```

The proc and endp directives indicate to the assembler the beginning and the end of the procedure, respectively. The ret instruction, during the execution of the procedure, indicates when to return to the calling program. Unlike many high-level language, the ret instruction does not return a value to the calling program but rather indicates that the execution of the program should return to the calling program. One of the most common errors made by beginning assembly language programmers is forgetting to include the ret instruction, allowing the execution of the program to continue past the end of the procedure and possibly into another procedure following the current procedure. Although there can be more than one ret instruction in a procedure, like in many high-level languages, it is recommended to include only one return statement in a procedure. This helps to keep the program structured with only one entry point and one exit point. Further, almost any procedure can be rewritten to contain only one ret instruction. For example, given the following procedure with two ret instructions:

```
sample1         proc
                .if eax == 0
                mov edx,1
                ret
                .else
                mov edx,0
                ret
                .endif
sample1         endp
```

it can be rewritten to utilize only one ret instruction:

```
sample1         proc
                .if eax == 0
                mov edx,1
                .else
                mov edx, 0
                .endif
                ret
sample1         endp
```

The result is cleaner code that is less prone to logic errors during modification. Also, it is usually best to be sure that the `ret` instruction is the last statement in a procedure prior to the `endp` directive. Can you determine what is wrong with the following procedure that is supposed to add all the registers together and return the value in `eax`?

```
; *** Caution: Contains a logic error ***
sample2     proc
            add eax, ebx
            add eax, ecx
            ret
            add eax, edx
sample2     endp
```

Yes, the value in the `edx` register is never added to the `eax` register, and `eax` only contains the sum of `eax`, `ebx`, and `ecx` upon return to the calling program. The `add eax, edx` instruction in the above procedure is sometimes referred to as "dead code," because although it takes up space in memory, it is never executed. In larger programs, whole sections of code might never be executed if the code is located incorrectly and it might create a difficult situation to debug. The correct procedure is given below:

```
; *** Note: Correctly implemented code ***
sample2     proc
            add eax, ebx
            add eax, ecx
            add eax, edx
            ret
sample2     endp
```

What if one wanted to implement the multiplication algorithm from Chap. 5 in two different locations? The code could be written twice in two different sections of the program, but instead of writing the code twice, it would be much easier to put the logic in a procedure and then call the procedure from two different locations in the main program:

```
  .
call mult
  .

  .
call mult
  .
```

Then after the main program, the code for the `mult` procedure could be written. Recall this algorithm from the end of Sect. 5.1 which used the `.while` directive. The variables x and y could still contain the two values to be multiplied, but instead of using the variables i and ans, the following procedure uses the ecx and eax registers, respectively, along with other minor changes:

```
mult    proc
        mov eax,0           ; initialize eax to 0
        .if x != 0
        mov ecx,1           ; initialize i to 1
        .while ecx<=y
        add eax,x           ; add x to eax
        inc ecx             ; increment i by 1
        .endw
        .endif
        ret
mult    endp
```

Is there a potential problem with the above procedure? Since ecx is being used as a temporary variable to implement the loop, the contents of ecx will be destroyed. If the main program is not using the ecx register, this would not be a problem. However, if ecx is being used to hold various values, such as a counter for another loop in the calling program, this routine could cause problems. It could be difficult to debug if a programmer did not know that ecx is being used by the procedure. Although it is fairly obvious in this case, it can be difficult to notice in larger procedures.

One solution is to document the procedure carefully and include a comment right at the beginning of the procedure indicating which registers are destroyed by the procedure to warn potential users of the procedure. The responsibility for saving the contents of the affected register then lies with the programmer of the calling program. Although for some small, seldom-used procedures, this effectively solves the problem, it is still possible that the programmer using the procedure might miss the warning. Further, if the procedure is going to be called many times, then the calling program needs to save and restore the affected registers many times, thus wasting memory. Also, the possibility of forgetting to save and restore the registers at some point in time is increased.

When writing procedures, it is often a good idea to have the procedure take the responsibility of saving and restoring any registers being destroyed. This saves memory, since there is only one copy of the code and also lessens the chance for error by the calling program. What is the best way to accomplish this task? Although a temporary variable could be used, this is an excellent situation to use the stack as discussed in Chap. 6. The following multiplication procedure includes the pushing and popping of the ecx register:

```
mult    proc
        push ecx        ; save ecx
        mov eax,0       ; initialize eax to 0
        .if x != 0
        mov ecx,1       ; initialize i to 1
        .while ecx<=y
        add eax,x       ; add x to eax
        inc ecx         ; increment i by 1
        .endw
        .endif
        pop ecx         ; restore ecx
        ret
mult endp
```

Although the act of calling and returning a procedure is a little slower than straight line code, it does save memory because the code needs to be written only once. Of course, the memory saving is compounded as the size of the procedure and the number of calls increase.

7.2 Complete Program: Implementing the Power Function in a Procedure

To illustrate a complete example, consider the problem of calculating x^n from Sect. 5.6. Instead of having the code to calculate x^n in the main program, it could be placed in a procedure. The procedure can then be invoked more than one time from the main program without having to duplicate the code each time. For the sake of simplicity both in the C program and more importantly in the subsequent assembly language program, power is implemented as a procedure (void function) and x, n, and ans are implemented as global variables. In addition to outputting a message in the case of an error, the procedure also returns a −1 in the variable ans:

```
#include <stdio.h>
int x,n,ans;
int main() {
    void power();
    printf("%s","Enter x: ");
    scanf("%d",&x);
    printf("%s","Enter n: ");
    scanf("%d",&n);
    power();
```

```
      printf("\n%s%d\n\n","The answer is: ",ans);
      return 0;
}
void power() {
   int i;
   ans=-1;
   if(x<0 || n<0)
      printf("\n%s\n","Error: Negative x and/or y");
   else
      if(x==0 && n==0)
         printf("\n%s\n","Error: Undefined answer");
      else {
         i=1;
         ans=1;
         while(i<=n) {
            ans=ans*x;
            i++;
         }
      }
}
```

As mentioned previously, global variables are used for x, n, and ans both in the C program above and in the assembly language below. Since i is declared as a local variable in the C code above and is not needed in the main program, ecx is used as the loop control variable in the assembly language procedure below:

```
                  .686
                  .model flat,c
                  .stack 100h
scanf        PROTO arg2:Ptr Byte, inputlist:VARARG
printf       PROTO arg1:Ptr Byte, printlist:VARARG
                  .data
in1fmt       byte "%d",0
msg1fmt      byte "%s",0
msg3fmt      byte "%s%d",0Ah,0Ah,0
errfmt       byte "%s",0Ah,0
errmsg1      byte 0Ah,"Error: Negative x and/or y",0
errmsg2      byte 0Ah,"Error: Undefined answer",0
msg1         byte "Enter x: ",0
msg2         byte "Enter n: ",0
msg3         byte 0Ah,"The answer is: ",0
x            sdword ?
n            sdword ?
```

```
ans           sdword ?
              .code
main          proc
              INVOKE printf, ADDR msg1fmt, ADDR msg1
              INVOKE scanf, ADDR in1fmt, ADDR x
              INVOKE printf, ADDR msg1fmt, ADDR msg2
              INVOKE scanf, ADDR in1fmt, ADDR n

              call power

              INVOKE printf, ADDR msg3fmt, ADDR msg3, ans
              ret
main          endp
power         proc
              push eax    ; save registers
              push ecx
              push edx
              mov ans,-1       ; default value for ans
              .if x<0 || n<0
              INVOKE printf, ADDR errfmt, ADDR errmsg1
              .else
              .if x==0 && n==0
              INVOKE printf, ADDR errfmt, ADDR errmsg2
              .else
              mov ecx,1        ; initialize ecx loop counter
              mov ans,1        ; initialize ans
              .while ecx <= n
              mov eax,ans    ; load eax with ans
              imul x         ; multiply eax by x
              mov ans,eax    ; sotre eax in ans
              inc ecx        ; increment eax loop countere
              .endw
              .endif
              .endif
              pop edx          ; restore registers
              pop ecx
              pop eax
              ret
power         endp
              end
```

Could the assembly language procedure above use registers instead of global variables to communicate back and forth between the procedure and the main program? Yes, but in the procedure above, x and y are checked to see if they are negative in the .if directive. Recall from Chap. 4 that the default in high-level directives is unsigned data unless a memory location declared as sdword is used.

Also, INVOKE directives are being used in the procedure to output error messages and remember from Chap. 2 that they destroy the contents of the eax, ecx, and edx registers. The result is that for smaller and simpler procedures the use of registers is probably the preferred method, but in instances like this, the use of global variables might be the better choice.

Note that the eax, ecx, and edx registers are saved at the beginning and restored at the end of the procedure. This is done not only because of the INVOKE directives but also because even if the procedure did not perform any output, the three registers should be saved and restored. It is obvious that eax is used in the mov instructions and the contents of ecx are destroyed when it is used for loop control. However, the edx register does not appear in the procedure, so why should it be saved and restored? Again, look carefully at the code and recall what happens with the imul instruction. The imul instruction extends the sign of the eax register into the edx register and destroys the contents of edx, so it should be saved and restored also. Even if the main program that called the procedure does not use the eax, ecx and edx registers, the procedure should save and restore them so that the procedure could easily be used by other programs that might use these registers. Lastly, as discussed in Chap. 6, be careful to insure that the pop instructions are in the correct order to properly restore the three registers.

7.3   Saving and Restoring Registers

Note that if registers are not being used to communicate back to the main program, it is possible to save and restore all the registers, whether they were altered or not. Although this might be an easy way to avoid having to think about whether a register is altered, it is a sloppy method and does not help other programmers understand what is happening in the procedure. In other words, even though it might be simpler for the person writing the code, it is not necessarily easier for subsequent people reading and modifying the code. By saving and restoring only the registers that are altered, it helps others understand which registers are being altered and also helps makes the code more self-documenting. Of course whether code appears to be self-documenting or not, documentation is always a good idea to supplement any code written.

However, what if a routine was altering all the registers and does not use a register to communicate back from a procedure to the main program? It could get a little messy trying to push and pop all the registers and further, there could be a chance for a logic error if the pop instructions were accidently written in the wrong order. Luckily it is possible to save the four general purpose registers (eax, ebx, ecx, and edx) along with the esi, edi, ebp, and esp registers with only one instruction. The pushad instruction pushes contents of all the above registers onto the stack and the popad instruction subsequently pops the values from the stack and puts them back into their respective register locations.

As an example, consider a procedure that outputs blank lines a variable number of times. It would be nice that it does not destroy the contents of any registers and also not use any global variables, both of which would make it a very portable procedure that could be used in many different programs. As is known, using the INVOKE directive to output the blank lines can cause the contents of the eax, ecx, and edx registers to be altered. Since global variables will not be used, the ebx register could be used to communicate to the procedure how many blank lines need to be output. At the same time, since ebx would not be destroyed by the INVOKE directive, it would also make a good candidate for a loop control variable. Given these circumstances in this example, all four registers should probably be saved and restored. In the first example, each of the four general purpose registers are saved and restored individually:

```
blankln     proc
            push eax
            push ebx
            push ecx
            push edx
            .repeat
            INVOKE printf, ADDR blnkfmt
            dec ebx
            .until ebx<=0
            pop edx
            pop ecx
            pop ebx
            pop eax
            ret
blankln     endp
```

Note the order of the push and pop instructions above to properly save and restore the contents of the four registers. In the example below, the four general purpose registers are saved all at once using the pushad and popad instructions:

```
blankln     proc
            pushad
            .repeat
            INVOKE printf, ADDR blnkfmt
            dec ebx
            .until ebx<=0
            popad
            ret
blankln     endp
```

As can be seen, clearly the second procedure is much cleaner than the first procedure. Since the above procedures do not return a value via a register and all four general purpose registers need to be saved and restored, this is a good example of when the `pushad` and `popad` instructions should be used. However, since most of the time the majority of the procedures in this text will be returning a value, the previously described method of saving and restoring registers individually will be used more frequently.

7.4 Macros

Another method to avoid having to write the same code again and again is the *macro*. However, be forewarned that even though it executes faster than a procedure, it tends to waste memory. Although most readers have probably not encountered macros in previous programming classes, they might have encountered the term in working with application software packages. Probably the most common occurrence of macros is in spreadsheet packages, where one can record a macro that consists of a series of steps performed by the user. Although a macro in assembler can contain a series of instructions, it is different from a macro in a spreadsheet, where the instructions are not recorded but rather need to be written by the programmer.

Like procedures, macros can be declared in many different places. Whereas procedures are usually declared after the main program, macros are usually written and located prior to the main program, just after the `.code` directive. This first writing of the macro is sometimes called the *macro definition* and does not take up any memory in the executable program. Further, a macro has a similar structure to a procedure, where on the first line the name of the macro is in the label field, indicated by `mname` below, and the `macro` directive is in the opcode field. The body of the macro follows, which is then followed by the `endm` directive which unlike an `endp` does not repeat the name of the macro in the label field as shown below:

```
mname     macro
          ; body of the macro
          endm
```

However, a question here might be, should there be a `ret` instruction just prior to the `endm` directive above? The answer is no, because there is not a set of instructions in a common place that are branched to and executed as with a procedure. Rather, a set of instructions exist only in the source code file (`.asm`), a copy of the instructions is inserted into the listing file (`.lst`), and the machine language equivalent is inserted into the execution file (`.exe`), wherever the macro is invoked.

Instead of a `call` instruction as with a procedure, a *macro invocation* is done by just using the name of the macro, `mname` in this instance, in the opcode field of the invoking program as demonstrated below:

```
    .
mname
    .

    .
mname
    .
```

Thus unlike a procedure, where the flow of executions jumps to the procedure and then returns back to the calling program, a copy of the macro is inserted into the program at each point where the macro is invoked. The result is that macros are faster because there is no calling or returning. Further, it is possible that if the macro is never invoked, it will never take up any memory because the code exists only in the source code file (`.asm`). However, usually macros tend to take up more memory due to the copying of the instructions at every location it is invoked and this is especially true when macros are large and/or invoked many times.

Consider an example of swapping two memory locations `num1` and `num2`, where a macro could be written as follows:

```
swap    macro
        mov ebx,num1     ; copy num1 into ebx
        xchg ebx,num2    ; exchange ebx and num2
        mov num1,ebx     ; copy ebx into num1
        endm
```

As mentioned above, notice the lack of a `ret` instruction in the macro declaration. The invoking of a macro is done by just specifying the macro name in the opcode field in the calling program, as shown below, where it can be assumed that the programmer wanted to swap `num1` and `num2`, and then turn around and swap them back to their original locations:

```
    .
swap
    .

    .
swap
    .
```

A common mistake made by beginning assembly language programmers is that they include the `call` instruction when trying to invoke the macro, where this should be avoided and would cause a syntax error. A question that many readers might have at this point is: Why haven't `push` and `pop` been included in the macro definition above? Couldn't there be the same problems with the calling program as with procedures, since the contents of the ebx register are being destroyed by the macro? The answer to the second question is yes, the same problem still exists. But in answer to the first question, the reason why the push and pop instructions have not been included is because they take up memory. One must remember that every time a macro is invoked, another copy of the macro is inserted into the code in the invoking program. As a result, many times the contents of registers are not saved in macros in order to save memory and a programmer needs to be extra careful whenever invoking a macro.

This can be especially confusing, because unlike the procedure which is invoked via the call instruction, a macro is invoked only by using the name of the macro. Many times the name of a macro almost appears to be like the name of an instruction, so the user of the macro might be lulled into believing it is an instruction and forget about the hidden instructions in the macro that might destroy the contents of the registers. Many a programmer has accidentally made this mistake and spent much time trying to subsequently debug a program.

To help illustrate how macros take up memory and remind programmers that they are not instructions, it is sometimes useful to examine the assembly listing file (.1st) to see what is known as the *macro expansion* and all the instructions from the macro that are inserted into the code. For example the above calling program that invokes the macro swap twice would look as follows in the .1st file:

```
                    swap
00000000  8B 1D 00000046 R  1   mov ebx,num1     ; copy num1 into ebx
00000006  87 1D 0000004A R  1   xchg ebx,num2    ; exchange ebx and num2
0000000C  89 1D 00000046 R  1   mov num1,ebx     ; copy ebx into num1
                    swap
00000012  8B 1D 00000046 R  1   mov ebx,num1     ; copy num1 into ebx
00000018  87 1D 0000004A R  1   xchg ebx,num2    ; exchange ebx and num2
0000001E  89 1D 00000046 R  1   mov num1,ebx     ; copy ebx into num1
```

In the above listing, both the relative memory address and machine language equivalent in hexadecimal can be seen to the left. However, since the .1st file can sometimes get rather messy and have a cluttered appearance when macros are expanded, the addresses and machine code have been removed to make this example easier to read in both the listing below and many subsequent listings (for more information on machine language, see Chap. 12):

```
swap
        mov ebx,num1        ; copy num1 into ebx
        xchg ebx,num2       ; exchange ebx and num2
        mov num1,ebx        ; copy ebx into num1
swap
        mov ebx,num1        ; copy num1 into ebx
        xchg ebx,num2       ; exchange ebx and num2
        mov num1,ebx        ; copy ebx into num1
```

A nice feature that should be noticed above is that any comments placed in the macro definition also appear in the macro expansion. Although the macro expansion might cause the program to appear more cluttered and also waste more paper when printing out the listing of the program, the possibility of avoiding errors during program development might well be worth it. It can also be especially helpful during the debugging process when trying to track down pesky logic errors.

A very useful feature when using macros is the ability to use arguments and parameters. Recall from high-level languages that the calling program sends arguments to procedures which correspond to parameters in the procedure. However, parameters in macros are different from many of the parameters that one may have encountered in various high-level languages. Depending on which language the reader has used previously, it should be recalled that reference and value parameters are used in C++ and that only value parameters are used in Java. Reference parameters refer to their corresponding arguments via an address and value parameters copy the values from the corresponding arguments. If the reader has had an upper-level course in programming languages, then name parameters might be familiar. Although name parameters are not used by very many modern programming languages, they were used in the past in languages such as Algol in the 1960s. For those who have not encountered them before, name parameters are essentially substitution parameters, where the names of the arguments are merely substituted in place of the parameter names.

For example, in the previous swap macro, what if one wanted to swap the contents of any two memory locations instead of just num1 and num2? The swap macro could be rewritten as follows, where p1 and p2 are the two name parameters:

```
swap    macro p1,p2
        mov ebx,p1          ; copy p1 into ebx
        xchg ebx,p2         ; exchange ebx and p2
        mov p1,ebx          ; copy ebx into p1
        endm
```

Now, the above macro would work with any two memory locations as arguments. For example,

```
        .
swap num1,num2
        .
        .
swap x,y
        .
```

Although at first glance the macro invocations look somewhat like memory to memory instructions, they are not. In order to understand how the above macros work it is best to look at the macro expansions. In the first swap, the code would look similar to the previous example without parameters because the argument

names are the same as the previously used variable names. However, the second
swap looks different because different memory locations are used in the arguments:

```
swap num1,num2
        mov ebx,num1        ; copy p1 into ebx
        xchg ebx,num2       ; exchange ebx and p2
        mov num1,ebx        ; copy ebx into p1
        .
        .
swap x,y
        mov ebx,x           ; copy p1 into ebx
        xchg ebx,y          ; exchange ebx and p2
        mov x,ebx           ; copy ebx into p1
        .
```

The above example shows the versatility of parameters, where different arguments can be used with each invocation. Although the comments from the macro
definition are included in the expansion, unfortunately the comments refer to the
parameter names rather than the argument names. Should one want to document the
macro definition using comments, but not see the comments in the macro expansion, double semicolons (;;) should be used prior to the comment in the macro
definition instead of the single semicolons (;) as used above.

What if a programmer left one or both arguments blank when trying to invoke
the swap macro? With this particular macro it is not much of a problem, because in
this instance a syntax error would occur from the instructions themselves in the
macro that are missing a required operand. However, there are a few instructions,
such as the imul instruction, that have optional operands and not requiring an
argument might cause a syntax error to be missed. As a result, it is good programming practice to indicate whether or not the arguments are required. This can
be accomplished by using the :REQ statement in the parameter list. Should a
required argument not be included, a syntax error would be generated regardless of
the instructions used in the macro. To require both arguments in the swap macro,
the resulting macro definition would look as follows:

```
swap    macro p1:REQ,p2:REQ
        mov ebx,p1          ;; copy p1 into ebx
        xchg ebx,p2         ;; exchange ebx and p2
        mov p1,ebx          ;; copy ebx into p1
        endm
```

Note also the comments above have been changed to use double semicolons
(;;) so that they do not appear in subsequent macro expansions. Although the
problem of a missing argument is solved, what would happen if an incorrect
argument was used? For example, what would happen if an immediate value was
inadvertently used as one of the arguments instead, as in swap num, 1? The result
is that this would cause a syntax error in the second instruction of the macro

expansion in the `.lst` file, because immediate values cannot be exchanged as illustrated below:

```
swap num1,1
     mov ebx,num1
     xchg ebx,1
error A2070: invalid instruction operands
     mov num1,ebx
```

In another potential problem, what if registers were used instead of memory locations? Would this cause a problem, especially if one of the registers was `ebx` as in the second example below?

```
swap eax,ecx
```

```
swap ebx,ecx
```

The above invocations would generate the following macro expansions. As an aside, note that comments are not generated in the macro expansion due to the use of the double semicolons (; ;) in the previous macro definition:

```
swap    eax,ecx
        mov ebx,eax
        xchg ebx,ecx
        mov eax,ebx
```

```
swap    ebx,ecx
        mov ebx,ebx
        xchg ebx,ecx
        mov ebx,ebx
```

Although both of the above work, they are very redundant. In the first example, the value of `eax` is placed into `ebx`, then swapped with `ecx`, and then the value originally in `ecx` is placed into `eax`, where just a simple `xchg eax,ecx` would have sufficed instead. The second example is even more redundant where the value of `ebx` is moved into itself, then `ebx` is exchanged with `ecx`, and then `ebx` is moved again back into `ebx`. Although both of these expansions are redundant, they are syntactically correct and logically harmless. But what would happen if the two registers in the last example were reversed, as in `swap ecx,ebx`? The answer can be found in the following macro expansion:

```
            .
swap    ecx,ebx
        mov ebx,ecx
        xchg ebx,ebx
        mov ecx,ebx
            .
```

As can be seen, the contents of ebx are wiped out by the contents of ecx in the first line of the macro expansion, then ebx is swapped with itself, and then ecx is reloaded with the results that were originally in ecx. The result is that both ebx and ecx would now contain the contents of ecx. Would this produce an error message? No, this is not a syntax or an execution error but rather a logic error and points to a problem with using parameters with macros. As a result, where some problems produced syntax errors and some produced redundant code, this last one is the most serious. Programmers must be very careful when using macros and be sure to understand how they work before invoking them. It might be argued that a mistake like this is solely the responsibility of the programmer using the macro and let the user beware. However, can the problem be fixed? Yes, where a possible solution to this problem will be addressed in Sect. 7.6.

7.5   Conditional Assembly

Conditional assembly can be a confusing topic to beginning assembly language programmers. It uses what looks like if statements so that it seems like it is altering the flow of control during the execution of the program, but it is not the same as the selection structures learned in Chap. 4. Instead, the key to understanding conditional assembly is from its name, where it is "conditional assembly," not "conditional execution." Specifically, conditional assembly controls the assembler, not the flow of execution. Instead of having one or two possible routes for the execution to follow as with an .if statement, conditional assembly tells the assembler whether to put in a possible instruction or a possible set of instructions into the program as opposed to other possible instructions or no instructions at all.

There are a number of ways that conditional assembly can work, and this section will look at a few of the more commonly used methods. Table 7.1 lists the conditional assembly directives used in this and subsequent sections. Probably the best way to illustrate the concept and the directives is through an example.

Although somewhat simplistic, the first method to be examined is whether or not there is an argument in a macro invocation. In other words, instead of causing an error from a :REQ or subsequent instruction in the macro expansion, whether caused by an intentional or an unintentional missing argument, alternative code can be generated.

For example, suppose one wanted to create a macro called addacc, that when invoked without an argument, the default is to add the number 1 to the eax register. Since the most efficient way to do that is to use the inc instruction, that is

Table 7.1 Conditional assembly directives

Directive	Meaning
if	If (can use EQ, NE, LT, LE, GT, GE, OR, AND)
ifb	If blank
ifnb	If not blank
ifidn	If identical
ifidni	If identical case insensitive
ifdif	If different
ifdifi	If different case insensitive

what the macro will use. However, when a number, a register, or a memory location is used as an argument, the macro will then add that number, register, or memory location to the eax register. Clearly the inc instruction would not work in this second instance, so an add instruction must be used. How would the conditional assembly work in this example? If the argument is blank, then the inc instruction would be inserted into the code, otherwise the add instruction with the appropriate argument would be inserted into the code. The macro would be written as follows:

```
addacc    macro parm
          ifb <parm>
          inc eax
          else
          add eax,parm
          endif
          endm
```

Note that :REQ is not used in the parameter list, because a blank argument is one of the options. The first directive in the macro is ifb, which stands for "if blank." Again, it is not an instruction, nor is it like one of the directives from Chap. 4 which generate the instructions like cmp and je. Rather as the assembler is inputting statement after statement from the assembly language source file (.asm), it checks to see if the argument from the macro invocation statement is blank. If it is blank, it inserts the inc eax instruction into the .lst file and the equivalent machine language instruction into the .exe file. Otherwise the mov eax,parm instruction after the else directive is inserted with the corresponding argument in place of the parameter parm. Lastly, the endif indicates the end of the ifb. It should be carefully noted that unlike the selection statements introduced in Chap. 4, none of these three directives have a decimal prior to the directive.

The following contains four different invocations of the preceding macro definition:

```
.
addacc
.

.
addacc 5
.

.
addacc edx
.

.
addacc num
.
```

The complete resulting code with the macro expansions is given below to show how it would actually look in the .lst file. Although it appears that there are a number of instructions, the only real lines of executable code that are generated are the ones that have addresses and machine code off to the left in hexadecimal (again see Chap. 12):

```
                                  addacc
                              1           ifb <>
0000000A 40                   1           inc eax
                              1           else
                              1           add eax,
                              1           endif
                                  addacc 5
                              1           ifb <5>
                              1           inc eax
                              1           else
0000000B 83 C0 05             1           add eax,5
                              1           endif
                                  addacc edx
                              1           ifb <edx>
                              1           inc eax
                              1           else
0000000E 03 C2                1           add eax,edx
                              1           endif
                                  addacc num
                              1           ifb <num>
                              1           inc eax
                              1           else
00000010 03 05 0000003A R     1           add eax,num
                              1           endif
```

The above code segment does save a little memory under some circumstances because as mentioned back in Chap. 3 and will be demonstrated in Chap. 12, the inc instruction takes up less memory. Although it is getting a little ahead here in the text, it is interesting to point out that depending on the argument, a different machine language instruction is generated based on the operand. To illustrate, the inc eax instructions generates at relative memory location 0000000A a hexadecimal 40 machine language instruction that is only 1 byte long and the add eax, num instruction generates at relative memory location 00000010 a hexadecimal 03 05 0000003A machine language instruction that is 6 bytes long (see Chap. 12). As before, since the above is rather cluttered, by eliminating the other lines of source code, the following shows a copy of each macro invocation followed by only the assembly instruction that would be generated and executed:

```
addacc
    inc eax
addacc 5
    add eax,5
addacc edx
    add eax,edx
addacc num
    add eax,num
```

Although the above cleaned up code segment seems relatively simple, it illustrates how different code can be used in place of other code when using conditional assembly, even though the source code containing the macro definition looks as though there might be more instructions. Again, there is only one actual assembly language instruction generated for each invocation in the above example.

7.6   Swap Macro Revisited Using Conditional Assembly

Returning to the swap example in Sect. 7.4, what would happen if invocations such as the ones on the left in Table 7.2 were used to invoke the previous definition repeated on the right?

The result would be that the following code would be generated:

Table 7.2 Macro invocations and definition

Invocations	Definition
.	`swap macro p1:REQ,p2:REQ`
`swap num1,num1`	`    mov ebx,p1        ;; copy p1 into ebx`
.	`    xchg ebx,p2       ;; exchange ebx and p2`
	`    mov p1,ebx        ;; copy ebx into p1·`
`swap eax,eax`	`    endm`
.	

```
        .
swap num1,num1
        mov ebx,num1
        xchg ebx,num1
        mov num1,ebx
        .
        .
swap eax,eax
        mov ebx,eax
        xchg ebx,eax
        mov eax,ebx
        .
```

As has happened before, redundant code is generated in both cases, but is there a possible solution to this problem? The answer is yes and it can be solved by using conditional assembly. As per Table 7.1, an ifidn (if identical) checks to see if the two arguments are equal using case sensitivity and an ifidni does the same thing but is case insensitive. The directive ifdif (if different) uses case sensitivity to check to see if the arguments are different and ifdifi does the same thing with case insensitivity.

The statement that can help in this instance is ifidni directive. For example, if the arguments are the same, then there is no need to swap the contents and thus no code needs to be generated as shown in the following macro definition:

```
swap    macro p1:REQ, p2:REQ
        ifdifi <p1>,<p2>
        mov ebx,p1
        xchg ebx,p2
        mov p1,ebx
        endif
        endm
```

The invocation of swap using various different scenarios is shown below:

```
swap num1,num2
swap num1,num1
swap eax,ecx
swap eax,eax
```

The resulting macro expansions are as follows:

```
swap    num1,num2
        mov ebx,num1
        xchg ebx,num2
        mov num1,ebx


swap    num1,num1


swap    eax,ecx
        mov ebx,eax
        xchg ebx,ecx
        mov eax,ebx


swap    eax,eax
```

Note that code is not generated in the second and fourth examples because of the ifdifi directive and thus the redundant code need not be generated. The swapping of two memory locations is carried out easily in the first example and although the third example is still redundant, there is no harm done. As can be seen, this helps clean up much of the redundant code but still allows for some redundant code as in the third case above. However, what about the more serious problem at the end of Sect. 7.4 when the ebx register was used as the second argument resulting in a logic error?

In addition to seeing if the two arguments are the same or different, the above directives can be used to see if the parameters are equal to a particular register. In other words, by putting a particular register in brackets in one of the two positions of the ifidni, and the name of the parameter in brackets in the other position, it can then compare the parameter to the particular register and generate the appropriate code.

```
swap    macro p1:REQ,p2:REQ
        ifidni <ebx>,<p2>
        xchg p1,ebx
        else
        mov ebx,p1
        xchg ebx,p2
        mov p1,ebx
        endif
        endm
```

In the code above, <p2> is compared to see if it is identical to <ebx>, and if so, different code can be generated, otherwise the original code is executed in the else section. The following invocations

```
.
swap ebx,eax
.

.
swap eax,ebx
.
```

show how the code is different when the ebx is in either of the argument positions:

```
swap    ebx,eax
        mov ebx,ebx
        xchg ebx,eax
        mov ebx,ebx

swap    eax,ebx
        xchg eax,ebx
```

Again, some of the code is still redundant, but the danger of the logic error has now been eliminated. Can this last bit of redundancy be eliminated? Yes, by nesting another set of if, else, and endif directives after the outer else directive. Even an elseif directive could be used as follows:

```
swap    macro p1:REQ,p2:REQ
        ifidni <ebx>,<p2>
        xchg p1,ebx
        elseifidni <p1>,<ebx>
        xchg ebx,p2
        else
        mov ebx,p1
        xchg ebx,p2
        mov p1,ebx
        endif
        endm
```

Using the same two swap invocations from above, the following code is generated:

```
swap    ebx,eax
        xchg ebx,eax

swap    eax,ebx
        xchg eax,ebx
```

If a macro is going to be used only a few times by knowledgeable programmers, does one need to create such an elaborate macro using conditional assembly? The answer is probably no, because the time and effort needed to create the macro is most likely not worth the savings in terms of memory and execution speed. However, if the macro will used a lot and by programmers with a variety of different skill levels, then the savings not only in terms of memory and execution speed might be worth it, but also the savings in terms of not having to correct syntax, redundancy, and logic errors may prove to be well worth the additional effort too.

7.7 Power Function Macro Using Conditional Assembly

In another example, what if one wanted to implement the power function in a macro? Recall from Chap. 6 the definition of the power function, which is reiterated below. For the sake of convenience, instead of outputting error messages, only a flag such as a -1 could be returned to indicate error had occurred:

$x^n =$ If $x < 0$ or $n < 0$, then -1
    Else if $x = 0$ and $n = 0$, then -1
      Else if $n = 0$, then 1
        Otherwise $1 * x * x * \ldots * x$ (n times)

Although the above definition would ideally be better implemented as a procedure because only one copy of it would be needed, it is a good example that can help illustrate some more important concepts concerning macros and conditional assembly. Of course, a macro could be written without conditional assembly, but then every time the code was generated, both the selection statements and loop would need to be inserted whether they were needed or not, which would be a waste of memory.

However, by using conditional assembly, not all of the if statements need to be included every time the macro is invoked. Further, in some of the cases a loop is not needed and the code for the loop would not need to be generated. For example, when n is 0, then the answer is 1, when n is 1 the answer is x, and when x is either 0 or 1, the answer is x. Thus, the above definition can be further revised as follows to better reflect how the macro could be written. Only when both x and n are greater than 1 would the code for the loop need to be generated. Below is the modified definition used in this example:

x^n = If $x < 0$ or $n < 0$, then -1
     Else if $x = 0$ and $n = 0$, then -1
      Else if $x = 0$ or $x = 1$, then x
       Else if $n = 0$, then 1
        Else if $n = 1$, then x,
             Otherwise $1 * x * x * \ldots * x$ (n times)

In addition to the directives used previously (ifb, inb, idif, etc.), it is possible to use just a simple if directive that can use the equivalent of relationals (eq, ne, lt, gt, le, ge) and logic (and, or) as shown in Table 7.1. The implementation of the above definition can then be accomplished as below. However, note that the simple if directive cannot contain memory locations or registers, but only constants. Also, it should be noted to use parentheses when using the logical operators as shown below. For this example, a constant for x will be passed as the first argument and a constant for the exponent n as the second argument, and the answer returned in the eax register:

```
power       macro x:REQ,n:REQ
            if (x lt 0) or (n lt 0)
            mov eax,-1
            elseif (x eq 0) and (n eq 0)
            mov eax,-1
            elseif (x eq 0) or (x eq 1)
            mov eax,x
            elseif n eq 0
            mov eax,1
            elseif n eq 1
            mov eax,x
            else
            mov eax,x
            mov ebx,eax
            mov ecx,n
            dec ecx
            .repeat
            imul ebx
            .untilcxz
            endif
            endm
```

When either x or n is less than 0, or if both x and n are equal to 0, the eax register is set to -1. Should x be equal to either 0 or 1, the result is x, if only n is 0, the answer is 1, or if n is 1, then the answer is x, where in all of these cases the loop does not need to be executed nor does it even need to be generated. Lastly, notice that the loop is implemented using a .repeat-.untilcxz directive instead of a while loop. Since the case when n is equal to one is already handled, the loop only needs to iterate n−1 times. Although the above code segment looks rather large, remember that not all of the code is used in each invocation. Only the last case is the largest and since it is generated only when x and n are greater than 1, it does not need to be generated for all of the other cases. Note that all the registers are used, so care must be used when invoking this macro. The following sample invocations test seven different cases:

```
    .
power 2,-1
    .
power 0,0
    .
power 0,2
    .
power 1,2
    .
power 2,0
    .
power 3,1
    .
power 2,3
    .
```

Given the invocations above, the following macro expansions would be generated in each of the seven cases. Note that it is in only the last case that the loop is actually generated, where the .repeat-.untilcxz directive is implemented as a loop instruction:

```
        .
power 2,-1
        mov eax,-1
        .
power 0,0
        mov eax,-1
        .
power 0,2
        mov eax,0
        .
power 1,2
        mov eax,1
        .
```

```
power 2,0
      mov eax,1
           .
power 3,1
      mov eax,3
           .
power 2,3
      mov eax,2
      mov ebx,eax
      mov ecx,3
      dec ecx
@C0001:
      imul ebx
      loop    @C0001
           .
```

7.8   Complete Program: Implementing a Macro Calculator

A nice way to illustrate the use of macros is to create what could be thought of as a macro calculator that simulates a one register (accumulator) computer. In a sense, the macros created and subsequently invoked almost appear to be a new set of instructions that can be used by the programmer. Although it somewhat looks like a new assembly language has been created and it is even sometimes mistakenly called an assembler, it is not really a new assembly language because that would require a separate program to assemble the instructions into the corresponding machine language. Instead, macros are used to create what looks like new instructions for the programmer and those macros in turn use existing assembly language instructions. Even though it is not really an assembler, it is still interesting to invoke the macros that appear to be like instructions that come from another hypothetical assembly language.

To implement this macro calculator, it is assumed that there is only one register called the accumulator. The eax register naturally can assume the role of this accumulator. As far as the macro calculator instruction set is concerned, there are no other registers. However, that does not mean that the other registers cannot be used on occasion as necessary to implement some of the other instructions. In a sense, the other registers are hidden from the macro calculator programmer. For those who are taking or have had a computer organization course, this is not unlike many processors that have registers that are not directly accessible by the programmers, such as the MAR (memory address register) and MDR (memory data register) in the CPU. The instructions for this macro calculator are given in Table 7.3.

Table 7.3 Macro calculator instructions

Instruction	Implemented as	Description
INACC	proc	Prompt for and input an integer into the accumulator
OUTACC	proc	Output message and integer in the accumulator
LOADACC	macro	Load the accumulator with the operand
STOREACC	macro	Store accumulator in the operand
ADDACC	macro	Add operand to the accumulator
SUBACC	macro	Subtract operand from the accumulator
MULTACC	macro	Multiply accumulator by the operand (iterative)
DIVACC	macro	Divide accumulator by the operand (iterative)

As mentioned above, the only register that should be modified is the eax register, which serves as the accumulator for the macro calculator. When implementing the various macros, care should be taken not to alter any of the other registers needlessly. For example, with the MULTACC macro, it will be necessary to alter at least one other register. As stated previously, macros typically do not save and restore the registers because that can take up time and memory. However, the purpose of this program is not necessarily to be efficient but rather to simulate a one accumulator machine where the only register that should be altered is eax and this will provide further practice in using the stack.

As mentioned previously in Chap. 6, a possible solution to saving and restoring registers is to use the pushad and popad instructions, but many of the above macros return a value via the eax register. Also, many of the macros will only alter a single register, so this method would almost be overkill. Another solution is that instead of trying to determine which registers are indeed altered, just save and restore all the other registers not being used to return values to insure that none of them will accidently be altered. Although this solution would work and is sometimes employed by some programmers, it is again overkill and also a sloppy solution. Instead, it is best to save and restore only those registers that are indeed altered, which helps other programmers examining the macros to understand the code and also helps cut down on the number of instructions necessary to implement the macro when saving and restoring registers.

In looking at a few of the above macros, the LOADACC macro simply loads the contents of the specified memory location into the accumulator. Obviously, this is like the mov instruction and it forms the body of the macro. The ADDACC macro is similarly just the implementation of the add instruction. In both cases, no other registers are altered, so there is no reason to save and restore any other registers. The implementation of each can be found below:

```
LOADACC    macro operand
           mov eax,operand
           endm


ADDACC     macro operand
           add eax,operand
           endm
```

The MULTACC macro could obviously be implemented using an imul instruction, but for the sake of practice the iteration method will be used. Again, since there is more than one instruction, it might be better to have it implemented as a procedure, but to allow for additional practice, a macro will be used. The algorithm presented here is somewhat similar to the algorithm presented in Sect. 5.1; however, the one presented here stresses some different concepts. Although there are some inefficiencies in the following algorithm, a more interesting concern here is the multiplying by a negative number which will allow another demonstration of conditional assembly.

If the multiplier in the operand is positive, there is no problem, because the loop will repetitively add the value of the multiplicand in the accumulator (eax) and whether the value in the accumulator is positive or negative does not matter. But if the multiplier in the operand is negative, it needs to be made positive in order to loop the correct number of times. Then if the value of the multiplicand in the accumulator is positive, the answer will need to be made negative and if the value of the multiplicand in the accumulator is negative, the answer will need to be made positive, because a negative number multiplied by a negative is positive. Table 7.4 illustrates these four possibilities.

Using the simple conditional if directive, the following can use only immediate integer values for the operand:

Table 7.4 Four possibilities

Accumulator	Operand	Iteration	Answer	Answer corrected
2	3	2 + 2 + 2	= 6	
−2	3	−2 + −2 + −2	= −6	
2	−3	2 + 2 + 2	= 6	−(6) = −6
−2	−3	−2 + −2 + −2	= −6	−(−6) = 6

```
MULTACC     macro operand
            push ebx                ;; save ebx and ecx
            push ecx
            mov ebx,eax             ;; mov eax to ebx
            mov eax,0               ;; clear accumulator to zero
            mov ecx,operand         ;; load ecx with operand
            if operand LT 0         ;; if operand is negative
            neg ecx                 ; make ecx positive for loop
            endif
            .while ecx >0
            add eax,ebx             ;; repetitively add
            dec ecx                 ;; decrement ecx
            .endw
            if operand LT 0   ;; if operand is negative
            neg eax                 ; negate accumulator, eax
            endif
            pop ecx                 ;; restore ecx and ebx
            pop ebx
            endm
```

Since the eax register is serving as the accumulator and it contains the value that needs to be returned as a result of the multiplication operation, note that the ebx and ecx registers are obviously saved and restored and that the eax register is not. Also notice the negation of ecx prior to the loop and the negation of eax after the loop are done using conditional assembly, where only if the operand is negative will these instructions be generated in the macro expansion. If the value of the operand is 0, then the loop will not iterate, but if the value in eax is 0, then the loop will iterate redundantly. Can this be solved using conditional assembly? Yes, and this is left as an exercise for the reader at the end of the chapter.

Obviously there is no single instruction to output the contents of the accumulator. Since the implementation of the output is really a call to a procedure via the INVOKE directive and to incorporate some procedures in this example, the OUT-ACC is implemented below as a procedure. Of course the format statements and the temporary memory location temp will need to be defined as is shown in the program skeleton shortly:

```
OUTACC      proc
            push eax     ; save eax, ecx, and edx
            push ecx
            push edx
            mov temp,eax
            INVOKE printf, ADDR msg1fmt, ADDR msg1, temp
            pop edx      ; restore eax, ecx, and edx
            pop ecx
            pop eax
            ret
OUTACC      endp
```

Why does the above code save and restore the contents of the eax, ecx, and edx registers? Again remember from Chap. 2 that the INVOKE directive destroys the contents of these three registers. Although the pushad and popad might have been able to be used here, only three registers are used, the code is more self-documenting, and since the above is implemented as a procedure, space is not as much of a concern.

The following is the skeleton of the program which loads the accumulator with the value 1, adds the number 2 to the accumulator, adds the contents of memory location three which contains a 3, multiplies the accumulator by 4, and then multiplies the accumulator by a −3. Lastly, it outputs the contents of the accumulator:

```
            .686
            .model flat,c
            .stack 100h
scanf       PROTO arg2:Ptr Byte, inputlist:VARARG
printf      PROTO arg1:Ptr Byte, printlist:VARARG

            .data
msg1fmt     byte 0Ah,"%s%d",0Ah,0Ah,0
msg1        byte "The contents of the accumulator are: ",0
temp        sdword ?
three       sdword 3
            .code
LOADACC     macro operand
            mov eax,operand    ;; load eax with the operand
            endm
```

```
ADDACC          macro operand
                add eax,operand    ;; add to eax the operand
                endm
MULTACC         macro operand
                push ebx           ;; save ebx and ecx
                push ecx
                mov ebx,eax        ;; mov eax to ebx
                mov eax,0          ;; clear accumulator to zero
                mov ecx,operand    ;; load ecx with operand
                if operand LT 0    ;; if operand is negative
                neg ecx            ; make ecx positive for loop
                endif
                .while ecx >0
                add eax,ebx        ;; repetitively add
                dec ecx            ;; decrement ecx
                .endw
                if operand  LT 0   ;; if operand is negative
                neg eax            ; negate accumulator, eax
                endif
                pop ecx            ;; restore ecx and ebx
                pop ebx
                endm
main            proc
                LOADACC 1
                ADDACC 2
                ADDACC three
                MULTACC 4
                MULTACC -3
                CALL OUTACC

                ret
main            endp
OUTACC          proc
                push eax     ; save eax, ecx, and edx
                push ecx
                push edx
                mov temp,eax
                INVOKE printf, ADDR msg1fmt, ADDR msg1, temp
                pop edx    ; restore eax, ecx, and edx
                pop ecx
                pop eax
                ret
OUTACC          endp

                end
```

What is interesting is that the main program above only contains the following macro invocations and procedure call. As alluded to at the beginning of this section, they almost look like a new assembly language has been created:

```
LOADACC 1
ADDACC 2
ADDACC three
MULTACC 4
MULTACC -3
CALL OUTACC
```

When the above macros are expanded, the following code is generated:

```
LOADACC 1
     mov eax,1
ADDACC 2
     add eax,2
ADDACC three
     add eax,three
MULTACC 4
     push ebx
     push ecx
     mov ebx,eax
     mov eax,0
     mov ecx,4

     jmp @C0001
@C0002:
     add eax,ebx
     dec ecx
@C0001:
     cmp ecx, 0
     ja @C0002
     pop ecx
     pop ebx
MULTACC -3
     push ebx
     push ecx
     mov ebx,eax
     mov eax,0
     mov ecx,-3
     neg ecx        ; make ecx positive for loop
     jmp @C0004
@C0005:
     add eax,ebx
     dec ecx
@C0004:
     cmp ecx, 0
     ja @C0005
     neg eax        ; negate accumulator, eax
     pop ecx
     pop ebx
     CALL OUTACC
```

When this program is assembled, it is advisable to get a copy of the assembly listing in the .lst file. As hinted at previously and to pique the reader's interest to read Chap. 12, although the instructions for the ADDACC macro are both add instructions, it is interesting to note that the machine code in hexadecimal is different. An add eax, 3 in machine language is 83 C0 02 and this is different than an add eax, three which in machine language is 03 05 00000032. When using different arguments for the parameter, the instructions are different as a result of using name parameters which use strict substitution. Another thing to note is the conditional assembly of the MULACC macro when the operand is negative, where the additional neg instructions are inserted along with their associated comments due to their single semicolons (;). Lastly, note the somewhat unusual way in which the .while directive is implemented with the comparison at the bottom. Although it appears to be implemented as a post-test loop where it seems possible that the loop will execute at least once, be sure to note the jmp instruction at the beginning of the loop that prevents that from happening.

The reader is encouraged to use this program to experiment with, by using the macros given. It also forms the skeleton to add the other macros listed previously which are a part of the exercises at the end of this chapter. The reader can also add other macros and procedures as requested by the instructor or can experiment on their own initiative.

7.9 Summary

- Procedures create only one copy of the code, whereas macros create a new copy of the code every time they are invoked.
- Procedures often save and restore registers, whereas macros often do not attempt to save and restore registers.
- Procedures tend to save memory, whereas macros tend to save execution time.
- To invoke a procedure, use the call instruction followed by the name of the procedure, whereas to invoke a macro, merely put the name of the macro in the opcode field.
- Always include a ret instruction in a procedure but do not include one in a macro.
- Although more than one ret instruction can be included in a procedure, it is best to have only one and include it as the last instruction in a procedure.
- Remember to include the name of a procedure in the label field of the endp statement but do not include the name of the macro in the label field of the endm statement.

- When arguments are required when invoking a macro, use :REQ after the parameter name in the macro definition.
- When using any of the conditional assembly directives, such as if, ifb, else, and endif, do not include a period prior to the directive.
- When using the conditional assembly directive if, do not use registers or memory locations for arguments in the macro, rather use only constants. Also, when using logical operators or and and, use parentheses as in if(x lt 0)or (y gt 0).
- Use the ifb conditional assembly directive to check for a blank matching argument and ifnb to check for a non-blank matching argument.
- Use the conditional assembly directive ifid to check if two items are identical and ifdif to check if they are different. Both of these are case sensitive, so to make them case insensitive, add the letter i to the end of the directive as in ifidi and ifdifi.

7.10 Exercises (Items Marked with an * Have Solutions in Appendix D)

1. Given the following assembly language statements and assuming memory locations and labels are properly declared, indicate whether they are syntactically correct or incorrect. If incorrect, indicate what is wrong with the statement:

*A. return	B. endm	*C. .ifb <parm>
C. ifdif <p>,<q>	*E. if eax lt 0	F. elseif
G. call dog	H. endif	I. ifne <p1>,<p2>

2. Write a procedure to implement the factorial function as defined in the exercise section of Chap. 5.
3. Write a procedure to implement the Fibonacci numbers as defined in the exercise section of Chap. 5.
4. Write a macro to implement the factorial function as defined in the exercise section of Chap. 5.
5. Write a macro to implement the Fibonacci numbers as defined in the exercise section of Chap. 5.
6. Using conditional assembly, modify the MULACC macro defined in this chapter to not only eliminate the redundant looping but also not generate the loop instruction itself in the case that the multiplier in the operand is 0 and the answer is 0, or when it is 1 and the answer is just the value in the accumulator. (Hint: Use the power macro as an example.)

7. Implement the following instructions as macros as part of the macro calculator
   problem in the last section of this chapter. For the division macro, use conditional assembly to solve any problems with negative numbers. Also, when
   dealing with the possibility of division by 0, a -1 should be returned from the
   macro to indicate an error:

```
INACC
STOREACC
SUBACC
DIVACC
```

Arrays

8

Up until this point, arrays have not been needed in the examples shown. However, this chapter will introduce the declaration of arrays, array access, indexing arrays, and how to input, process, and output arrays. Although there are many ways one can index an array, this text will present only two of them. This chapter will be concerned with the declaration of arrays of signed double words (sdword), while the declaration of an array of bytes will be introduced in the next chapter on strings. Lastly, this chapter will illustrate the use of arrays in a number of examples.

8.1 Array Declaration and Addressing

There are a couple of different ways to declare an array based on the data and the needs of the programmer. The simplest way to declare an array is to list memory location after memory location. In fact, it is entirely possible to address the next memory location after any other memory location by adding a constant to the address. For example, given the following two memory locations, it is possible to address the memory location result when referring to memory location number:

```
        .data
number  sdword 2
result  sdword 7
```

In other words, instead of an instruction such as mov eax, result, which would move the integer 7 into the eax register, mov eax, number+4 could also be written which would accomplish that exact same thing. Note that the +4 does not add 4 to the contents of number, rather an add instruction would be needed to accomplish that task. Instead, it adds a 4 to the address of number. However, one might ask isn't result only one memory location away from number? That

© Springer Nature Switzerland AG 2020
J. T. Streib, *Guide to Assembly Language*, Undergraduate Topics
in Computer Science, https://doi.org/10.1007/978-3-030-35639-2_8

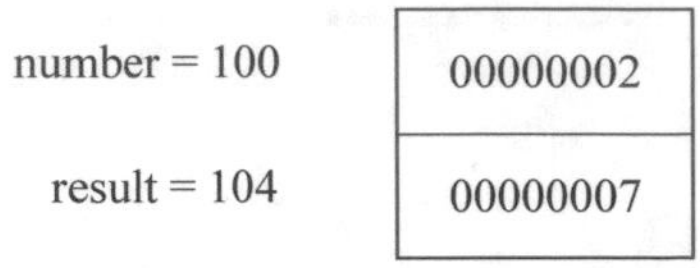

number = 100 | 00000002 |

result = 104 | 00000007 |

Fig. 8.1 Signed double words

would be true if `number` was declared as a `byte`, but note that `number` is declared as an `sdword` which takes up 4 bytes as shown in Fig. 8.1.

Although the above form of addressing memory is allowable and useful in specific situations, trying to address memory locations by another variable name other than the variable name assigned to it is known as *aliasing*. It is not considered to be very good programming practice because it can make programs very difficult to debug and maintain, where a program that uses two different variable names for the same memory location can cause difficultly when trying to make updates to a program. To help illustrate the sort of problems that might be encountered, what if one added another variable between the variables `number` and `result` above, such as demonstrated below?

```
        .data
number  sdword 2
answer  sdword 5
result  sdword 7
```

The problem would be that when the previous instruction `mov eax, number+4` is used, the number 5 would be moved into the `eax` register instead of the number 7. Although in small programs, it might be relatively easy to find all such references, it would be very difficult in large programs. This is the reason why this method should be avoided when addressing individually declared variables.

However, it is also possible to create an array as follows, where it should be noticed that the subsequent memory locations do not have variable names attached to them:

```
numary  sdword 2
        sdword 5
        sdword 7
```

Although using offsets should be avoided when addressing individual labeled memory locations, it is necessary when dealing with arrays. In the case above, the programmer has no choice but to use the variable name `numary` to access the subsequent memory locations in the array and since there are no other variable names, each of the subsequent memory locations would not be referred to via an alias. However, what if there were many entries in the above array? It could take up quite a few lines of code to create the array. Luckily, MASM has an easier way to declare the above on just one line, where the directive `sdword` need to appear only

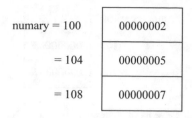

numary = 100   00000002

= 104   00000005

= 108   00000007

Fig. 8.2 Array of signed double word

once, and each of the entries would appear on the same line, each separated by a comma as follows:

```
numary    sdword 2,5,7
```

In both cases, the array would appear in memory as shown in Fig. 8.2.

Continuing, what if each element of an array were to be initialized to the same number, such as 0, or what if each memory location in the array did not need to be initialized? Each of the following could be used, respectively:

```
zeroary    sdword 0,0,0
empary     sdword ?,?,?
```

Although the above works okay for small arrays, what if there were hundreds of elements needed to be declared? Then clearly the above method would be cumbersome. Instead, the dup operator is very convenient, where the above would be rewritten as follows:

```
zeroary    sdword 3 dup(0)
empary     sdword 3 dup(?)
```

With only three elements the previous method of individually listing each element is sufficient, but as the number of elements increases, using the dup operator is obviously more convenient.

Given the above, how does one access individual elements of an array? For example, assume that the last element of the previously declared numary needed to be moved to the first element of numary. Remembering that arrays in C start with the zeroth element, the C equivalent of this operation would be numary[0] =numary[2]; and the equivalent assembly code would be as follows:

```
mov eax,numary+8    ; load eax with third element
mov numary+0,eax    ; store eax in first element
```

and would appear in memory as shown in Fig. 8.3.

Of course, regardless of whether one is dealing with a single memory location or with the elements of an array, memory to memory transfer needs to go through a register. As with C, the first element in an array is the zeroth element. Also, since numary is two memory locations away, the offset needs to be multiplied by 4 to determine the correct address because as mentioned previously, each memory

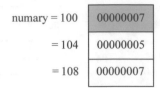

numary = 100 | 00000007
= 104 | 00000005
= 108 | 00000007

Fig. 8.3 Copying individual elements of an array

location is 4 bytes long. Lastly, numary in the second mov statement technically does not need to have the +0, since by default the offset of a stand-alone memory location is +0. However, including the +0 is a nice way of indicating to others who might read the program that the memory location specified is part of an array instead of a stand-alone memory location.

8.2   Indexing Using the Base Register

Although occasionally only access to a single element of an array is needed, more often than not access to many elements of the array is necessary and simply accessing them one at a time would prove to be inefficient. As mentioned at the outset of this chapter, there are two major ways of indexing an array. The first one is similar to indexing an array using subscripts in a high-level language, whereas the second one is similar to using pointers and is helpful when trying to process strings as discussed in the next chapter.

Although high-level languages typically use a variable as an index when indexing arrays, in assembly language indexing is accomplished using registers. Recall from Chap. 1 that the ebx register is known as the base register and is very useful when indexing arrays. Although it is a register, it is used much like an index variable in the C programming language.

How would one use the ebx register to index an array? As an example, what if one wanted to sum all the elements of an array? To make things simpler at first, assume that the array already contains values as introduced in the last section and as shown below:

```
numary    sdword       2,5,7
sum       sdword       ?
```

In C, the variable sum would first need to be initialized to 0. Further, since there are a fixed number of items to be summed, a for loop would be the best choice. Lastly, for each iteration of the for loop, the *i*th element of the numary would need to be added to sum using sum=sum+numary[i];. Optionally, the summation could be done using the shorthand notation sum+=numary[i]; as shown below:

```
sum = 0;
for(i=0;  i<3;  i++)
    sum += numary[i];
```

Of course since the `for` loop is the best choice as used above, the equivalent code in assembly language would be the use of the `.repeat-.untilcxz` directive. Unlike C code, where the variable i is being used both as a loop counter and as an index, in assembly language, two separate registers need to be used. So in addition to using the `ebx` register for indexing, the `ecx` register would be used for loop control. Lastly, since `sum` was not initialized in the data section, it must be initialized to 0 during execution time. The resulting code is as follows:

```
mov sum,0              ; initialize sum to 0
mov ecx,3              ; initialize ecx to 3
mov ebx,0              ; initialize ebx to 0
.repeat
mov eax,numary[ebx]    ; load eax with element of numary
add sum,eax            ; add eax to sum
add ebx,4              ; increment ebx by 4
.untilcxz
```

As discussed in the previous section, note that a 4 needs to be added to the `ebx` register to access the next signed double word. Also, do not forget that the `ecx` register should not be altered, since the `.untilcxz` directive decrements the `ecx` register by 1 automatically. After walking through the above code segment, the contents of the registers and memory locations would be as shown in Fig. 8.4, where all values are in hexadecimal.

Why does the `ebx` register have the hexadecimal number 0000000C (decimal 12) in it? Could it not end up addressing the memory location `sum`? Prior to the loop, the `ebx` register is initialized to 0 to access the first element in the array. After accessing and summing the current element in the array, the value in `ebx` is incremented by 4 in anticipation of accessing the next element in the array the next time through the loop. To answer the first question, during the last iteration of the loop and after the third memory location has been accessed, `ebx` is incremented by 4 to 0000000C in anticipation of accessing the next element in the array. The answer to the second question would then be yes, where the memory location `sum`

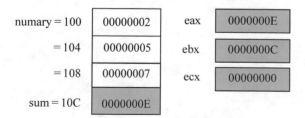

Fig. 8.4 Using ebx for array processing

could be accessed via ebx upon completion of the loop. Would this have caused an execution or run-time error if the contents of sum were accessed via ebx? As discussed in the previous section, accessing another memory location like this is possible, and no, it would not cause an error. However, it is not advisable and the result is that extra care must be taken when addressing arrays in assembly language.

In all of the previous examples, the array already contains data. How can one input data into an array? To add a small twist, how could the array also be output in reverse order? Obviously this problem will require the I/O capabilities learned in Chap. 2 and will require two non-nested loops. Furthermore, assume that the user will need to first be prompted and will then enter the number of integers to be input. The code in C is as follows:

```c
int arry[20],n,i;
printf("\n%s","Enter the number of integers to be input: ");
scanf("%d",&n);
if (n>0){
    for (i=0; i<n; i++){
        printf("\n%s","Enter an integer: ");
        scanf("%d",&arry[i]);
    }
    printf("\n%s\n\n","Reversed");
    for (i=n-1;i>=0;i--)
        printf("     %d\n\n",arry[i]);
}
else
    printf("\n%s\n\n","No data entered.");
```

The user is first prompted to enter the number of integers to be input followed by prompts to enter the integers themselves. After the integers have been placed into the array, a loop then outputs the array in reverse order. In the event that a 0 or a negative number is entered for the first prompt, a message stating that no data was entered is displayed. The above C code can then be implemented as follows in the partial .data and .code segments below:

```
                .data
msg1fmt         byte 0Ah,"%s",0
msg2fmt         byte 0Ah,"%s",0Ah,0Ah,0
msg3fmt         byte "     %d",0Ah,0Ah, 0
in1fmt          byte "%d",0
msg1            byte "Enter the number of integers to be input: ",0
msg2            byte "Enter an integer: ",0
msg3            byte "Reversed",0
msg4            byte "No data entered."
n               sdword ?
arry            sdword 20 dup(?)

                .code
                INVOKE printf, ADDR msg1fmt,ADDR msg1
                INVOKE scanf, ADDR in1fmt, ADDR n
                mov ecx,n               ; initialize ecx to n
                mov ebx,0               ; initialize ebx to 0
                .if ecx>0
                .repeat
                push ecx                ; save ecx
                INVOKE printf, ADDR msg1fmt, ADDR msg2
                INVOKE scanf, ADDR in1fmt, ADDR arry[ebx]
                pop ecx                 ; restore ecx
                add ebx,4               ; increment ebx by 4
                .untilcxz
                INVOKE printf, ADDR msg2fmt, ADDR msg3
                mov ecx,n               ; initialize ecx to n
                sub ebx,4               ; subtract 4 from ebx
                .repeat
                push ecx                ; save ecx
                INVOKE printf, ADDR msg3fmt,arry[ebx]
                pop ecx                 ; restore ecx
                sub ebx,4               ; decrement ebx by 4
                .untilcxz
                .else
                INVOKE printf, ADDR msg2fmt, ADDR msg4
                .endif
```

   Notice in the assembly code segment that the use of the .if directive to check whether n is greater than 0 is not only helpful in outputting a message that no data was entered but also necessary to help insure that the value of the ecx register does not start off at 0 or a negative number for the .repeat-untilcxz directives that follow. Also, note that the ecx register is saved and restored before and after the INVOKE directives in the body of the loop so that the count is not destroyed. Should the contents of the ebx register also be saved and restored in the loop? No, because it is the only register that is not altered by the INVOKE directive.

8.3 Searching

As another example of using the `ebx` register for indexing, there are two main searches that the reader has probably heard about in a previous high-level programming course: the sequential search and the binary search. The former works with either unordered or ordered data, whereas the latter works with only ordered data. Since the binary search is the more complicated of the two, it is probably best to leave that to be implemented in a high-level language and this text will examine only the sequential search.

Assuming that the data has already been entered into an array, that the number of elements in the array is known, and that there are no duplicates in the array, the first thing that should be done is to request from the user what data needs to be found. Then a flag must be initially cleared indicating the data has not yet been found. Next the program should loop through the array to determine whether the data being searched for is in the array. If the data is found, the flag must be set to indicate that it was found, the index set to the location of the data, and the rest of the array need not be searched. The following C program is one way of solving this problem:

```c
int arry[20],n=20,i,number,found;
printf("\n%s","Enter the integer to be found: ");
scanf("%d",&number);
i=0;
found=0;
while(i<n && !found)
   if(number==arry[i])
       found=-1;
   else
       i++;
if (found)
   printf("\n%s\n\n", "The integer was found");
else
   printf("\n%s\n\n","The integer was not found");
```

Note that the code was written using a `while` loop instead of a `for` loop. The use of a `for` loop would require the code to branch out of the middle of the loop and in C this would require the use of a `break` statement. This would be the equivalent of a "goto" or a jump statement in assembly language and could cause unstructured code to be written which this text has been trying to avoid. Assuming that the PROTO statements have already been written correctly, the following partial `.data` and `.code` segments implement the preceding C program:

```
                  .data
msg1fmt    byte "%s",0
msg2fmt    byte 0Ah,"%s",0Ah,0Ah,0
in1fmt     byte "%d",0
msg1       byte "Enter the integer to be found: ",0
msg2       byte "The integer was found",0
msg3       byte "The integer was not found",0
arry       sdword 20 dup(?)
n          sdword 20
number     sdword ?
found      sbyte ?


                  .code
                  INVOKE printf, ADDR msg1fmt,ADDR msg1
                  INVOKE scanf, ADDR in1fmt, ADDR number
                  mov ebx,0           ; initialize ebx to 0
                  mov ecx,0           ; initialize ecx to 0
                  mov edx,number      ; load edx with number
                  mov found,0         ; initialize found to 0
                  .while(ecx<n && !found)
                  .if(edx==arry[ebx])
                  mov found,-1        ; set found to -1
                  .else
                  add ebx, 4          ; increment ebx by 4
                  .endif
                  inc ecx             ; increment ecx by 1
                  .endw
                  .if(found)
                  INVOKE printf, ADDR msg2fmt, ADDR msg2
                  .else
                  INVOKE printf, ADDR msg2fmt, ADDR msg3
                  .endif
```

In the above code segment, note that since only single byte is needed instead of 4 bytes to create a flag, so the found flag is only a signed byte (sbyte) instead of a signed double word (sdword). Also, notice that the ecx register is used instead of the memory location i. Although i could be used, it could not be easily used in the .while because memory to memory comparisons are not allowed. Since it would need to be transferred to a register anyway and ecx is also known as the counter register, it did not hurt to somewhat mimic the .repeat-.untilcxz directives and use the ecx register. The primary difference is that the count is going forward instead of backward and the increment of the ecx register should not be forgotten at the bottom of the loop. The other difference is the .repeat-.untilcxz directive is a post-test loop structure and the .while directive is a pre-test loop structure, and if n was equal to 0, the .while loop would not loop at all.

8.4   Indexing Using the `esi` and `edi` Registers

Although the use of the base register `ebx` is fairly straightforward, being limited to a single register can prove to be somewhat restrictive. To help with this matter, there are two index registers `esi` and `edi`, where the `esi` register is known as the source index register and `edi` is known as the destination index register. The subtle difference between the use of the `ebx` register and the `esi` and `edi` registers is that the former is used with the name of the array as an index and the latter are used more like pointers. In this latter case, the address of the array is first loaded into the register and the name of the array is not subsequently used. Also, these two registers are very useful when manipulating strings, as will be discussed in the next chapter.

To demonstrate the different way of addressing using these registers, it is easier to examine the addressing of only a single element of an array first. For example, if only the second element of an array needed to be moved into the `eax` register, the instruction `mov eax,numary+4` could be written as done in the first section of this chapter. However, could the contents of `numary+4` be moved into `eax` without using +4 attached to the name of the array? Yes, the same thing could be accomplished by using a register as an index. The following code segment would work the same assuming the existence of the previous array, `numary`:

```
mov ebx, 4
mov eax,numary[ebx]
```

Although a bit cumbersome compared to using `numary+4`, this code segment should make sense given the previous section, where `ebx` contains a 4, and `numary` indexed by `ebx` would be the address of the second element of `numary`. The dashed arrows in Fig. 8.5 show how the address of `numary`, which is 100, is added to or indexed by the 4 in the `ebx` register to create the address 104, which is the address of the second element of the array `numary`. The solid arrow in Fig. 8.5 shows the contents of memory location 104 being copied into the `eax` register.

Using the `esi` register could accomplish the same task in the following code segment which introduces the new `offset` operator:

```
mov esi,offset numary+4
mov eax,[esi]
```

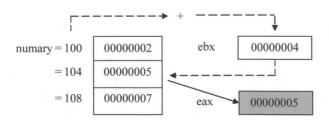

Fig. 8.5 Using `ebx` register to access a single element

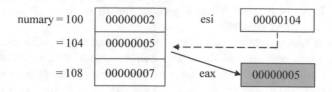

Fig. 8.6 Using esi to access a single element

Instead of causing the "contents" of numary+4 to be loaded into the esi register, the word offset causes the "address" of numary+4 to be loaded into the esi register. In the second statement, notice that there is no reference to numary because the address of numary+4 was loaded into the esi in the first line. Now the address in esi can be used like a pointer, indicated by the square brackets, to point to the data in the second element in the array, where its contents are transferred to the eax register. The dashed arrow in Fig. 8.6 shows the esi register pointing to the second element of numary at memory location 104 and the solid arrow in Fig. 8.6 shows the contents of memory location 104 being copied into the eax register.

Care must be taken when using this form of indexing. If the word offset was not included on the first line, then the "contents" of memory location numary+4, which is a 5, would be loaded into the esi register instead of the "address" of numary+4. This would have caused havoc on the second line of code because the unknown contents of memory location 5 would be loaded into the eax register. Further, if the square brackets were accidently omitted on the second line of code, then the 104 in the esi register would be transferred to the eax register, and this is clearly not what is intended in this example.

In addition to using the offset operator, there is an alternative method. Instead of using the mov instruction with the word offset, the lea instruction, which stands for "load effective address," can be used as follows:

```
lea esi,memory + 4
mov eax,[esi]
```

Although in these two instances, the end results are the same, there is a subtle difference between these two ways of getting an address. In a sense, using offset is *static* and lea is *dynamic*. When using offset, the address is calculated at assembly time, and with lea, the address is calculated at run-time. The only time the latter would need to be used is when there is a register in the second operand, where the register value could change during the course of the execution of the program and the address would need to be recalculated. Since in the above example there is no register as part of the second operand and a recalculation of the address is not necessary, either the mov and offset or the lea can be used. Further, since the use of registers in a second operand will not be used in this text, either method is acceptable. This text will use both methods interchangeably to allow readers to get use to both methods. Although the offset operator can be used with the lea instruction it is not needed, nor is it recommended, in order to keep these two methods separate and distinct.

The above shows the use of the `esi` register, but what of the `edi` register? Actually, the `edi` register could have been used equally well in the above example. However, as will be seen in the next chapter, some string instructions have specific uses for each register and substituting one for the other would not work. In the above case; however, if both could have been used equally well, why should one be used over the other? The answer can be found in the names of the registers mentioned above, where `esi` is the source index register and `edi` is the destination index register. As a general rule, when retrieving data from memory, it is best to use the `esi` register because memory is the source from which the data is coming. When storing data back into memory, the `edi` register indicates the destination where the data will be placed. This use of these registers corresponds to how the string instructions work and it provides a common way of using the registers to help programmers who might look at the code in the future.

As should be recalled from Chap. 1, data can be moved from one memory location to another by simply moving the contents of one memory location to a register and then from that register to the other memory location as follows:

```
mov eax,num1
mov num2,eax
```

Although the following example is clearly less efficient than the above, it helps demonstrate how the `esi` and `edi` registers can be used to transfer data between memory locations and will be helpful in subsequent examples of array processing:

```
lea esi,num1    ; load the address of num1 into esi
lea edi,num2    ; load the address of num2 into edi
mov eax,[esi]   ; move contents of where esi is pointing into eax
mov [edi],eax   ; move contents of eax to where edi is pointing
```

Instead of having the memory locations as part of the two latter `mov` statements, they appear in the first two `lea` instructions, where the addresses of num1 and num2 are transferred into the `esi` and `edi` registers, respectively. Then instead of moving the contents of num1 into `eax`, the contents of where `esi` is pointing to, which is num1, are moved to `eax`, and then the contents of `eax` are moved to where `edi` is pointing, which is num2 as shown in Fig. 8.7.

As discussed previously, note that `esi` points to the source of the transfer, num1, and `edi` points to the destination of the transfer, num2. Could one have saved an extra instruction and just coded `mov [edi],[esi]`? At first, the answer may appear to be yes because it looks like a simple register-to-register `mov` instruction. However, if one thinks about it for a moment, this is not a simple register transfer, rather those registers are pointers to memory locations, and as learned in Chap. 1, memory to memory `mov` instructions are not allowed. As always with this form of addressing, care must be taken. For example, if the brackets around `esi` and `edi` were left off, then a 100 would be moved into `eax`

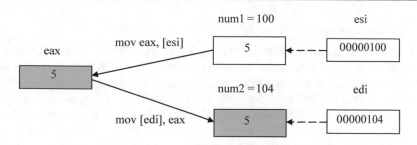

Fig. 8.7 Using esi and edi to move data from memory to memory

and the 100 would then be moved into the edi register, which is not the intended goal.

Clearly the first example is simpler, but the code above accomplishes the same task and can be expanded to transferring elements of an array. Given how the esi and edi registers work, can they be used to implement some of the array functions introduced previously? The answer is yes. As an example, consider the previous C segment which summed the elements of an array,

```
sum = 0;
for(i=0; i<3; i++)
    sum += numary[i];
```

which can be implemented in assembly language using the esi register as follows:

```
mov sum,0          ; initialize sum to zero
mov ecx,3          ; initialize ecx to 3
lea esi,numary+0   ; load the address of numary into esi
.repeat
mov eax,[esi]      ; move contents of where esi pointing to eax
add sum,eax        ; add eax to sum
add esi,4          ; increment esi by 4 to next element
.untilcxz
```

In comparison to the previous version, notice that instead of initializing the ebx register to 0, the esi register is initialized to the address of numary+0. As mentioned previously, the +0 alerts other programmers that numary is not just a simple variable, but rather is an array. The other change is that instead of accessing numary indexed by [ebx], only [esi] is used. Lastly, esi instead of ebx is incremented, but regardless of which index is used, it is incremented by 4 to access the next sdword in the array.

What if one wanted to reverse the contents of an array? Instead of trying to just write in assembly language, first think through the problem in a high-level language. Also, it is a good idea to expand the array from 3 to 5 elements so that more of a pattern can be seen:

```
n          sdword    5
numary     sdword    2,4,7,9,12
```

One of the common mistakes to be made here is an assumption that a fixed-iteration loop structure that loops five times is needed. What often happens in such circumstances is that the array is returned back to its original order. Instead, by drawing arrows to indicate which elements need to be swapped as shown in Fig. 8.8, it should be noticed below that only approximately half the elements in the array need to be swapped. Since in this example there are an odd number of items, the middle element does not need to be swapped. Integer division can then be used to determine the number of items that need to be swapped, where in this case 5 divided by 2 is 2. The result is that the loop should iterate a fixed number of times as $n/2$.

Although this algorithm can be implemented with just one index, the i and j indexes are helpful in this example and will lend themselves to the use of the esi and edi registers in the subsequent assembly language program:

```
j=n-1;
for(i=0; i<n/2; i++){
    temp=numary[i];
    numary[i]=numary[j];
    numary[j]=temp;
    j--;
}
```

However, the only major change that will probably be needed is to remember that esi and edi are initially loaded with the appropriate addresses of the array, as can be seen prior to the .repeat-.untilcxz loop below. The esi register is loaded with the address of the first element of the array, numary+0. To calculate the address of the last element of the array, the number of elements in the array is first decremented by 1 and then multiplied by 4. As seen in Fig. 8.8, 5 minus 1 is 4, times 4 is 16, which when added to 104 is 120 in decimal or 114 in hexadecimal:

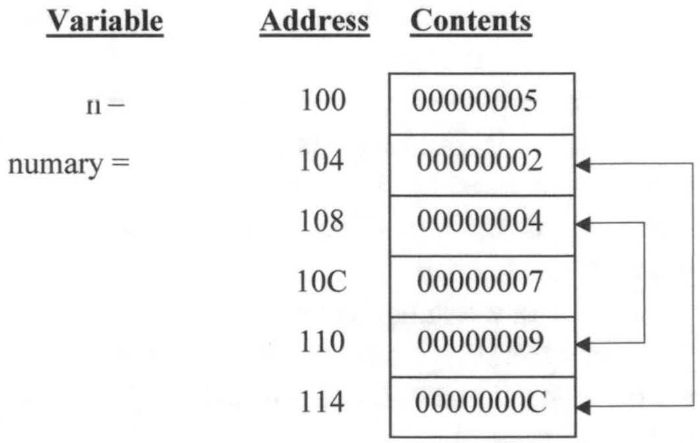

	Variable	Address	Contents
	n −	100	00000005
	numary =	104	00000002
		108	00000004
		10C	00000007
		110	00000009
		114	0000000C

Fig. 8.8 Swap routine

```
mov ecx,n            ; load ecx with contents of n
sar ecx,1            ; divide ecx by 2, number of times to loop
lea esi,numary+0     ; load address of numary into esi
mov edi,esi          ; move contents of esi to edi
mov eax,n            ; load eax with contents of n
dec eax              ; decrement eax by one
sal eax,2            ; multiply eax by 4
add edi,eax          ; add eax to edi for ending address of array
.repeat
mov eax,[esi]        ; move contents where esi is pointing to eax
xchg eax,[edi]       ; exchange eax and where edi is pointing
mov [esi],eax        ; move eax to where edi is pointing
add esi,4            ; add four to esi for next element
sub edi,4            ; subtract four from edi for next element
.untilcxz
```

Note that the `idiv` instruction is not used in the code segment above. Since the n needs to be divided by 2, arithmetically shifting `ecx` one bit position to the right accomplishes the same task. Likewise, when calculating the ending address of the array, after subtracting 1, multiplication by 4 is needed, so a 2-bit arithmetic shift to the left is a simple solution (see Chap. 6). Of course, both `esi` and `edi` need to be adjusted by 4 each time through the loop. Lastly, would `xchg [esi],[edi]` have worked in the above segment? Although it would be nice if it did, remember that the `xchg` instruction cannot work between two memory locations as mentioned in Chap. 7. Also as discussed earlier in this chapter, just because it seems that two registers are being exchanged, `[esi]` and `[edi]` are actually pointing to two memory locations and thus at most only one of the operands in the exchange instruction can reference a memory location.

8.5 Lengthof and Sizeof Operators

In the previous example, the following declarations were used to declare the array and indicate its length:

```
n          sdword    5
numary     sdword    2,4,7,9,12
```

Putting the number of elements in a variable is clearly a better choice than to leave the number of elements as an immediate value in an instruction. The advantage of using a variable is that any time the number of elements in the array is changed, the programmer can easily change the variable n, which is hopefully declared in close proximity to the declaration of the array.

Although this method works and is better, it is still rather clumsy. Consider if the number 15 was added to the end of numary and the number of elements in the array changed from 5 to 6. In addition to adding the extra element to the array, the value for n would also need to be changed as follows:

```
n          sdword   6
numary     sdword   2,4,7,9,12,15
```

What would happen if one forgot to update the value of n from 5 to 6? In this case, the previous swapping program would process only the first five elements of the array. Now consider instead of adding an additional element to the original array, an element was removed from the array as in the following:

```
n          sdword   4
numary     sdword   2,4,7,9
```

What would happen if one forgot to decrease the value of n in this case? The previous swapping program code segment would still attempt to process five elements, and whatever memory location was declared after numary would also be involved in the swap routine, which is clearly incorrect.

The solution to this problem is to neither leave the length of the array as an immediate value in an instruction nor leave it in a variable, but rather declare it using the lengthof operator. This operator instructs the assembler to calculate the length of the array at assembly time. For example, in the previous code segment from the end of the last section that reverses an array, the instruction mov ecx, n could be replaced with mov ecx, lengthof numary. Then every time the length of the array is changed, the assembler would recalculate the length of the array.

Whereas the lengthof operator indicates how many elements there are in an array, the sizeof operator indicates how many bytes there are in an array. So if with a five-element array of sdword the lengthof operator would return a 5, what would the sizeof operator return? Since there are 4 bytes in a sdword and there are 5 elements in the array, the answer would be 20.

Although the mov eax, n instruction in the program in the previous section could also be replaced with a mov eax, lengthof numary instruction, there is an even better way. Since the purpose of that section of the code segment was to calculate the number of bytes to determine the address of the last element in the array to be stored in the edi register, the sizeof operator could be utilized. The result is that the following code segment

```
mov eax,n         ; load eax with contents of n
dec eax           ; decrement eax by one
sal eax,2         ; multiply eax by 4
```

could be replaced with

```
mov eax,sizeof numary    ; load eax with the size of numary
sub eax,4                ; decrement eax by four
```

In the first case, eax is decremented by 1, where the 4 times 4 bytes per sdword would be 16. Then the 16 needs to be added to the beginning address of the array to calculate the address of the last element of the array. In the second example, the size of numary is 20, where 4 is subtracted to get 16, which again is used to calculate the address of the last element of the array. Using both the lengthof and sizeof operators, the previous code segment could be rewritten as follows:

```
mov ecx,lengthof numary   ; load ecx with length of numary
sar ecx,1                 ; divide ecx by 2, of times to loop
lea esi,numary+0          ; load address of numary into esi
mov edi,esi               ; move contents of esi to edi
mov eax,sizeof numary     ; load eax with size of numary
sub eax,4                 ; decrement eax by four
add edi,eax               ; add eax to edi for ending address of array
.repeat
mov eax,[esi]             ; move contents where esi is pointing to eax
xchg eax,[edi]            ; exchange eax and where edi is pointing
mov [esi],eax             ; move eax to where edi is pointing
add esi,4                 ; add four to esi for next element
sub edi,4                 ; subtract four from edi for next element
.untilcxz
```

8.6 Complete Program: Implementing a Queue

A common structure that sometimes needs to be implemented in assembly language is the *queue*. As learned in a second semester computer science course, a queue is known as a *FIFO* data structure, where the first item put into the queue is the first item taken out. The operation used to put an item in a queue is often called enqueue and the operation to remove an item from a queue is known as dequeue. Although the Intel processor has instructions to push and pop items from a stack, it does not have instructions to enqueue and dequeue items from a queue.

A queue is especially helpful when there is a faster process trying to communicate with a slower process, where data can be placed into a queue by a faster process and the slower process can then remove that data from the queue at a later time. A common example is when a fast processor needs to send something to a slow printer and data is placed in a print queue. In another example, when an interrupt occurs in a processor, it must be attended to immediately in what is known as the foreground environment. However, the foreground environment may not have time to completely process the interrupt, so the information is placed in a queue, sometimes called a foreground/background queue. Then when there are no pending interrupts, the background environment will complete the processing of the information that was previously placed in the foreground/background queue. Although the implementation of interrupts is beyond the scope of this text, the implementation of a queue provides an excellent opportunity to demonstrate the use of an array and indexing.

Before looking at assembly code, it might be helpful to be reminded how queues can be implemented in a high-level language. Although ideally it would be best to use parameters, the following code again uses global variables to mimic the subsequent assembly language program. The main program uses a sentinel-controlled loop to continue to iterate until the letter s is input, which stands for stop. Then for each iteration of the loop, it checks for the letter e for enqueue or d for dequeue, otherwise an appropriate error message is output.

The enqueue routine should look somewhat familiar to those who have taken a second semester computer science course in data structures. Although there can be some complex ways to determine whether a queue is full, the simplest method is to use a counter such as count, which is checked to see if it is less than the length of the queue, n in this case. If so, number is placed in the rear of the queue. The variable rear is incremented by 1. The mod function (%) is used to cause rear to be reset to 0 should it exceed the length of the queue (n). For example, if rear is equal to 3, the 3%3 is equal to 0. The dequeue routine is similar and it is left for the reader to walk through the procedure:

```
#include <stdio.h>
const int n=3;
int queue[3],number,front=0,rear=0,count=0;
char command;
int main() {
    void enqueue();
    void dequeue();
    printf("\n%s","Enter a command, e, d, or s: ");
    scanf("%s",&command);
    while (command != 's'){
        if (command=='e'){
            printf("\n%s","Enter a positve integer: ");
            scanf("%d",&number);
            enqueue();
        }
```

```c
        else
           if (command=='d'){
               dequeue();
               if (number>0)
                  printf("\n%s%d\n","The integer is: ",number);
               }
           else
               printf("\n%s","Invalid entry, try again");
           printf("\n%s","Enter a command, e, d, or s: ");
           scanf("%s",&command);
        }
        printf("\n");
        return 0;
    }
void enqueue(){
    if (count<n){
        count++;
        queue[rear]=number;
        rear=(rear+1)%n;
    }
    else
        printf("\n%s\n","Error: Queue is full");
    }
void dequeue(){
    if (count>0){
        count--;
        number=queue[front];
        front=(front+1)%n;
    }
    else{
        printf("\n%s\n","Error: Queue is empty");
        number =-1;
    }
}
```

Since there needs to be a pointer for both the front and the rear of a queue, the use of the esi and edi registers, respectively, makes an excellent choice. Although procedures are often used for the enqueue and dequeue operations, the use of macros will mimic the push and pop instructions and also provide another opportunity to reinforce the concept of macros. Although not very versatile, global variables are used to communicate between the main program and the macros as with the previous C program:

```
                .686
                .model flat,c
                .stack 100h
scanf           PROTO arg2:Ptr Byte, inputlist:VARARG
printf          PROTO arg1:Ptr Byte, printlist:VARARG


                .data
in1fmt          byte "%s",0
in2fmt          byte "%d",0
msg1fmt         byte 0Ah,"%s",0
msg3fmt         byte 0Ah,"%s%d",0Ah,0
msg4fmt         byte 0Ah,0
errfmt          byte 0Ah,"%s",0Ah,0
msg1            byte "Enter a command, e, d, or s: ",0
msg2            byte "Enter a positive integer: ",0
msg3            byte "The integer is: ",0
errmsg1         byte "Error: Invalid entry, try again",0
errmsg2         byte "Error: Queue is full",0
errmsg3         byte "Error: Queue is empty",0
queue           sdword 3 dup(?)
command         sdword ?
number          sdword ?
count           sdword 0

                .code
enqueue         macro
                .if count < lengthof queue
                 inc count              ; increment count
                 mov eax,number         ; load eax with number
                 mov [edi],eax          ; store eax in rear
                 mov eax,edi            ; copy edi (rear) to eax
                 sub eax,offset queue   ; subtract address of queue
                 add eax,4              ; increment eax by 4
                 cdq                    ; convert double to quad
                 mov ecx,sizeof queue   ; get size of queue (bytes)
                 idiv ecx               ; divide
                 mov edi,offset queue   ; load address in rear
                 add edi,edx            ; add remainder to rear
                .else
                INVOKE printf, ADDR errfmt, ADDR errmsg2
                .endif
                endm
dequeue         macro
                .if count > 0
```

```
                  dec count                 ; decrement count
                  mov eax,[esi]             ; load eax from front
                  mov number,eax            ; store eax in number
                  mov eax,esi               ; copy esi (front) to eax
                  sub eax,offset queue      ; subtract address of queue
                  add eax,4                 ; increment eax by 4
                  cdq                       ; convert double to quad
                  mov ecx, sizeof queue     ; get size of queue (bytes)
                  idiv ecx                  ; divide
                  mov esi,offset queue      ; load address in front
                  add esi,edx               ; add remainder to front
                  .else
                  INVOKE printf, ADDR errfmt, ADDR errmsg3
                  mov number,-1             ; store -1 (flag) in number
                  .endif
                  endm
main              proc
                  mov edi,offset queue+0 ; use edi as front of queue
                  mov esi,offset queue+0 ; use esi as rear of queue
                  INVOKE printf, ADDR msg1fmt, ADDR msg1    ; priming
                  INVOKE scanf, ADDR in1fmt, ADDR command  ; read
                  .while command != "s"  ; while not stop
                  .if command=="e"        ; enqueue?
                  INVOKE printf, ADDR msg1fmt, ADDR msg2
                  INVOKE scanf, ADDR in2fmt, ADDR number
                  enqueue                   ; enqueue number
                  .elseif command=="d"   ; dequeue?
                  dequeue                   ; deque number
                  .if number >0             ; not -1 (flag)?
                  INVOKE printf, ADDR msg3fmt, ADDR msg3, number
                  .endif
                  .else
                  INVOKE printf, ADDR errfmt, ADDR errmsg1
                  .endif
                  INVOKE printf, ADDR msg1fmt, ADDR msg1
                  INVOKE scanf, ADDR in1fmt, ADDR command
                  .endw
                  INVOKE printf, ADDR msg4fmt
                  ret
main              endp
                  end
```

Although much of the assembly code is similar to its C counterpart, there are a few sections that might need some explanation, such as the enqueue routine. As previously indicated, the edi register is used to point to the rear of the queue. However, instead of merely adding a 1 to rear as with the previous C code, a 4 needs to be added for the sdword elements of queue. Also note that offset queue is subtracted from edi prior to the division and then offset queue is added back to edi after the division. This is because edi does not contain a simple index within queue as in the previous C program but rather edi is acting as a pointer to queue and the address of queue needs to be removed before the division can take place and then added back afterward.

8.7   Complete Program: Implementing the Selection Sort

Although sorting could be done more easily in a high-level language, it provides an excellent opportunity to examine nested loops, ifs, and again the use of the esi and edi registers. As should be recalled from a first-year sequence in computer science, there are a number of sorts called in-place sorts, which can sort the contents of an array. These sorts typically use two loops and on average if the array contains n elements, they have a time complexity of $O(n^2)$. Compared to other sorts, these are relatively slow but are acceptable with smaller sets of data and are relatively easy to learn. Three common $O(n^2)$ sorts are the selection sort, the bubble sort, and the insertion sort, of which the bubble sort is one of the more popular. Although all three sorts have a number of similarities, the selection sort tends to be a little easier to understand and a little simpler to implement, especially when trying to implement a sort in assembly language. Since many students may have already implemented a bubble sort previously in a high-level language, the implementation of the bubble sort in assembly language is left as an exercise at the end of this chapter.

The implementation of the selection sort (and the bubble sort for that matter) can be implemented in two different ways. The first method is what could be called the simplified method, where only the two loops, an if structure, and a swap routine need to be written. In this form, the sort is very inefficient but the technique of accessing various elements in the array is made quite clear. The second method of implementing the sort could be called the modified method, where the sort is modified to be more efficient and avoid any unnecessary swapping of elements or passes through the data in the array. The simplified method of the selection sort will be presented first and then it will be subsequently modified. Should the reader already be familiar with the selection sort, the following paragraph could be skipped, but it could also serve as a quick refresher as to how the sort works.

The simplified way of implementing the selection sort is to perform n-1 passes through the array. During the first pass, the first element of the array will be compared with each of the subsequent elements in the array. If the array is to be sorted in ascending order (smallest to the largest) and if a subsequent element is smaller than the first element, a swap occurs. Comparison continues on through all of the subsequent elements. After comparing the first element with all the subsequent elements on the first pass, the smallest element will be in the first position. The process then continues on with the second element being compared to all the subsequent elements, the third element being compared to all subsequent elements, and so on until the second to the last element is compared to the last element, where the entire array will be sorted. Notice that the number of elements that need to be compared in each pass decreases by one with each subsequent pass.

The simplified selection sort can be implemented as follows in C:

```
// number of passes
for(i=0; i<n-1; i++)
   //number of comparisions
   for (j=i+1; j<n; j++)
      // compare the ith and jth element
      if (arry[j]<arry[i]) {
         // swap the elements
         temp=arry[j];
         arry[j]=arry[i];
         arry[i]=temp;
      }
```

Note that the outer for loop iterates n-1 times for the number of passes needed through the array and that the inner for loop starts at the i+1 position to compare to the subsequent number of elements. The if statement compares the subsequent element to the current element, and if it is smaller, it swaps the subsequent element with the current element as shown in Fig. 8.9.

However, the above algorithm is somewhat inefficient because it keeps swapping each time it finds a smaller number. Wouldn't it be easier to only swap once? The

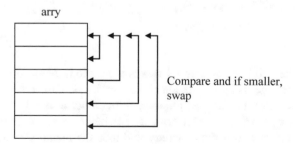

arry

Compare and if smaller, swap

Fig. 8.9 Simplified selection sort

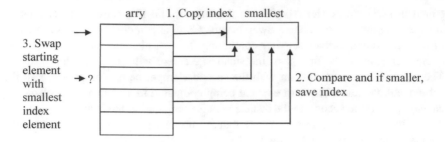

Fig. 8.10 Modified selection sort

answer is yes. First, the index of the starting element would be copied into a variable called `smallest`. Second, should a smaller element be found, its index is copied into `smallest`. Third, at the end of the pass the element that contains the smallest number indicated by the index in `smallest` is swapped with the element in the starting element. Now instead of a potential swap with every comparison, there is only one swap at the end of each pass as illustrated in Fig. 8.10.

The C code implementing the above algorithm can be found below:

```
// number of passes
for(i=0; i<n-1; i++) {
    // save index of first element of pass in smallest
    smallest= i;
    //number of comparisions
    for(j=i+1; j<n; j++)
        // compare jth elelemnt with smallest
        if(arry[j]<arry[smallest])
            // save new smallest element
            smallest=j;
    // swap first element of pass with smallest
    temp=arry[i];
    arry[i]=arry[smallest];
    arry[smallest]=temp;
}
```

The use of the two indexes `i` and `j` makes it easy to implement these two loops in assembly language using the `esi` and `edi` registers. Conversely, the use of `i` and `j` as loop counters makes it a little more difficult because only the `ecx` register can be used as a counter in nested `.repeat-.untilcxz` loops. One solution is to use the equivalent of two while structures and thus the memory locations `i` and `j`

could easily be used as loop counters. However, the alternative is to use two
.repeat-.untilcxz loops and to be careful to save and restore the contents of
the ecx register at the beginning and end of the outer loop structure. In the code
below, the esi register in a sense does double duty. At the beginning and the end
of the sort, it points to the starting element, but in the middle part of the sort, it
points to the smallest element. To be consistent, the input and the output also use
the esi and edi registers:

```
                .686
                .model flat,c
                .stack 100h
scanf           PROTO arg2:Ptr Byte, inputlist:VARARG
printf          PROTO arg1:Ptr Byte, printlist:VARARG

                .data
msg1fmt         byte 0Ah,"%s",0
msg2fmt         byte "%s",0
msg3fmt         byte 0Ah,"%s",0Ah,0Ah,0
msg4fmt         byte "    %d",0Ah,0
msg5fmt         byte 0Ah,0
in1fmt          byte "%d",0

msg 1           byte "Enter the number of integers to be input: ",0
msg2            byte "Enter an integer: ",0
msg3            byte "Sorted",0
n               sdword ?
arry            sdword 20 dup(?)
temp            sdword ?

                .code
main            proc
                INVOKE printf,ADDR msg1fmt,ADDR msg1
                INVOKE scanf,ADDR in1fmt,ADDR n
                INVOKE printf,ADDR msg5fmt
                .if n>0                 ; if n <= 0, don't continue
                mov ecx,n               ; load ecx with n
                mov edi,offset arry+0   ; load address of arry into edi
                .repeat
                push ecx                ; save ecx
                INVOKE printf,ADDR msg2fmt,ADDR msg2
                INVOKE scanf,ADDR in1fmt,ADDR [edi]
                add edi,4               ; incrment edi by 4
                pop ecx                 ; restore ecx
                .untilcxz
                .if n>1                 ; check >1 elements in array
                mov ecx,n               ; load ecx with n
                dec ecx                 ; loop n-1 times
                mov esi,offset arry+0   ; load esi with address of arry
                .repeat
```

```
        push ecx                    ; save ecx
        push esi                    ; save address, esi now smallest
        mov edi,esi                 ; load address of esi in edi
        add edi,4                   ; move edi to the next element
        .repeat
        mov eax,[esi]               ; move smallest to eax to compare
        .if [edi]<eax               ; compare smallest to next
        mov esi,edi                 ; save the new smallest in esi
        .endif
        add edi,4                   ; move to next element to compare
        .untilcxz
        mov edi,esi                 ; edi points to smallest element
        pop esi                     ; esi points to the start element
        mov eax,[esi]               ; move start element to temp
        xchg eax,[edi]              ; exchange start and smallest
        mov [esi],eax               ; move smallest back to start
        add esi,4                   ; move start index to next
        pop ecx                     ; restore ecx to be decremented
        .untilcxz
        .endif
        INVOKE printf, ADDR msg3fmt, ADDR msg3
        mov ecx, n                  ; load ecx with n
        mov esi,offset arry+0       ; load esi with address of arry
        .repeat
        push ecx                    ; save ecx
        mov eax,[esi]               ; load eax with element from arry
        mov temp,eax                ; store eax in temp for output
        INVOKE printf, ADDR msg4fmt, temp
        add esi,4                   ; increment esi to next element
        pop ecx                     ; restore ecx
        .untilcxz
        INVOKE printf, ADDR msg5fmt
        .endif
        ret
  main  endp
        end
```

Notice that edi is used on input because the array is the destination of the data and esi is used on output because the source of the data is the array. Again, esi does double duty, where at the beginning and the end of the sort, it points to the starting element, but in the middle part of the sort, it points to the smallest element.

The push and pop instructions are carefully used when making the transition between these two tasks. Lastly, note that a temporary memory location is used to help output the array.

8.8 Summary

- The dup operator allows for the declaration of large initialized or uninitialized arrays.
- The ebx register can be used as an index for an array, much like a variable such as i in a high-level language.
- The esi and edi registers are known as the source index register and destination index register, respectively. They work like pointers and are especially useful with strings.
- When dealing with arrays of sdword, remember to increment by 4 instead of 1, because a signed double word takes up 4 bytes.
- The mov instruction and offset operator, or the lea instruction, allows for getting the address of a variable, where the former is static and the latter dynamic.
- Use square brackets [] around the ebx, esi, and edi registers, not to get the contents of the register, but rather to get the contents of the memory location to which they are indexing or pointing.
- The lengthof operator returns how many elements are in an array, whereas the sizeof operator returns how many bytes there are in an array.

8.9 Exercises (Items Marked with an * Have Solutions in Appendix D)

1. Given the following assembly language statements, indicate whether they are syntactically correct or incorrect. If incorrect, indicate what is wrong with the statement:

 *A. x sdword ?,?,? B. y sdword 3 dup(0) *C. mov eax,x+8
 D. mov eax,y[ebx] *E. mov esi,edi F. mov [esi],[edi]

2. Given the contents of the following memory location, what is stored in the eax register at the end of each segment?

$$temp = 200 \quad \boxed{00000005}$$
$$= 204 \quad \boxed{00000007}$$

[*]A. `mov eax,temp`   B. `mov eax,offset temp`
[*]C. `lea eax,temp`   D. `mov eax,offset temp+4`
[*]E. `mov esi,offset temp`   F. `mov edi,offset temp`
   `mov eax,esi`   `mov eax,[edi]`
 G. `lea esi,temp`   H. `mov esi,offset temp+4`
   `lea edi,temp+4`   `mov eax,2`
   `mov eax,[esi]`   `imul [esi]`
   `add eax,[edi]`

3. Implement the following C instructions using assembly language. Assume all variables are declared as sdword:

  [*]A.   `num[0] = 1;`
   B.   `x[1] = x[2];`
  [*]C.   `y[i+1] = y[i];`
   D.   `z[i] = z[j];`

4. Given the declarations below, indicate what would be stored in the eax register for each of the following instructions. Note that oarray is of type sword, not sdword (hint: see Chap. 1):

```
narray sdword 1,2,3,4,5
marray sdword 10 dup(?)
oarray sword  15,20,25
```

  [*]A. `mov eax,lengthof narray`   [*]B. `mov eax,sizeof narray`
   C. `mov eax,lengthof marray`   D. `mov cax,sizeof marray`
  [*]E. `mov eax,lengthof oarray`   F. `mov eax,sizeof oarray`

5. Write both the C code and the assembly code to transfer the contents of a 20-element array of integers to a second 20-element array of integers.

6. Just as there is a simple and modified version of the selection sort, so is there both a simple version and a modified version of the bubble sort. The simple version in C is the same length as the simplified version of the selection sort presented in Sect. 8.6.

a. Write both the C code and the assembly code to implement the simplified version of the bubble sort which compares every element of every pass through the array whether there was a swap on the previous pass or not.

b. First write the C code for the modified version of the bubble sort and then write the modified version in assembly language. With the modified version, if there is not a swap on the previous pass through the array, the array is in order and there is no need to make any subsequent passes through the array.

Strings

9

9.1 Introduction

This chapter concerns string processing. Specifically it examines various string processing instructions that are available in MASM. Continuing on with the last chapter, it also examines the manipulation of arrays of strings.

In its simplest case, a string is nothing more than an array of bytes as opposed to an array of signed double words. So, it is possible to use all of the techniques for arrays introduced in the last chapter with strings. For example, what if one wanted to copy the contents of one string to another string? As with arrays, the `ebx` register could be used an index for both strings. However, there are a couple of subtle but important changes in the following code:

```
                .data
string1         byte "Hello World!",0
string2         byte 12 dup(?),0

                .code
                mov ecx,12              ;load ecx with 12
                mov ebx,0              ;load ebx with 0
                .repeat
                mov al,string1[ebx]    ;load al with string1[ebx]
                mov string2[ebx],al    ;store al in string2[ebx]
                inc ebx                ;increment ebx by 1
                .untilcxz
```

First, note that the strings are declared as `byte` instead of `sdword`. As a result, notice that the `mov` instructions are using only a 1-byte register, `al`, instead of a 32-bit register `eax`, where it should be recalled from Chap. 1 that `al` is the rightmost byte of the `eax` register. Lastly, instead of incrementing `ebx` by four, it is

© Springer Nature Switzerland AG 2020
J. T. Streib, *Guide to Assembly Language*, Undergraduate Topics
in Computer Science, https://doi.org/10.1007/978-3-030-35639-2_9

incremented only by one to account for the size of `byte` as opposed to the size of a `sdword`.

Just as arrays can be indexed using the `esi` and `edi` registers, so too can strings be indexed using these registers. The `esi` register can be used for `string1` as the source of the transfer, and the `edi` can be used for the destination of the transfer to `string2`:

```
          .data
string1   byte "Hello World!"
string2   byte  12 dup(?)
          .code
          mov ecx,12          ; load ecx with 12
          lea esi,string1     ; load esi with address of string1
          lea edi,string2     ; load edi with address of string2
          .repeat
          mov al,[esi]        ; load al with [esi]
          mov [edi],al        ; store al in [edi]
          inc esi             ; increment esi by 1
          inc edi             ; increment edi by 1
          .untilcxz
```

As with the `ebx` register previously, `esi` and `edi` are incremented by one instead of four. As seen in the previous chapter, arrays are typically drawn vertically, and in representing how strings are processed, they are typically drawn horizontally. This is especially helpful when trying to represent arrays of strings later in this chapter. The above code could be illustrated just prior to the `mov al, [esi]` instruction the second time through the loop as shown in Fig. 9.1, where b represents a blank or a space.

First, the letter H has been transferred from the first byte in `name1` to the first byte in `name2`. Also, the `ecx` register has been decremented by one from 12 to 11, `0000000B` in hexadecimal. Lastly, the `esi` and `edi` registers have been incremented by one and are pointing to the next byte in each of the strings.

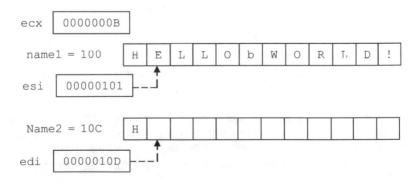

Fig. 9.1 Using `esi` and `edi` to move a string

In looking at the above code, it seems to be more complicated than its previous `ebx` counterpart. Although, if the array were to be transferred in reverse order, then clearly using `esi` and `edi` would be easier because there are two registers available to accomplish the task. But in a purely simple transfer, `ebx` has the advantage because the same register can be used as both the source and the destination. However, as alluded to in Chap. 8, the use of `esi` and `edi` in the above example is a good preview of some of the string processing instructions that use these two registers.

9.2   String Instructions: Moving Strings (movsb)

Since there are a number of functions that need to be performed on strings, many high-level languages include specialized libraries with instructions that perform many of the unique functions that help in string processing. Although assemblers usually do not come with a library of string functions, that does not prevent users from creating their own libraries. Whether or not a library of string functions is created, or code for string processing is written on an as-needed basis, creating the code needed using the same instructions that can be used for arrays can be tedious and cumbersome. Luckily, there are some instructions provided in the Intel architecture that help to make the task a little easier.

Before looking at these instructions, it should be pointed out that some of the instructions are designed to help with array processing as well. But since the needs when processing an array tend to be different, programmers often times use the mechanisms described in the previous chapter and use the following instructions primarily for string processing. As will be shown later, having the ability to use both techniques can be helpful in some instances. As with previous instructions, there are many different options available, but only the basic and most useful ones will be discussed here.

Instruction	Meaning
movsb	Move string byte
cmpsb	Compare string byte
scasb	Scan string byte
storsb	Store string byte
lodsb	Load string byte

Although the above instructions have their word and double word counterparts, which can be created by substituting the letter b in the instructions with the letters w and d, respectively, only the byte instructions are listed above. One of the most useful instructions listed above to be discussed in this section is the `movsb` instruction which is used to move a string of bytes. This instruction is not a simple instruction because it does more than one thing. In particular, the `movsb` instruction does two things. First, it moves the contents of the byte pointed at by the `esi` register to the byte in memory pointed at by the `edi` register. Then it decrements the `ecx` register and either increments or decrements the `esi` and `edi` registers by 1. So, for example, if one wanted to move only a single byte, then whether the `esi` and `edi` registers are incremented or decremented would not matter and one could write the following code segment:

```
        .data
letter1 byte 'a'
letter2 byte ?

        .code
        lea esi,letter1   ; load esi with address of letter1
        lea edi,letter2   ; load edi with address of letter2
        movsb             ; move string byte from [esi] to [edi]
```

However, obviously the above code segment could be written much easier by simply writing the following:

```
    mov al,letter1    ; load al with letter1
    mov letter2,al    ; store al in letter2
```

As can be seen, by itself the `movsb` instruction is not terribly useful, but when used in conjunction with some other instructions, it becomes a fairly powerful instruction. The fact that the `movsb` instruction can alter `esi` and `edi` can be very useful when moving a number of bytes. The way to determine which way `esi` and `edi` will be altered is based on the direction flag (mentioned previously in Chap. 4). The direction flag can be cleared or set by using the `cld` or `std` instructions, which stand for clear direction flag or set direction flag, respectively. If the `esi` and `edi` registers need to be incremented, the direction flag then needs to be cleared (`cld`), otherwise the direction flag needs to set (`std`) to cause the registers to be decremented. Using this information, the `movsb` instruction could be used to simplify the loop used in the previous section and relisted below on the left, where the modified code using the `movsb` instruction is listed on the right:

```
mov ecx,12                     mov ecx,12
mov esi,offset string1         mov esi,offset string1
mov edi,offset string2         mov edi,offset string2
.repcat                        cld
mov al,[esi]                   .repeat
mov [edi],al                   movsb
inc esi                        .untilcxz
inc edi
.untilcxz
```

Note that `ecx`, `esi`, and `edi` all need to be initialized as before, but notice that the body of the loop is much smaller because of the power of the `movsb` instruction. An intermediate general purpose register is not needed to move from one memory location to another. Also note that it is not necessary for the programmer to increment the esi and edi registers, because it is automatically done by the movsb instruction. The only thing that needs to be done is to clear the direction flag using the cld instruction to cause the two registers to be incremented as opposed to being decremented, which only needs to be done once prior to the loop.

To help with making string processing even simpler, the above code can be further simplified by using a prefix. There are three prefixes that are useful here as listed below:

Prefix	Meaning
rep	Repeat
repe	Repeat while equal
repne	Repeat while not equal

The rep prefix works just like the .repeat-.untilcxz directives, where it decrements the ecx register until it reaches 0. Unlike the .repeat-.untilcxz directives which can have any number of instructions in the body of the loop, the rep prefix works only in conjunction with instructions like movsb. Thus the above code on the right and shown again below on the left can be further simplified as follows on the right:

```
mov ecx,12              mov ecx,12
lea esi,string1         lea esi,string1
lea edi,string2         lea edi,string2
cld                     cld
.repeat                 rep movsb
movsb
.untilcxz
```

As mentioned previously, the movsb instruction is not very useful when used as a stand-alone instruction, but when used in conjunction with other instructions, its power is evident. However, as with any instruction that has a lot of power, it loses some of its versatility. If each character needed to be processed as it was moved from one string to another, then the movsb instruction is not very useful. Since all it does is move bytes, which it does very well, it cannot do much of anything else. This is not to disparage the power of the movsb, but rather to show its limitations. For example, if each letter moved from one string to the other needed to be changed from lowercase to uppercase, the movsb would not be as useful and the following code segment would instead accomplish this task. For the sake of convenience in the example below, it is assumed that each character in the variable name1 is a letter of the alphabet:

```
            .data
name1       byte "MaryJo"
name2       byte 6 dup(?)


            .code
            mov ecx,lengthof name1        ; load ecx with length

            lea esi,name1                 ; load esi with address of name1
            lea edi,name2                 ; load edi with address of name2
            .repeat
            mov al,[esi]                  ; load al with [esi]
            and al,11011111b              ; convert lower to upper case
            mov [edi],al                  ; store al in [edi]
            inc esi                       ; increment esi by 1
            inc edi                       ; increment edi by 1
            .untilcxz
```

9.3   String Instructions: Scanning (scasb), Storing (stosb), and Loading (lodsb)

The scasb instruction is a fairly useful instruction when used with either the repe or repne prefixes. For example, what if one wanted to scan a string of bytes to find whether there was a particular character in a string, such as a blank? First, the al register is loaded with the character that needs to be found. Then the edi register is loaded with address of the string to be scanned. And lastly, the ecx register needs to be loaded with the number of characters to be scanned in the string. Then each time a character is scanned in the string, the ecx register is decremented by 1 and the edi register is incremented by 1. Using the repne prefix, the string will be scanned until the character is found or until the ecx is equal to 0:

```
            .data
name1       byte "Abe Lincoln"

            .code
            mov al,' '                    ; load al with a space
            mov ecx,lengthof name1        ; load ecx with length
            lea edi,name1                 ; load address of name1
            repne scasb
```

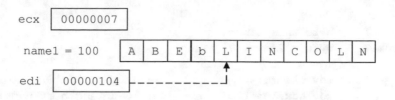

Fig. 9.2 Using repne scasb

In the above code segment, ecx is initially loaded with the length of name1, which is 11 (B in hex). After scanning for a space, or in other words, a blank as indicated by a lowercase b in Fig. 9.2, the ecx register will have been decremented to 7, which is how many characters are left to be scanned in name1, and the edi register would be pointing to the next character in the string as shown.

The stosb instruction is useful to store the contents of the al register at the location in a string pointed at by the edi register. The lodsb instruction loads the al register with the contents of the string pointed at by the esi register. In both cases the edi or the esi register is incremented after their respective operations. The semantics of each instruction is shown below using equivalent mov and inc instructions.

String instruction	Equivalent
stosb	mov al,[edi] inc edi
lodsb	mov [esi],al inc esi

As can be seen, the string instructions are a little cleaner and have the option of using the rep prefix. Although both instructions could be used with a rep prefix, only the stosb instruction would benefit the most by its use when initializing a string to blanks or some other character. As an example of how many of the above instructions might be used, consider the task of taking someone's name in the normal first name followed by last name order and then reversing it so that the last name is first, followed by a comma, followed by a space, and then followed by the last name:

```
            .data
name1       byte "Abe Lincoln"
name2       byte  12 dup (?)
            .code
            mov al,' '                  ; load al with space
            mov ecx,lengthof name1      ; load length of name1
            lea edi,name1               ; load address of name1
            repne scasb                 ; find space in name1
            push ecx                    ; save ecx
            mov esi,edi                 ; move edi to esi
            lea edi,name2               ; load adress of name2
            rep movsb                   ; copy last name to name2
            mov al,', '                 ; load al with comma
            stosb                       ; store comma in name2
            mov al,' '                  ; load al with comma
            stosb                       ; store space in name2
            mov ecx,lengthof name2      ; store length of name2
            pop eax                     ; restore ecx into eax
            sub ecx,eax                 ; sub length of last name
            dec ecx                     ; decrement ecx for space
            lea esi,name1               ; load address of name1
            rep movsb                   ; copy first name to name2
```

In the above program, first the space needs to be found between the first and the last name in name1 using the scasb instruction. After ecx is saved for subsequent processing, the last name from name1 would be copied to name2 using the movsb instruction. A comma and a space then need to be inserted into name2 using the stosb instruction. Then using the previously saved value of ecx to determine the length of the first name, the first name can be copied from name1 to name2 using the movsb instruction.

9.4   Array of Strings

What if one wanted to move an array of strings to another array of strings? It is possible that one could just treat the entire array of strings as one giant string and use a single rep movsb instruction. Given the following array of strings,

```
names1    byte "Abby","Fred","John","Kent","Mary"
```

it could be viewed as shown in Fig. 9.3.

names1

Fig. 9.3 Strings viewed as a single string

Fig. 9.4 Strings viewed as
an array of strings

names1	A	b	b	y
	F	r	e	d
	J	o	h	n
	K	e	n	t
	M	a	r	y

Although using only a `rep movsb` would work, the disadvantage of this approach is, what if one wanted to process each string individually? Instead it is helpful to not view `names1` as just a single string but rather to view it as an array of strings as shown in Fig. 9.4.

Although the following solution to the problem does not address the issue of processing each string separately, it lays the groundwork for that in a future problem and illustrates a more versatile way to process an array of strings. What are needed are two loops: one to control the array of strings and the other for each character in the string:

```
        .data
names1  byte "Abby","Fred","John","Kent","Mary"
names2  byte 20 dup(?)

        .code
main    proc
        mov ecx,5       ; load ecx with 5
        lea esi,names1  ; load esi with address of names1
        lea edi,names2  ; load edi with address of names2
        cld             ; clear direction flag
        .repeat
        push ecx        ; save ecx
        mov ecx,4       ; load ecx with 4
        rep movsb       ; move string from names1 to names2
        pop ecx         ; restore ecx
        .untilcxz
```

Note that the value of ecx needs to be pushed and popped prior to and after the rep movsb instruction since the rep prefix uses the ecx register too. Further, the cld could have been placed in the loop prior to the rep movsb instructions, but since the value of the direction flag does not change, there is no need to clear it each time and it can be placed just prior to the outer loop. Again, although the above code could have been done with only a rep movsb instruction, it lays the foundation for a problem in a subsequent section.

9.5   String Instructions: Comparing Strings (cmpsb)

What if one wanted to compare two strings to see if they are equal? As might be suspected, this can be done with a loop and an if structure, but the code for this is rather ungainly. Instead of showing this option, it is much easier to go straight to the instruction designed for this task, which is the cmpsb instruction used to compare a string of bytes. It is very similar to the movsb instruction, where it performs two major tasks. First, it compares the two bytes pointed to by the esi and edi registers and sets the appropriate flags such as the zero and sign flags. It then decrements the ecx register, and increments or decrements the esi and edi registers as indicated by the direction flag, just like with the movsb instruction. Also, similar to the rep operator with the movsb, a repe prefix can be added to allow loop control. The repe repeats, while the two characters being compared are equal. For example, given the following declaration with equal length strings, what would happen in the following code segment?

```
        .data
name1   byte "James"
name2   byte "James"

        .code
        mov ecx,lengthof name1   ; load ecx with length
        lea esi,name1            ; load address of name1
        lea edi,name2            ; load address of name2
        cld                      ; clear direction flag
        repe cmpsb               ; repeat while equal
```

First, upon completion of the segment, ecx would be 0. Assuming that name1 was at memory location 100 and name2 was at memory location 105 as in the drawing in Fig. 9.5, the final values of esi and edi would be 105 and 10A (in hex), respectively.

But what if name1 and name2 contained James and Jamie, respectively?

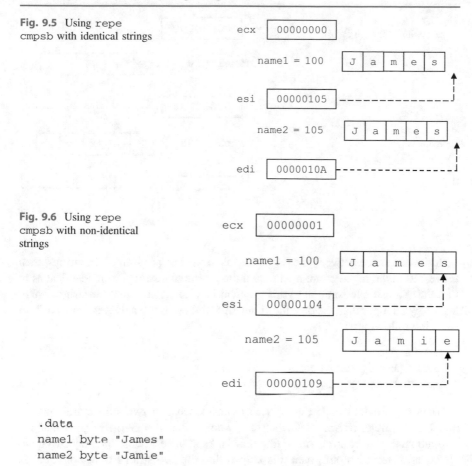

Fig. 9.5 Using repe cmpsb with identical strings

Fig. 9.6 Using repe cmpsb with non-identical strings

```
.data
name1 byte "James"
name2 byte "Jamie"
```

Since the repe cmpsb instructions stop after a difference is found, the value of ecx would be 1, after being decremented four times for the four characters that were compared. The value of esi and edi would be 104 and 109, respectively, as shown in Fig. 9.6.

At first, it would seem that the final two values of the ecx register would be useful in determining whether two strings are equal or not. However, what if the difference between the two strings was only in the last position as in the following?

```
.data
name1 byte "Marci "
name2 byte "Marcy "
```

Again, since repe cmpsb stops when a difference is found, the value of ecx would be 0 after being decremented five times, the value of esi would be 105, and edi would be 10A, as shown in Fig. 9.7.

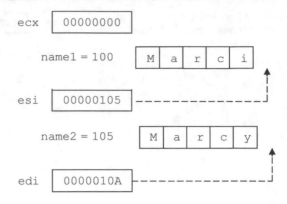

Fig. 9.7 Using repe cmpsb with difference in last character

If the difference between the two strings is in the last position of the strings, then the results in the registers are no different than if the two strings were identical as in Fig. 9.5. The simple solution to this problem is to make sure that the strings are at least 1 byte longer than the data they contain and there is a blank in the last position as in the following:

```
.data
name1 byte "Marci "
name2 byte "Marcy "
```

Then the previous code can be used to check whether two strings are equal or not. For example, if ecx is 0, then it is known that the repe cmpsb made it throughout the entire string, including the blanks at the end, and that they are equal. However, if ecx is not 0, then it is known that the two strings were not equal as shown in Fig. 9.8.

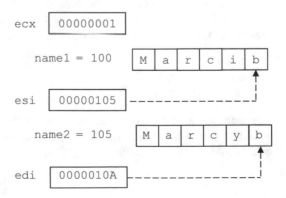

Fig. 9.8 Using repe cmpsb with extra blanks

So after the `repe cmpsb` instructions in the code segment above, an `.if` directive could be added to test the contents of the `ecx` register and act accordingly. However, what if adding extra bytes to the string is not a possibility? What would happen if the difference occurred in the last element of the string and `ecx` was a 0? Returning to the previous example which did not contain the extra spaces,

```
.data
name1 byte "Marci"
name2 byte "Marcy"
```

the code would still need to check to see if `ecx` was 0, but there would need to be an additional check to determine whether there was a difference between the last two characters. Since the values of `esi` and `edi` would be one beyond the last character as they are in Fig. 9.7, they would need to be "backed up" or decremented by 1 to determine whether there was a difference in the last character as illustrated in Fig. 9.9.

Modifying the previous code segment above to include input and output, the following complete program illustrates how this would work. Should `ecx` be greater than 0, then the two strings are different. However, if `ecx` is equal to zero, then `esi` and `edi` would need to be decremented to determine whether the strings are same. Note that this program assumes that equal length strings will be input:

Fig. 9.9 Using `repe` cmpsb and backing up one character

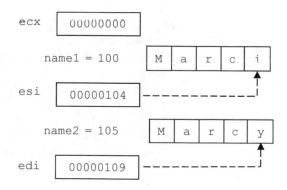

```
                    .686
                    .model flat,c
                    .stack 100h
scanf               PROTO arg2:Ptr Byte, inputlist:VARARG
printf              PROTO arg1:Ptr Byte, printlist:VARARG
                    .data
msg1fmt             byte "%s",0
msg2fmt             byte 0Ah,"%s",0Ah,0Ah,0
in1fmt              byte "%s",0
msg1                byte "Enter a first name: ",0
msg2                byte "Enter another first name: ",0
msg3                byte "The names are not the same.",0
msg4                byte "The names are the same.",0
name1               byte 6 dup(" ")
name2               byte 6 dup(" ")
                    .code
main                proc
                    INVOKE printf, ADDR msg1fmt, ADDR msg1
                    INVOKE scanf, ADDR in1fmt, ADDR name1
                    INVOKE printf, ADDR msg1fmt, ADDR msg2
                    INVOKE scanf, ADDR in1fmt, ADDR name2
                    mov ecx,lengthof name1    ; load ecx with length
                    lea esi,name1             ; load address of name1
                    lea edi,name2             ; load address of name2
                    cld                       ; clear direction flag
                    repe cmpsb                ; compare while equal
                    .if ecx > 0               ; check if ecx > 0
                    INVOKE printf, ADDR msg2fmt, ADDR msg3
                    .else
                    dec esi                   ; back up esi one position
                    dec edi                   ; back up edi one position
                    mov al,[esi]              ; load al with [esi}
                    .if al != [edi]           ; if not equal
                    INVOKE printf, ADDR msg2fmt, ADDR msg3
                    .else
                    INVOKE printf, ADDR msg2fmt, ADDR msg4
                    .endif
                    .endif
                    ret
main                endp
                    end
```

Looking carefully at the declaration of name1 and name2, it should be noted that they have been declared to be 6 bytes long instead of 5 bytes. Is the reason for adding the extra byte to make the comparisons easier as discussed previously? The answer is no, because the data is not a pre-defined string, but rather it is being input via an INVOKE scanf instruction. When the user keys in a string, the last thing they do is press the Enter or Return key at the end of the string. The Enter key appears at the end of the string as a binary zero, not unlike the 0 that appears at the end of a string such as msg3 and msg4 in the .data section in the above program. The result is that space needs to be made for the binary zero, otherwise it could spill over into other memory locations and could cause various logic errors.

What if one wanted to determine if the content of one string is less than or greater than another string? For example, what if one wanted to put the names in alphabetical order? Unfortunately, an instruction does not exist for this, but looking back at the previous program, there is a hint of a possible solution to the problem. Previously, when ecx was 0, esi and edi needed to be backed up to determine whether or not the strings were equal. What would need to happen if ecx was not 0 in the previous case as shown below?

```
.data
name1 byte "James"
name2 byte "Jamie"
```

The repe cmpsb instruction stopped after a difference was found and in this case the value of ecx was 1 after being decremented four times for the four comparisons. However, to determine whether the character is less than or greater than the other, the values of the esi and edi registers would again need to be backed up in this case to 103 and 108, respectively, as shown in Fig. 9.10.

In other words, regardless of whether ecx is 0 or not, esi and edi need to be backed up so that the last two characters can be compared to determine whether they are the same, or whether one is larger or smaller. Using some of the same code from the previous example, where it is assumed that equal length strings for name1 and name2 have already been prompted for and input, it can be modified as follows:

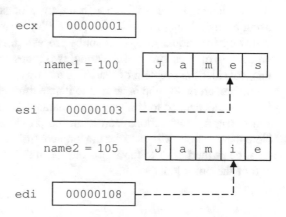

Fig. 9.10 Backing up to determine name1 is greater than or less than name2

```
            ; *** assume previous INVOKEs, prompts, and formats
msg3    byte "The names are the same.",0
msg4    byte "The first name is less than the second.",0

msg5    byte "The first name is greater than the second.",0
name1   byte 6 dup(" ")
name2   byte 6 dup(" ")
        .code
main    proc
        ;*** assume previous prompts and input
        mov ecx,lengthof name1   ; load ecx with length
        lea esi,name1            ; load address of name1
        lea edi,name2            ; load address of name2
        cld                      ; clear direction flag
        repe cmpsb               ; compare while equal
        dec esi                  ; back up esi one position
        dec edi                  ; back up edi one position
        mov al,[esi]             ; load al with [esi}
        .if al == [edi]          ; if equal
        INVOKE printf, ADDR msg2fmt, ADDR msg3
        .else
        .if al < [edi]           ; if less than
        INVOKE printf, ADDR msg2fmt, ADDR msg4
        .else
        INVOKE printf, ADDR msg2fmt, ADDR msg5
        .endif
        .endif
```

9.6 Complete Program: Searching an Array of Strings

As mentioned previously, although an array of strings can be moved by simply using a single loop or by using merely a rep movsb instruction, the disadvantage is that the individual strings cannot be processed. In order to accomplish individual processing of each string in the array, two loops should be employed. To illustrate this, consider the problem of searching an array of fixed length strings sequentially. As before, an outer loop is needed to iterate through each string in the array and an inner loop is needed to compare each character in the string. For this latter task, the repe cmpsb instructions learned in the previous section is the obvious choice. Note that since ecx is used for the loop control variable of the outer loop, its value must be pushed prior to the repe cmpsb instruction and then popped prior to the end of the outer loop:

```
            .686
            .model flat,c
            .stack 100h
Scanf    PROTO arg2:Ptr Byte, inputlist:VARARG
printf   PROTO arg1:Ptr Byte, printlist:VARARG
            .data
msg1fmt byte 0Ah,"%s",0
msg2fmt byte 0Ah,"%s",0Ah,0Ah,0
in1fmt  byte "%s",0
msg1     byte "Enter the state to be found: ",0
msg2     byte "The state was found.",0
msg3     byte "The state was not found.",0
arrystr byte "Illinois ","Michigan","Iowa       ",
             "Missouri ","Arkansas ","Tennessee",
             "Louisiana","Arizona ","Montana    ",
             "Ohio       "
n        sdword 10
string   byte 10 dup(?)
found    sdword ?
            .code
main     proc
            INVOKE printf, ADDR msg1fmt,ADDR msg1
            INVOKE scanf, ADDR in1fmt, ADDR string
            mov ecx,0              ; initialize ecx to 0
            mov found,0           ; initialize found to 0
            lea edi,arrystr+0     ; load edi with address
            .while(ecx<n &&  found != -1)
            push ecx              ; save ecx
            lea esi,string+0     ; load address of string
            cld                  ; clear direction flag
            mov ecx,lengthof string ; load length of string
            repe cmpsb           ; compare while equal
            dec esi              ; decrement es1
            dec edi              ; decrement edi
            mov al,[esi]         ; load al with [esi]
            mov ah,[edi]         ; load ah with [edi]
            .if (al==0)&&(ah==" ") ; compare for 0 and space
            mov found,-1          ; if yes, found
            .endif
            inc edi                    ; increment edi back
```

```
            add edi,ecx                ; adjust edi to next string
            pop ecx                    ; restore ecx
            inc ecx                    ; increment ecx
            .endw
            .if (found == -1)
            INVOKE printf, ADDR msg2fmt, ADDR msg2
            .else
            INVOKE printf, ADDR msg2fmt, ADDR msg3
            .endif
            ret
    main    endp
            end
```

Although each string in the array of strings in the above program is of equal
length, each string entered is of variable length. Again these strings are terminated
by the pressing of the Enter key which appears at the end of the string as a binary 0.
In the case where the input string is equal to the fixed length string in the array,
repe cmpsb will stop because the binary 0 will not equal the space in the array.
For example, "Tennessee", 0 will not be equal to "Tennessee ". So, the esi
and edi registers are backed up to check for the 0 and the space, and if they are
there, the string has been found.

However, in the case that the strings are different, such as "Tennessea", 0, the
difference will occur before the binary 0, and thus when backing up the esi
register, the binary 0 will not be found. In the case where the string that is input is
longer, such as "Ioway", 0 as compared to "Iowa", again the difference would
occur before the binary 0 is encountered. However, if all these cases are caught by
checking for the binary 0, why check for the space? If the presence of the space was
not checked for, then "Iow", 0 would end up being equal to "Iowa", which is
clearly incorrect.

Also notice that when the string is not found in the array, the value edi will be
incorrect, so it is necessary to adjust the values to point to the beginning of the next
string in the array. This is accomplished by first incrementing edi back to its
original location to account for the decrement discussed in the previous paragraph.
Then, the number of characters left in the string needs to be added, which is the
value in the ecx register, to the edi register.

9.7 Summary

- The movsb instruction moves a string of bytes from where the esi register is
  pointing to where the edi register is pointing. The registers are then incremented
  or decremented based on the direction flag.
- The cmpsb instruction compares a byte in a string pointed to by the esi and
  edi registers. The registers are then incremented or decremented based on the
  direction flag.

- Do not forget to clear the direction flag using cld to increment esi and edi or set the direction flag using std to decrement esi and edi prior to either the cmpsb or movsb instructions.
- The rep prefix prior to movsb loops the number of times indicated by the ecx register, decrements the ecx register by 1, and continues until ecx is 0.
- The repe prefix prior to cmpsb works like the rep prefix in that it will quit looping when ecx equals 0, but it will also quit looping when the 2 bytes pointed to by esi and edi are not equal. The repne prefix is like repe but will instead quit looping when the 2 bytes are equal.
- The scasb instruction will scan a string for the character located in the al register and the edi register will point 1 byte after the location it is found. The stosb instruction will store the character in the al register in a string at the location pointed at by the edi register. And the lodsb instruction will load the character in a string pointed to by the esi register into the al register.

9.8 Exercises (Items Marked with an * Have Solutions in Appendix D)

1. Given the following assembly language statements, indicate whether they are syntactically correct or incorrect. If incorrect, indicate what is wrong with the statement:

   *A. movesb B. cmpsb *C. scasb
   D. stosb *E. rept strsb F. loadsb

2. Given the following declarations, walk through the following code segments and indicate the contents of the ecx, esi, edi, and al registers upon completion of each segment. You may assume that string1 starts at memory location 100 and string2 at memory location 105. With problem D, in addition to the registers, what would be the contents of string2?

```
string1 byte "abcde"
string2 byte "abcyz"
```

*A.
```
mov ecx,5
mov al,"c"
mov edi,offset string1
rep scasb
```

B.
```
mov esi,offset string1+3
Lodsb
```

*C.
```
mov ecx,5
mov esi,offset string1
mov edi,offset string2
repe cmpsb
```

D.
```
mov ecx,5
mov esi,offset string1
mov edi,offset string2
repne cmpsb
```

E.
```
lea edi,string2
mov al,"d"
stosb
```

3. Using the `esi` and `edi` registers and a `.repeat-untilcxz` loop, determine whether the word in a string is a palindrome. For the sake of convenience, assume that the string is 10 elements long and all the words in the string are also 10 characters long. Do not use a stack.

Floating-Point Instructions

10

This chapter introduces the fundamentals of floating-point instructions. This includes registers, memory storage, input/output, the instructions needed to perform arithmetic, and basic control structures. In order to learn the concepts in this chapter one should understand how floating-point numbers are represented in memory from a computer organization class or text. Alternatively, one can review or learn the basic concepts needed as presented in Appendix B.7 of this text. Also, one should have knowledge of stacks usually discussed in a second semester computer science course or text such as *Guide to Data Structures* [3].

10.1 Memory Storage

In addition to integer, string, and Boolean data, programs can be written to store and process floating-point data. For example, in the C programming languages, floating-point data can be stored as a `float` which takes up 32 bits, as a `double` which uses 64 bits, or a `long double` which uses 80 bits. Using more bits allows for a larger range and more precision, but takes up more memory. In assembly language these three types can be declared as `real4`, `real8`, and `real10`, respectively, where the number indicates the number of bytes. Examples of declaring each are as follows:

```
x       real4      ?
y       real8      3.14
z       real10     -27.1
```

© Springer Nature Switzerland AG 2020
J. T. Streib, *Guide to Assembly Language*, Undergraduate Topics
in Computer Science, https://doi.org/10.1007/978-3-030-35639-2_10

10.2   Floating-Point Register Stack

As with integers, data must be loaded into a register from memory, processed, and then stored back into memory. However, instead of using the four general purpose registers eax, ebx, ecx, and edx, an eight-element floating-point register stack is used. The registers in the stack are called ST(0) through ST(7), where ST(0) is the top of the stack as illustrated below:

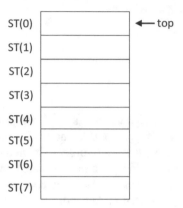

This stack is different from the stack discussed in Chap. 6, where that stack is created in memory, can be declared to be different lengths, and to hold different types of data. The floating-point register stack is not declared in memory but is rather composed of registers in the CPU. Further it is used to store floating-point numbers of type real4, real8, and real10, and the stack has a fixed length of eight elements.

10.3   Pushing and Popping

Note that the instructions used to push and pop floating-point numbers cannot use immediate operands, so to illustrate these instructions, assume that the following have been declared:

```
num1 real4   2.71
num2 real4   3.14
num3 real4   ?
num4 real4   ?
```

First, it should be noted that all instructions that will be used to process floating-point data begin with the letter f. Initially, this may seem a little strange, but it helps distinguish the floating-point instructions from the instructions used with integers. In order to push the contents of a memory location onto the stack, a floating-point load instruction, `fld`, must be used. There are many variations on this instruction, but for the purposes of this text only this simple one will be used.

To demonstrate how to take a copy of the contents of memory location `num1` and load, or push, it onto the stack the following would be used:

    fld num1

which would cause the stack to appear as follows with the change indicated in green:

If `num2` needed to be pushed onto the stack, the following would be used,

    fld num2

and the stack would look as follows:

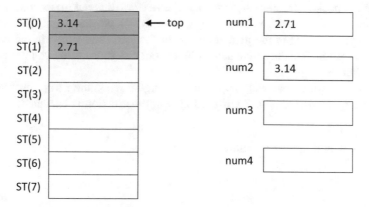

Note that the 2.71 is pushed further down on the stack and the 3.14 is now at the top of the stack. At first, the use of a floating-point load instruction may seem a little confusing because it might seem that a push instruction should be used instead. But if one thinks of the process as loading a register which just happens to be the first position on a stack of registers, then with time it becomes a little more natural.

What if one wanted to copy or pop a number off the top of a stack? Again, there are many variations, but two instructions will be shown here. The first is a floating-point store instruction which makes a copy of the number at the top of the stack and stores it in a memory location. For example, to make a copy of the number 3.14 at the top of the stack and store in num3, the following would be used,

```
fst num3
```

and the stack would look as follows:

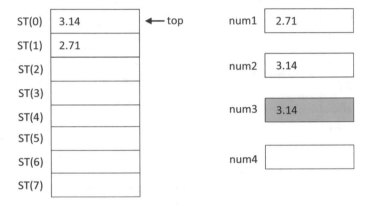

Notice that there is no change on the stack and the number 3.14 is still at the top. This is because the fst instruction is not really a true pop instruction but is rather like a peek instruction that one might have learned about in a second semester computer science course or text. The number is not popped from the stack, but rather a copy is made of the item at the top of the stack and stored in the specified memory location. This is convenient at times, but can cause some confusion if one isn't careful.

Should one want to actually pop an item from the stack, the fstp must be used, where the p stands for pop. So, if the following instruction is executed:

```
fstp num3
```

the results would appear as follows:

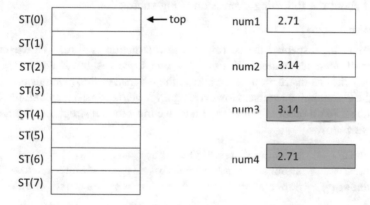

In this example, note that the 3.14 is no longer on the stack and the 2.71 has moved up to the top. Lastly, executing the following,

```
fstp num4
```

would cause the stack to be empty as shown below:

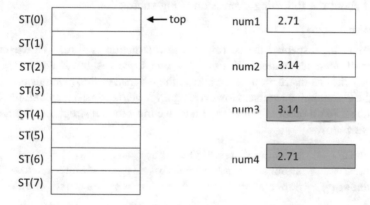

This is the typical result that one often expects when removing items from a stack and is also the instruction that will be used most often in this chapter.

10.4 Simple Arithmetic Expressions

In order to perform addition, the floating-point add instruction is used. As with the `fld` and `fstp` there are a number of variations but only the simplest ones will be shown here. The first is `fadd` which will take a number from memory and add it to the number at the top of the stack.

Given the previously declared variables with new values and an additional variable called `answer` as declared below,

```
num1     real4   2.5
num2     real4   3.5
num3     real4   4.0
num4     real4   5.5
answer   real4   ?
```

how could the following be implemented?

```
answer = num1 + num2;
```

First, num1 would need to be pushed onto the stack. Could num2 be pushed instead? Yes, but it is much more convenient to keep the order from left to right to help with readability and consistency. Then using the fadd instruction, num2 would be added to the number at the top of the stack. Lastly, the sum would be popped off the stack and stored in answer. The resulting code would be as follows:

```
fld  num1     ; push num1 onto the stack
fadd num2     ; add num2 to the first element on the stack
fstp answer   ; pop the sum off the stack into answer
```

What about the following expression using subtraction?

```
answer = num1 - num2;
```

As might be suspected the corresponding instruction is fsub. However, does the order of operands matter in this case? In one sense yes, but in another no. Note that there exists an instruction which allows the reversal of the operands call fsubr where the r stands for reverse. However, again it helps consistency and readability to use the standard order of left to right and use the fsub instruction. The resulting code is as follows:

```
fld  num1     ; push num1 onto the stack
fsub num2     ; subtract num2 from the first element on the stack
fstp answer   ; pop the difference off the stack into answer
```

Multiplication works as addition but instead uses the fmul instruction. So, the following expression,

```
answer = num1 * num2;
```

would result in the following code segment:

```
fld  num1     ; push num1 onto the stack
fmul num2     ; multiply num2 to the first element on the stack
fstp answer   ; pop the product off the stack into answer
```

Likewise, division is similar to subtraction but instead the `fdiv` instruction is used. However, note that there is no reverse instruction, so care must be taken with the order of the operands and the following expression:

```
answer = num1 / num2;
```

would be implemented as follows:

```
fld   num1     ; push num1 onto the stack
fdiv  num2     ; divide num2 into the first element on the stack
fstp  answer   ; pop the quotient off the stack into answer
```

10.5 Complex Arithmetic Expressions

As done in the previous examples, one can take each equation encountered and proceed directly to trying to create the necessary assembly language code. With simple examples this might be acceptable, but with more complicated expressions, the chances of making mistakes increase dramatically. A far more efficient method is to first convert the expression to postfix as might have been discussed when learning about stacks from a second semester course or text. Then the postfix expression can be easily written in the necessary floating-point instructions.

At first the extra step of converting to postfix might seem to be slowing down the process since code is not being written immediately. However, the time needed to produce the code is quicker and much less prone to time-consuming debugging. Using the following variables and values,

```
w         real4    2.5
x         real4    3.5
y         real4    4.0
z         real4    5.25
answer    real4    ?
```

consider the following C-like statement:

```
answer = w + x + y;
```

Recall that to do the conversion, first the variables are placed in the same order that they appeared in the original expression. Then since the addition on the left is done first, it is placed immediately after the two variables w and x. Then the second addition is placed after the variable y to add the sum of w and x and the variable y. The postfix equivalent of the right side of the expression is as follows:

w x + y +

Now to write the code of the corresponding expression going from left to right, the first step is to push any operands onto the stack. In this case the first two variables are pushed onto the stack as follows:

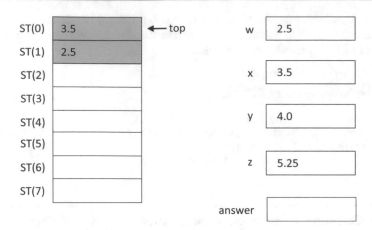

When encountering an operator, the operation should be performed on the top two numbers on the stack and the results pushed back onto the stack. To accomplish this task, the `fadd` instruction without an operand can be used. It takes the item on the top of the stack in ST(0) and adds it to the second item on the stack in ST(1). Then the first item is popped off the stack and the sum now occupies ST(0).

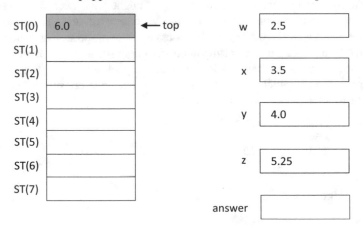

A question that might be asked at this point is what happened to the 3.5 that was popped off the stack? Where did it go? Since there is no operand in which to put the item, it simply is discarded.

Continuing, next the value in y is pushed onto the stack

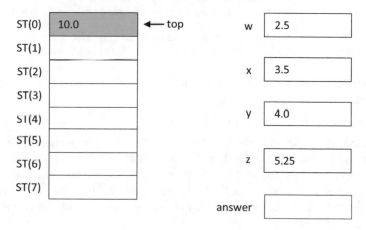

Then as before when the `fadd` instruction is executed, the item at the top of the stack in ST(0) is added to the item in the second element in the stack in ST(1). Then the item at the top of the stack in ST(0) is popped off the stack and the second item in the stack in ST(1) moves up to the position in ST(0).

Lastly, the item on the top of the stack is popped off the stack and put into `answer` as follows:

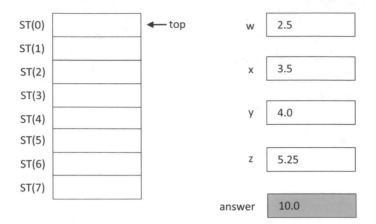

Putting all the above together results in the following assembly language code segment:

```
fld  w        ; push w onto the stack
fld  x        ; push x onto the stack
fadd          ; add the top two items leaving the sum at the top
fld  y        ; push y onto the stack
fadd          ; add the top two items leaving the sum at the top
fstp answer   ; pop the result off the stack into answer
```

In another more complex example that uses other operations, consider the following:

```
answer = w / x - y * z;
```

Remembering that multiplication and division have a higher priority than addition and subtraction and that in a tie the order is from left to right, the division is performed first, then the multiplication, and lastly the subtraction. The resulting postfix expression has the division after w and x, the multiplication after the y and z, and the subtraction is last after the quotient and product of the previous two operations as follows:

```
w x / y z * -
```

The resulting assembly code derived from the postfix expression is given below:

```
fld  w        ; push w onto the stack
fld  x        ; push x onto the stack
fdiv          ; divide leaving quotient at top of the stack
fld  y        ; push y onto the stack
fld  z        ; push z onto the stack
fmul          ; multiply leaving product at top of the stack
fsub          ; subtract leaving difference at top of the stack
fstp answer   ; pop the result off the stack into answer
```

As should be seen, the conversion from the postfix expression to the assembly language code is rather straight forward. However, if one is having difficulty converting an expression to postfix, be sure to go back to the text from a second semester course to review the process. Also, there are various practice exercises at the end of this chapter to help reinforce the process.

10.6   Mixing Floating-Point and Integers

Although it might be easier to not usually mix integers with floating-point numbers, on occasion it might be necessary. This section is not a comprehensive discussion of the matter, but gives a basic introduction so that one can be aware of some of the potential pitfalls when mixing these two types.

Since a floating-point number cannot be used with the general-purpose registers such as eax, it is instead necessary to use integers with the floating-point stack. In order to do so, the letter i (for integer) must be used after the letter f in a floating-point instruction. For example, instead of fld, the fild instruction would be used, and instead of fstp, the fistp instruction would be used, and so on. To illustrate how these instructions work, assume the existence of the following declarations:

```
one     sdword 1
one2    real4  1.2
one5    real4  1.5
one7    real4  1.7
two5    real4  2.5
three   sdword 3
ansint  sdword ?
ansflt  real4  ?
```

So, to transfer the integer contents of the variable one to the integer variable ansint using the floating-point stack, the following instructions would work:

```
fild one
fistp ansint
```

Although it would be much easier to use the eax register and mov instructions to transfer an integer, the above illustrates how the fild and fistp instructions work. Continuing, how could one move an integer to a floating-point variable? As one might suspect, the i is removed from the fistp instruction as follows:

```
fild one
fstp ansdbl
```

When moving a floating-point number to an integer, one needs to be careful with respect to rounding. Consider the following two sets of instructions from left to right that move the floating-point numbers 1.2 and 1.7, respectively.

```
fld one2                          fld one7
fistp ansint                      fistp ansint
```

As one might suspect the rounded results from left to right would be 1 and 2, respectively. What about moving the number 1.5 as follows?

```
fld one5
fistp ansint
```

As many have been taught, if the number is a 1.5, it should be rounded upwards. The result in the above example is 2, but not necessarily for the reason one might expect. Continuing, consider moving the number 2.5 in the following:

```
fld two5
fistp ansint
```

It would seem that the result in `ansint` would be 3, but in reality, it would be 2. Why? The reason is that the floating-point default mode for rounding a 0.5 is to round up or down to the nearest even number. In the case above the nearest even number to 2.5 is 2 and in the previous example that the nearest even number to 1.5 is 2. Although this may seem strange to some, it is a commonly used way of rounding numbers to avoid the accumulation of rounding errors and is known as *bankers rounding*. For example, adding the following numbers:

$$1.5 + 2.5 + 3.5 + 4.5 + 5.5$$

the answer would be 17.5. But what if all the above numbers were rounded up? The numbers would then be as follows:

$$2 + 3 + 4 + 5 + 6$$

The answer would be 20 which is significantly different than 17.5. But what if bankers rounding was used? The 1.5 would be rounded to 2 and the 2.5 would be rounded to 2, and so on, as follows:

$$2 + 2 + 4 + 4 + 6$$

The sum would be 18, which is much closer to the original answer of 17.5. Although this is a short list of numbers, the difference between using numbers that are rounded-up and the original numbers could be quite significant and the bankers rounding method helps mitigate this difference.

What if one didn't want to use rounding, but rather just truncate all numbers? This can be done by altering the floating-point control word, but this is beyond the scope of this text. Another solution is to use instructions that truncate, and this is accomplished by inserting the letter t just prior to the letter p in the fistp instruction so that it becomes the fisttp instruction. Taking the four real4 numbers previously declared above and using them from left to right with the fisttp instruction results in the following:

```
fld one2          fld one7          fld one5          fld two5
fisttp ansint     fisttp ansint     fisttp ansint     fisttp ansint
```

Instead of resulting in the answers 1, 2, 2, and 2 as would have happened with the fistp instruction, the above fisttp instruction would result in 1, 1, 1, and 2, respectively. Which instruction should be used? It depends on the application; however, rounding using the fistp instruction is probably going to be more useful.

How does all this affect arithmetic? Consider the following three code segments:

```
fld two5          fld two5          fld one5
fiadd three       fiadd three       fiadd three
fstp ansflt       fistp ansint      fistp ansint
```

The first one on the left adds 2.5 and 3, stores the result using ftsp, and the floating-point answer is 5.5. The second example uses the same numbers, uses the integer fistp instruction instead, and the answer is 6 which is the closest even number to 5.5. However, the answer to the third one on the right adding 1.5 and 3 also using the integer fistp instruction rounds the 4.5 to 4 since it the closest even integer.

The result is that when mixing integers and floating-point numbers, it must be done carefully. If one is just placing some integer values into floating-point variables, then there probably isn't as much of a problem, but if floating-point results are being placed into integer variables, then extra care must be taken. The problem can only be exacerbated in more complex arithmetic expressions with intermediate results stored in integer variables. Instead of just coding and excepting the answers to be correct, it is important to walk through the code with key examples to ensure that the answers are what are expected. Of course, the simplest way to avoid many of these problems is to use just floating-point numbers with floating-point numbers, but when integers need to be used along with floating-point numbers, careful coding and testing is necessary.

10.7   Input/Output

Before continuing with some more complex code examples that utilize control structures and a complete program, the topic of input and output should be discussed. As with integer input and output, it is helpful to first look at how floating-point input and output work in a C program.

10.7.1   float and real4

First, consider a simple program that inputs, transfers, and outputs a number of type float:

```
#include <stdio.h>
int main() {

        float x,y;

        printf("\n%s", "Enter a float for x: ");
        scanf_s("%f", &x);

        y = x;

        printf("\n%s%6.4f\n\n", "The float in y is: ", y);

        return 0;
}
```

If the number 3.14159 were input, the output would be as follows:

```
The float in y is: 3.1416
```

Note that in the scanf_s the %f indicates that a number of type float will be input. Also recall that just as with integers discussed in Chap. 2, an ampersand, &, must proceed the variable x on input to indicate the address where the number being input will be stored. On output the first number in the format prior to the decimal point indicates the total number of positions allocated to output the number, in this case 6. The second number after the decimal point indicates the number of positions that will be after the decimal point, in this case 4. Notice that since there are only four positions available for the five digits after the decimal point, the fourth position is rounded on output.

Although in assembly real4 numbers can be input, they need to be moved to a real8 variable before they can be output, as can be seen in the corresponding assembly code that follows:

```
            .686
            .model flat,c
            .stack 100h

printf      PROTO arg1:Ptr Byte, printlist:VARARG
scanf       PROTO arg2:Ptr Byte, inputlist:VARARG

            .data
in1fmt      byte "%f",0
msg0fmt     byte 0Ah,"%s",0
msg1fmt     byte 0Ah,"%s%6.4f",0Ah,0Ah,0
msg0        byte "Enter a float for x: ",0
msg1        byte "The float in y is: ",0

x           real4 ?
y           real8 ?

            .code
main        proc

            INVOKE printf, ADDR msg0fmt, ADDR msg0
            INVOKE scanf, ADDR in1fmt, ADDR x
            fld x
            fstp y
            INVOKE printf, ADDR msg1fmt, ADDR msg1, y

            ret
main        endp
            end
```

The above is all rather similar to integer input and output. Again, as a reminder, notice the ADDR prior to the variable x in the scanf statement. Also, in the msg1fmt note the %6.4f formatting for the output. Further, notice that x is declared as real4 and y as real8 and the transfer of x to y via the stack to allow for the output of the floating-point number.

10.7.2   **double and real8**

Given this need to move from a real4 to a real8 for output, it might be more convenient to just use real8 numbers for both input and output unless there is a concern for conserving memory, especially with arrays. Consider the following C program using type double:

```
#include <stdio.h>
int main() {

    double x,y;

    printf("\n%s", "Enter a double for x: ");
    scanf_s("%lf", &x);

    y = x;

    printf("\n%s%6.4f\n\n", "The double in y is: ", y);

    return 0;
}
```

Notice above that to input a number of type double, 1f is used. However, 1f is not needed for output and a simple f is sufficient. Although the transfer from x to y is not really needed and the contents of x could be output, the assignment statement remains for consistency between the preceding and subsequent programs. The equivalent code in assembly language is as follows:

```
                .686
                .model flat,c
                .stack 100h

printf          PROTO arg1:Ptr Byte, printlist:VARARG
scanf           PROTO arg2:Ptr Byte, inputlist:VARARG

                .data

in1fmt          byte "%lf",0
msg0fmt         byte 0Ah,"%s",0
msg1fmt         byte 0Ah,"%s%6.4f",0Ah,0Ah,0
msg0            byte "Enter a double for x:  ",0
msg1            byte "The double in y is: ",0
msg2fmt         byte 0Ah,"%s",0Ah,0Ah,0

x               real8 ?
y               real8 ?

                .code
main            proc
                INVOKE printf, ADDR msg0fmt, ADDR msg0
                INVOKE scanf, ADDR in1fmt, ADDR x
                fld x
                fstp y
                INVOKE printf, ADDR msg1fmt, ADDR msg1, y

                ret
main            endp
                end
```

Again, as with the C program, the important thing to notice is that lf is used for input and f is used for output.

10.7.3 `long double` and `real10`

Although `real8` numbers should be sufficient for most processing, the input and output of `real10` numbers are discussed in passing should they be needed. As done previously, first consider a C program using the `long double` type below:

```c
#include <stdio.h>
int main() {

    long double x,y;

    printf("\n%s", "Enter a long double for x: ");
    scanf_s("%Lf", &x);

    y = x;

    printf("\n%s%6.4Lf\n\n", "The long double in y is: ", y);
    return 0;
}
```

Probably the most important thing to notice in the above C program is that for both input and output the Lf format must be used. Also note that it uses an upper-case L and not a lower-case l. Since the code for `real10` in assembly language would be very similar to the previous two examples, it is left as an exercise at the end of this chapter. Again, since type `real8` is more convenient to use in output than type `real4` and has close to the same precision as `real10`, the type `real8` will be used in subsequent examples.

10.7.4 Inline Assembly

As will be seen in the next chapter, unfortunately inline assembly does not work with 64-bit integers. However, it can be used with all three floating point numbers: `float`, `double`, and `long double`. For example, the program from Sect. 10.7.2 can be rewritten using inline assembly for the transfer of x to y as follows:

```
#include <stdio.h>
int main() {

    double x,y;

    printf("\n%s", "Enter a double for x: ");
    scanf_s("%lf", &x);

    __asm {
        fld x
        fstp y
    }

    printf("\n%s%6.4f\n\n", "The double in y is: ", y);

    return 0;
}
```

As can be seen, the assembly code pushes the value of x onto the floating-point stack and then the value is popped off the stack into y. Although high-level control structures cannot be used with inline assembly, the advantage of inline assembly is that floating-point instructions and formatting can be tested without having quite the intricacy of assembly language input and output. Once they have been tested and debugged, they can be transferred and converted to an assembly language program.

10.8   Comparisons and Selection Structures

When comparing floating-point numbers using the 586 and earlier processors, there were various instructions, including the fcom, fcomp, fcompp instructions, which were rather cumbersome to use. However, starting with the 686 processors the additional less cumbersome fcomi and fcomip instructions were introduced. Whereas the original instructions needed to have the condition codes C0, C2, and C3 copied into the Carry, Parity, and Zero flags, respectively, the new instructions set the flags automatically. Due to this advantage, these new instructions are the ones will be discussed in this text.

Starting with a simple comparison using an if-then structure, consider the following C program segment:

```
if(x > y)
    printf("\n%s\n", "x is greater than y");
```

The segment simply compares to floating-point numbers, x and y, and if x is greater than y it outputs the corresponding message. First, it should be noted that unfortunately the previous high-level control structures used with integers introduced in Chap. 4 cannot be used with floating-point numbers. This is because the high-level structures use the cmp instruction which uses implied integer subtraction. However, this should not pose too much of a problem because the fcomi and `fcomip` instructions can be used with the label names such as `if01:` that were also introduced in Chap. 4. Another consideration is that although floating-point values are signed, instead of using signed conditional jumps such as `jg`, `jge`, `jl`, and `jle`, unsigned conditional jumps such as `ja`, `jae`, `jb`, and `jbe` are used which branch based on the contents of the flags set by the `fcomi` and `fcomip` instructions.

So, how do these instructions work? Looking first at the `fcomi` instruction, the two values that need to be compared are loaded onto the floating-point register stack. For example, using the C program from above the values x and y are loaded as follows:

```
fld y
fld x
```

Does it matter which value is loaded first? The answer is again yes and no. If the value on the right side of the conditional in the if statement is pushed on first, then the conditional jump statement that follows the `fcomi` statement will need to be reversed as was done back in Chap. 4 when dealing with integers. However, if the order in which the two values are pushed onto the stack is opposite from the above order, then writing the unconditional jump statement will unfortunately tend to be more complicated. So, although reversing the order might initially seem to be more confusing, the resulting code is simpler and will be more consistent with the previous technique used with integers. Assuming x and y contained a 5.0 and 7.0, respectively, then the stack would look as follows:

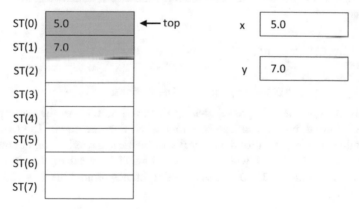

Next the `fcomi` has the following form:

```
fcomi st(0),st(i)
```

It compares the zeroth item at the top of the stack with the ith item on the stack. Although any item on the stack can be used for the second parameter, this text will use the second item on the stack, which is `st(1)` as shown below:

```
fcomi st(0),st(1)
```

However, one problem with the above code is that although it would work correctly, it does not pop the values off the stack. This might not be a problem with a small program with only a few numbers on the stack, but if there are more than 8 items loaded onto the stack an exception can occur. So, it makes more sense to get into the habit of popping the values off the stack using the `fcomip` instruction as follows:

```
fcomip st(0),st(1)
```

Then since the original code in the C program was,

```
if(x > y)
```

then reversing the condition as has been done previously with integers, the corresponding conditional jump statement is as follows:

```
jbe endif01
```

Putting all of the above pieces together along with the corresponding labels and output statement, the assembly code segment would be as follows:

```
             ;if x > y
if01:        fld y
             fld x
             fcomip st(0), st(1)
             jbe endif01
then01:      INVOKE printf, ADDR msg2fmt, ADDR msg2
endif01: nop
```

In another example, consider the nested if-then-else-if structure in the following C code segment:

```
if (x > y)
   printf("\n%s\n", "x is greater than y");
else
   if(x < y)
       printf("\n%s\n", "x is less than y");
```

In this example, if x is greater than y or x is less than y, the corresponding message is output, but no message is output when they are equal. The first part of the assembly code segment for the outer if will be the same as before, but instead of branching to `endif01`, it will branch to `else01`. Instead of the then section falling through to the `endif01`, it will need to branch around the `else01` section to the `endif01`.

```
             ;if x > y
if01:        fld y
             fld x
             fcomip st(0), st(1)
             jbe else01
then01:      INVOKE printf, ADDR msg2fmt, ADDR msg2
             jmp endif01
else01:      nop

             ; nested if to be inserted here

endif01: nop
```

In the else section there will be the nested if-then structure as follows:

```
           ;if x < y
if02:      jae endif02
then02:    INVOKE printf, ADDR msg2fmt, ADDR msg3
endif02: nop
```

Does there need to be another comparison in the nested if? And if so since the values were popped of the stack, do they need to be pushed back on the stack? In this case the answer to both questions is no because the flags are still set the same from the previous comparison. However, if the flags are altered by other instructions prior to the second if in the outer else section, then the answer would be yes to both questions. When in doubt, it doesn't hurt to reload and compare the values as part of the second if structure and this is done in the following segment:

```
           ;if x > y
if01:      fld y
           fld x
           fcomip st(0), st(1)
           jbe else01
then01:    INVOKE printf, ADDR msg2fmt, ADDR msg2
           jmp endif01
else01:    nop

           ;if x < y
if02:      fld y
           fld x
           fcomip st(0), st(1)
           jae endif02
then02:    INVOKE printf, ADDR msg2fmt, ADDR msg3
endif02:   nop

endif01:   nop
```

10.9 Complete Program: Implementing an Iteration Structure

Having looked at a couple of selection structures, it is time to examine a loop structure using floating-point numbers as part of a complete program. First, are there any changes needed with respect to loops that use a counter for loop control such as the .repeat-.untilcxz, .repeat-.until, or .while-.endw? The answer is not really because typically floating-point numbers are not used as loop control variables, but rather integers are used. However, one might use floating-point numbers with a sentinel-controlled loop, but a .while-.endw cannot be used because it is implemented using a cmp instruction which uses implicit integer subtraction. Again, the while loop will need to be implemented using labels and the `fcomip` instruction. Starting with a C program, consider the following which continues to sum values until a zero or negative number is entered:

```c
#include <stdio.h>
int main() {

    double x, sum;

    sum = 0.0;
    printf("\n%s", "Enter a positive double for x:");
    scanf_s("%lf", &x);

    while (x > 0.0) {

        sum = sum + x;
        printf("\n%s", "Enter a positive double for x: ");
        scanf_s("%lf", &x);
    }

    printf("\n%s%6.1f\n\n", "The sum is: ", sum);

    return 0;
}
```

First looking at just the while loop, the values to be compared must be loaded into the floating-point register stack. Again, the second value is loaded first and the conditional jump is reversed. Also, there needs to be an unconditional jump back to the beginning of the loop.

```asm
            ;while x > 0.0
while01:    fld zero
            fld x
            fcomip st(0), st(1)
            jbe endw01

            ; body of loop

            jmp while01
  endw01:   nop
```

Of course, without a change in the loop control variable, there would be an infinite loop. As discussed in Sect. 5.4 previously and shown in the C program above, there will be a priming read prior to the loop and it will be repeated as the last instruction in the body of the loop. Putting all the pieces together results in the following complete program:

```
               .686
               .model flat,c
               .stack 100h

printf    PROTO arg1:Ptr Byte, printlist:VARARG
scanf     PROTO arg2:Ptr Byte, inputlist:VARARG

               .data
in1fmt    byte "%lf",0
msg0fmt   byte 0Ah,"%s",0
msg1fmt   byte 0Ah,"%s%6.1f",0Ah,0
msg0      byte "Enter a positive double for x: ",0
msg1      byte "The sum is: ",0

x         real8 ?
sum       real8 ?
zero      real8 0.0

               .code
main      proc
               ;sum = 0.0
               fld zero
               fstp sum

               INVOKE printf, ADDR msg0fmt, ADDR msg0
               INVOKE scanf, ADDR in1fmt, ADDR x

               ;while x > 0.0
while01:  fld zero
               fld x
               fcomip st(0), st(1)
               jbe endw01
               ;sum = sum + x
               fld sum
               fadd x
               fstp sum
               INVOKE printf, ADDR msg0fmt, ADDR msg0
               INVOKE scanf, ADDR in1fmt, ADDR x
               jmp while01
  endw01: nop

               INVOKE printf, ADDR msg1fmt, ADDR msg1,
sum

               ret
main      endp
               end
```

10.10   Complete Program: Implementing an Array

Just as with integers, it is possible to create an array of floating-point numbers. To keep the complete program simple, assume the existence of the following five-element array:

```
array     real8 1.0, 2.3, 3.7, 4.9, 5.1
```

The array could have been declared as follows:

```
array     real8 5 dup(?)
```

and then the data could be input, but this is left as an exercise at the end of the chapter. In either case, in order to output the contents of the array, the number of elements could be stored in a variable n and since there is a fixed number of elements a post-test .repeat-.untilcxz loop could be used. Using the esi register, the address of the array would need to be placed into that register prior to the loop. Also, instead of incrementing the esi register by 4, it would need to be incremented by 8 because each element of the array is eight bytes long. The basic loop structure is as follows:

```
lea esi,array
mov ecx,n
.repeat

; body of loop

add esi,8
.untilcxz
```

An INVOKE statement can be used to output the contents of each element. However, one cannot just output the contents of [esi]. Instead the INVOKE printf statement needs to know the size of each element so real8 ptr [esi] must be used as follows:

```
INVOKE printf, ADDR msg2fmt, real8 ptr [esi]
```

Lastly, recall that the INVOKE statement destroys a number of registers including the ecx register, so it must be saved before and restored after the call. A temporary variable could be used or it could be pushed onto the stack which is what is done in the instance. The code segment is as follows:

```
lea esi,array
mov ecx,n
.repeat
push ecx
INVOKE printf, ADDR msg2fmt, real8 ptr [esi]
add esi,8
pop ecx
.untilcxz
```

Could the same be done with the `ebx` register? Yes, where the loop control is the same, but instead `ebx` is initialized to a zero and the `INVOKE` statement uses `array[ebx]` instead. As before `ebx` is incremented by eight and the `ecx` still needs to pushed and popped as shown in the following segment:

```
mov ebx,0
mov ecx,n
.repeat
push ecx
INVOKE printf, ADDR msg2fmt, array[ebx]
pop ecx
add ebx,8
.untilcxz
```

Of the two methods the second one is probably the simpler due to the less complicated `INVOKE` statement and mimicking the more common indexing method used in high-level languages. The complete program outputting the array twice using the two different registers and including headings prior to the two sets of output is shown below:

```
.686
.model flat, c
.stack 100h

printf    PROTO arg1:Ptr Byte, printlist:VARARG

.data
msg1fmt   byte 0Ah,"%s",0Ah,0Ah,0
msg2fmt   byte " %3.1f",0Ah,0
msg1      byte "Array",0
n         sdword 5
array     real8 1.0, 2.3, 3.7, 4.9, 5.1

.code
main proc

INVOKE printf, ADDR msg1fmt, ADDR msg1
lea esi,array
mov ecx,n
.repeat
push ecx
INVOKE printf, ADDR msg2fmt, real8 ptr [esi]
pop ecx
add esi,8
.untilcxz
```

```
            INVOKE printf, ADDR msg1fmt, ADDR msg1
            mov ebx,0
            mov ecx,n
            .repeat
            push ecx
            INVOKE printf, ADDR msg2fmt, array[ebx]
            pop ecx
            add ebx,8
            .untilcxz

            ret
     main endp
            end
```

10.11   Summary

- Use f for outputting Real4 and Real8 numbers, and use Lf for outputting Real10 numbers.
- Just like with integers, use an & prior to the variable when inputting floating-point numbers.
- Remember to use f for inputting Real4 numbers, lf for Real8 numbers, and Lf for Real10 numbers.
- Remember when using the fistp instruction the answer is rounded to the nearest even number and when using the fisttp instruction the answers are truncated.
- Although the fsubr instruction could be used when performing subtraction with numbers in reverse order, it is easier to push the numbers onto the floating-point stack from left to right and use the fsub instruction instead.
- Note that floating-point variables cannot be used to control high-level structures because the cmp instruction uses implied integer subtraction, so the floating-point compare (fcompi) and unsigned conditional jumps (ja, jb, etc.) must be used to create the control structures.
- Although the order of pushing numbers onto the floating-point stack is not really important when using the fcompi instruction, the resulting code is easier to write when the second number being compared is pushed on first and the conditional jump is reversed as done previously with integers.
- Depending on which is used to declare an array, real4, real8, real10, be sure to increment the index by 4, 8, or 10, respectively.

10.12   Exercises (Items Marked with an * Have Solutions in Appendix D)

1. Given the following variables, what are the results in the variable z for each of the following code segments?

```
w  real8 2.0
x  real8 5.5
y  real8 6.5
z  sdword ?
```

*a. fld w	b. fld y	c. fld y	d. fld w
fld y	fld w	fld w	fld y
fadd	fdiv	fsub	fadd
fistp z	fld x	fistp z	fist z
	fadd		fld w
	fisttp z		fadd
			fistp z

2. Convert the following C-like arithmetic instructions into post-fix form and then write the corresponding assembly language instructions. Assume that all variables are of type real8.

```
*a.  answer = x - y + z;
 b.  result = (w + x) / (y - z);
 c.  info = a / b * c - d;
 d.  data = i * j + (k / (m - n));
```

3. Can pre-fix form of an arithmetic statement be used to create the corresponding assembly language instructions? If not, why not? If so, how? For either answer, show how it can or cannot be done by giving an example of a conversion to pre-fix and the corresponding assembly instructions.

4. Write the equivalent assembly language code segment for the C program in Sect. 10.7.3 (which uses type long double).

5. Given the code using inline assembly in Sect. 10.7.4, rewrite it to work with float and long double types (Hint: For type float, see Sect. 10.7.1).

6. Alter the if-then code segment at the begining of Sect. 10.8 to implement an if-then-else structure to output the message "x is less than or equal to y" in the else section.

7. Alter the if-then-else-if code segment in Sect. 10.8 to add an else section to the nested if statement to output the message "x and y are equal".

8. Change the complete program in Sect. 10.9 to implement a do-while structure (post-test loop) instead of while structure (pre-test loop). Make sure that it works properly for 0.0 and negative numbers.
9. Change the complete program in Sect. 10.10 to instead prompt for and input the five numbers.

64-Bit Processing

11

To store larger 64-bit numbers in a high-level language such as Java, variables are declared as `long`, or in the C programming language `long long` is used. In assembly language a quad word, `qword`, or signed quad word, `sqword`, is used. Just as a 32-bit double word is twice as big as a regular 16-bit word, a 64-bit quad word is two times larger than a 32-bit double word or four times larger than a 16-bit word, thus the name quad word. In comparison with double words, Table 11.1 indicates the range of numbers that are capable of being stored in quad words.

Note that in comparison with a 32-bit double word which can store a signed positive number of approximately two billion, a 64-bit quad word can store a signed positive number of approximately 9 quintillion. Of course, with the advantage of being able to store larger numbers, there is the disadvantage of using more memory. Although using a single variable of 8 bytes instead of 4 bytes does not seem to be much of a disadvantage, this increase in memory is especially noticeable when using large arrays.

There are two other disadvantages of using 64-bit registers. First is that they cannot be used in in-line assembly. Although this presents some inconvenience, the focus of this text has been to use stand-alone assembly. A greater inconvenience is that the high-level directives such as `.if`, `.while`, and so on, cannot be used in 64-bit mode. However, as discussed in Chap. 4, it is possible to mimic high-level language structures and some examples will be given in Sect. 11.6.

11.1 Four General Purpose Registers

Of course, without registers to store 64-bit numbers, 64-bit processing would be difficult. Just as the letter `e` was added to indicate the 32-bit version of the `ax` register, the letter `r` is added to the `ax` register to indicate the 64-bit version. The

© Springer Nature Switzerland AG 2020
J. T. Streib, *Guide to Assembly Language*, Undergraduate Topics
in Computer Science, https://doi.org/10.1007/978-3-030-35639-2_11

Table 11.1 Types, number of bits, and range of values

Type	Number of bits	Range (inclusive)
sqword sdword	64	−9,223,372,036,854,775,808 to +9,223,372,036,854,775,807
qword	64	0 to +18,446,744,073,709,551,615
sdword	32	−2,147,483,648 to +2,147,483,647
dword	32	0 to +4,264,967,295

following is a variation of Fig. 1.4 to show the relationship between the 8-bit `al` register, 16-bit `ax` register, 32-bit `eax` register, and 64-bit `rax` register.

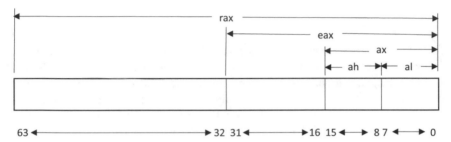

As before, the same diagram could be used to show the relationship with the `rbx`, `rcx`, and `rdx` registers by substituting the letters b, c, and d in place of the letter a.

Although the above appears fairly-straight forward, there are some interesting similarities and differences in the relationship between the different size registers. Recall that in 32-bit mode when the `al` register is altered, it does not alter the upper bits of the `ax` register and when the `ax` register is altered, the upper bits of the `eax` register are not altered. The same is true for these registers in 64-bit mode. For example, assuming that the `ax` register contained the following in hexadecimal,

ax | F7E5 |

and the following instruction was executed,

mov al,00h

then only the lower 8 bits would be altered as follows:

ax | F700 |

Likewise, if `eax` contained the following,

eax | FEDCBA98 |

and the following instruction was executed,

```
mov ax,0
```

the eax register would look as follows:

```
eax │ FEDC0000
```

However, when altering eax, the equivalent is not true in rax. If the rax register contained the following,

```
rax │ 0123456789ABCDEF
```

and the following instruction clearing eax to 0 was executed:

```
mov eax,0
```

the entire rax register would be cleared to 0 as follows:

```
rax │ 0000000000000000
```

What has happened is that zero was moved into the eax register which is the lower 32 bits of the rax register, and then the upper 32 bits are cleared to zero. Using the original number in the rax register from above, consider the following example:

```
mov eax,-1
```

Since a negative one is represented as FFFFFFFFh in oax, the contents of eax are copied into the lower 32 bits of rax and the upper 32 bits are of the rax register are again cleared to zero as shown below:

```
rax │ 00000000FFFFFFFF
```

What if one wanted to have the above result in all F's in hex to indicate a negative one? To accomplish this task the movsxd instruction would be used. It copies from a 32-bit memory location or register to the lower 32 bits of a 64-bit register and then extends or propagates the sign-bit from the leftmost position of the lower 32 bits into the upper 32 bits of the 64-bit register. Further, instead of initially placing the data into eax as in this case, it could be placed into another register such as ebx. From there the movsxd would copy the contents of ebx into rax as follows:

```
mov ebx,-1
movsxd rax,ebx
```

This would result in the following:

```
rax   │ FFFFFFFFFFFFFFFF │
```

What would happen with the segment below?

```
mov ebx,0
movsxd rax,ebx
```

In this case the results would look the same as when using the mov instruction, although the process is different. In the case of the mov instruction the upper bits are cleared to zero and in the movsxd case the sign-bit is propagated into the upper 32-bits. If the end result is the same, why would one use movsxd? The reason is that if there is unknown data in a 32-bit register or memory location then the movsxd would extend the sign-bit, whether a zero or a one, accordingly. For example, assume the variable num32 contains a signed integer:

```
mov ebx,num32
movsxd rax,ebx
```

Then regardless of what is in the sign-bit in num32, it will be extended into the upper 32 bits of rax. This principle also applies to the other three general purpose registers as well: rbx, rcx, and rdx.

Does the default of clearing the upper 32 bits of a 64-bit register cause any difficulties? If one is using just 32 bits in a 64-bit environment, then there is really no concern what is happening in the upper 32 bits of rax or the other registers. And if one is using only 64-bit registers and instructions then again this should be of no concern. Only if one is moving from the 32-bit environment to the 64-bit environment and is accustomed to the upper bits of a register being maintained or if one is mixing 32-bit and 64-bit registers and processing, then it could cause some difficulties. However, provided one is aware of the differences and is careful when choosing the correct instructions such as movsxd, then it should not pose much of a problem.

11.2   Other 64-Bit Registers

In addition to the four general purpose registers, other registers also have 64-bit variations. These include the index registers esi and edi which are available as rsi and rdi, and the stack registers esp and ebp as rsp and rbp, respectively. The eflags register also has a 64-bit counterpart as rflags, but although this could allow for more error flag bits in the future, at present the upper 32 bits of this register are not used. Also, the instruction pointer register eip has a corresponding 64-bit register rip.

Table 11.2 Summary of 64-bit registers

64-bit registers	Name	32-, 16, and 8-bit sub-registers	Brief description and/or primary use
rax	Accumulator	eax, ax, al	Arithmetic and logic
rbx	Base	ebx, bx, bl	Arrays
rcx	Counter	ecx, cx, cl	Loops
rdx	Data	edx, dx, dl	Arithmetic
rsi	Source index	esi, si	Strings and arrays
rdi	Destination index	edi, di	Strings and arrays
rsp	Stack pointer	esp, sp	Top of stack
rbp	Base pointer	ebp, bp	Stack base
rip	Instruction pointer	eip, ip	Points to next instruction
rflags	Flag	eflags, flags	Status and control flags
r8 – r15	Numbered	r8d – r15d	General use (where
		r8w – r15w	d = double word, w = word, and b = byte)
		r8b – r16b	

Lastly, in addition to the 64-bit variations of the previous 32-bit registers, there are also eight new numbered 64-bit registers available. They are r8 through r15, which each have corresponding sub-registers. These registers include the 32-bit double word registers r8d through r15d where the d stands for double word, the 16-bit word registers r8w through r15w where the w stands for word, and the 8-bit byte registers r8b through r15b where the b stands for byte.

Note that whereas the upper 8 bits of the original 16-bit registers are directly accessible, such as ah in the ax register, there is no name for the upper 8 bits in the corresponding r8w through r15w registers. Given this, how does one access these bits if there is no corresponding name? It is no different than when there is no name for the upper 16 bits of a 32-bit register or no name for the upper 32 bits of a 64-bit register. The solution is to use logic and shifting instructions.

Also, note that although registers such as r8b can be used with registers such as al, they cannot be used in the same instruction with registers such as ah. Then, how does one move information from ah to r8b? Again, the answer is logic and shifting instruction from Chap. 6 and as will be shown in Sect. 11.5 of this chapter. For convenience, all the registers discussed in this section are summarized in Table 11.2.

11.3 64-Bit Integer Output

As was mentioned earlier, 64-bit processing cannot be used with in-line assembly. This is unfortunate because it would make it easy to use C input/output instructions to test various 64-bit code segments. Further, the technique for inputting and outputting 64-bit integers is also different than the one used previously for 32-bit integers and this section gives examples of simple I/O to facilitate testing of code presented in this chapter.

As before, a simple program to output a 64-bit integer in C is given first followed by the equivalent program in assembly language. Consider the following C program which is similar to the program at the end of Sect. 2.3 except the variables are declared as type long long instead of type int and formatting using %lld instead of %d, respectively:

```
#include <stdio.h> int main(){
    long long num1=5, num2=7;
    printf("\n%lld%s%lld\n\n",num1," is not equal to ",num2);
    return 0;
}
```

In order to implement the above program using 64-bit output, there have been some changes made compared to 32-bit processing. Along with other important information in the directions for using Visual Studio in Appendix A.3, be sure to change the Solutions Platforms in the ribbon in from *x86* to *x64*.

In the program itself, note that the following statements are no longer needed and can simply be deleted from the program.

```
.686
.model flat, c
.stack 100h
```

As will be discussed shortly, input and output is no longer done via parameters, so it is not necessary to include the parameter list after the PROTO statements as done previously and the new statements are as shown below:

```
printf PROTO
scanf  PROTO
```

The data segment is similar to what has been used previously and appears as follows:

```
msg1fmt   byte 0Ah,"%lld%s%lld",0Ah,0Ah,0
msg1      byte " is not equal to ",0
num1      sqword 5
num2      sqword 7
```

The only change to notice is that instead of the variables being defined as sdword, they are defined as sqword. Also note the change in formatting from %d to %lld.

If parameters are not used as mentioned above, then how is information communicated to the input and output procedures? The information is sent either through registers or the stack, where it is more convenient to use registers. This is because the stack needs to be adjusted before and after calling a printf or scanf to allow for what is known as shadow space. This space is used for storing parameters and should be at least 32 bytes in length although larger amounts to ensure sufficient space can be used such as the 64 bytes in this text. This is accomplished by adjusting the stack pointer by subtracting 64 (40 h) from the stack pointer prior to the call and adding back 64 (40 h) after the call. Also note that the INVOKE statement is not used but rather the CALL statement is used instead. So, a call to a printf statement will appear as follows:

```
sub rsp,40h
CALL printf
add rsp, 40h
```

To communicate with the printf routine using registers, the information is sent via the rcx, rdx, r8, and r9 registers. Since these registers are being used for communications, any information in these registers can be lost during the I/O process. Further, the contents of the rax and r9 through r11 are altered by the printf statement. So if these registers are being used, it is important to save their contents prior to any I/O and have them returned to the registers afterwards. However, recall back in Sect. 1.6 that unless speed is a very important concern, it was recommended not to keep data in the registers in the first place and that it be returned to memory to avoid such complications. Again, it is easier to optimize a correctly implemented program than to get a supposedly optimized program to work correctly.

Prior to calling the printf statement, the registers need to be loaded with the format and data in the same order that was used previously with parameters. Instead of sending the address of the format statement or strings using ADDR, the address is loaded into the registers using mov and offset or using the lea instruction. In this first example mov offset is used but in later examples lea is used. So, the format statement can be loaded first into rax followed in order with the data in the subsequent registers. The resulting code would look as follows:

```
mov rcx,offset msg1fmt
mov rdx,num1
mov r8,offset msg1
mov r9,num2
```

Putting everything together results in the following program:

```
printf      PROTO
scanf       PROTO

            .data
msg1fmt     byte 0Ah,"%lld%s%lld",0Ah,0Ah,0
msg1        byte " is not equal to ",0
num1        sqword 5
num2        sqword 7

            .code
main        proc

            mov rcx,offset msg1fmt
            mov rdx,num1
            mov r8,offset msg1
            mov r9,num2

            sub rsp, 40h
            CALL printf
            add rsp, 40h

            ret
main        endp
            end
```

But what if more items need to be output in one line and only four registers are being used? For example, consider the following modification of the preceding C program code segment which outputs three numbers instead and uses " ! = " to save space:

```
#include <stdio.h> int main(){
   long long num1 =  5, num2 =  7, num3 = 9;
   printf("\n%lld%s%lld%s%lld\n\n",num1," != ",num2," != ",num3);
   return 0;
}
```

The problem is that in addition to the format there are five additional items to output on one line and there are only four registers. Although the stack could be used, it is easier to move the last two items and their formatting along with the "\n \n" to a second printf statement so that all of the output stays on one line as follows:

```
#include <stdio.h>
int main(){
   long long num1 =  5, num2 =  7, num3 = 9;
   printf("\n%lld%s%lld",num1," != ",num2);
   printf("%s%lld\n\n"," != ",num3);
   return 0;
}
```

The corresponding assembly code would be as follows:

```
printf   PROTO
scanf    PROTO

         .data
msg1fmt byte 0Ah,"%lld%s%lld",0
msg2fmt byte "%s%lld",0Ah,0Ah,0
msg1     byte " != ",0
num1     sqword 5
num2     sqword 7
num3     sqword 9

         .code
main     proc

         mov rcx,offset msg1fmt
         mov rdx,num1
         mov r8,offset msg1
         mov r9,num2

         sub rsp, 40h
         CALL printf
         add rsp, 40h

         mov rcx,offset msg2fmt
         mov rdx,offset msg1
         mov r8,num3

         sub rsp, 40h
         CALL printf
         add rsp, 40h

         ret
main     endp
         end
```

Although this takes up a little more code, it is relatively simple to implement and avoids any complications that might occur when using the stack. As an aside, all of the other types of formats in C can be used by attaching the letters ll after the % and before the format letter. For example, should one want to output the contents of a 64-bit memory location as unsigned, %llu should be used, and to output in hexadecimal, %llx should be used.

11.4   64-Bit Integer Input

Input is similar to output and using a C program that is similar to the one at the end of Sect. 2.4, consider the following program that inputs number, adds 1 to it, and then outputs number:

```
#include <stdio.h>
int main(){
    long long number;
    printf("\n%s","Enter an integer: ");
    scanf("%lld",&number);
    number++;
    printf("\n%s%lld\n\n","The integer is: ",number);
    return 0;
}
```

As before, there needs to be a prompt prior to the input and also the number input needs to be output, both of which are relatively simple given in the last section. The new part of interest here is the scanf. First, the address of the input format is loaded into rcx and then the address of the location number loaded into the rdx register. In both cases, the mov and offset or the lea instruction should be used. Notice that the stack has to be adjusted before and after the call just as it was with the printf statement all as shown below:

```
lea rcx, in1fmt
lea rdx, number
sub rsp,40h
CALL scanf
add rsp, 40h
```

The instruction to increment number by 1 is the same as with the 32-bit instruction as follows:

```
inc number
```

In fact, many of the instructions will be very similar between 32-bit and 64-bit processing as will be discussed in the next section. Further, it should be noted that the scanf alters the same registers, rax, rcx, rdx, and r8 through r11, as the printf. So again, care must be taken by the programmer to not leave any relevant data in these registers. The program to implement the above C program can be found below:

```
printf      PROTO
scanf       PROTO

            .data

in1fmt      byte "%lld",0
msg0fmt     byte 0Ah,"%s",0

msg1fmt     byte 0Ah,"%s%lld",0Ah,0Ah,0
msg0        byte "Enter an integer: ",0
msg1        byte "The integer is: ",0
number      sqword ?

            .code
main        proc
```

```
            lea rcx, msg0fmt
            lea rdx, msg0

            sub rsp,40h
            CALL printf
            add rsp,40h

            lea rcx, in1fmt
            lea rdx, number

            sub rsp,40h
            CALL scanf
            add rsp, 40h

            inc number

            lea rcx, msg1fmt
            lea rdx, msg1
            mov r8,number

            sub rsp, 40h
            CALL printf
            add rsp, 40h

            ret
    main    endp
            end
```

11.5   Logic and Arithmetic Applications

Although as seen in the previous section, much of the processing using 64-bit registers and memory locations are the same as with 32-bit registers, it does not hurt to give some examples of code to illustrate this similarity. Also, of particular interest is to show some applications and the interaction between 32-bit and 64-bit processing.

11.5.1   Shift and Rotate

As discussed in Sect. 11.2, instructions cannot access both a register such as ah in the rax register and r8b in the r8 register. In other words, the instruction mov r8b, ah is illegal. Although it would be nice to have such an instruction for the relatively rare occurrences that this type a transfer is necessary, it is really just a minor inconvenience. Since such an instruction does not exist, how would one accomplish it? Remembering various instructions from Chap. 6, shifting or rotating could be used. First the data in ah, which are bits 8 through 15 of the rax register, would need to be moved to the al register. A simple mov al, ah could be used, but this would destroy the contents of the al register. If that data is no longer needed then this method would not be a problem.

However, what if that data needed to be kept? It could be stored in another register or a memory location, but that might destroy other data or require the use of memory. So, how could it be done without having to use any other registers or memory locations? An alternative is to shift the contents of the rax register 8 bits to the right. But again, the data that was previously in al would be destroyed. The solution is to rotate the contents of the rax register to the right 8 bits, which would cause the contents of the lower 8 bits to be rotated to the upper 8 bits in bit positions 56 through 63 of rax. For example, if rax originally contained the following:

rax | 0123456789ABCDEF

And the instruction ror rax, 8 was executed, then rax would look as follows:

rax | EF0123456789ABCD

Then, the contents of al could be transferred to r8b. Further, if the contents of rax could be restored back by rotating it to the left 8 bits. This set of instructions is as follows:

```
ror  rax,8
mov  r8b,al
rol  rax,8
```

But why rotate all 64 bits of the rax register? Alternatively, only the ax subset of the rax register could be rotated by 8 bits as shown below:

rax | 0123456789ABEFCD

Then the contents of ax could be rotated back and the code for this is solution is as follows:

```
ror  ax,8
mov  r8b,al
rol  ax,8
```

11.5.2 Logic

Also as discussed in Sect. 11.1, two alternatives of moving 32 bits into a 64-bit register resulted in either the upper-32 bits becoming all zeros or extending the sign bit into the upper 32 bits. What if one did not want to alter the upper 32 bits of a 64-bit register?

The way this can be accomplished is by using various logic instructions. This would involve clearing out the lower 32 bits of the 64-bit register to zero, creating a mask to not alter the upper 32 bits, and using an `and` instruction to put the new data into the lower 32 bits. Again, assume the data in the `rax` register is as follows:

rax | 0123456789ABCDEF |

The mask necessary to clear out the lower 32 bits yet maintain the upper 32 bits is as follows:

| FFFFFFFF00000000 |

At first, one might be tempted to put the above in an operand of an `and` instruction, but it is too large. Instead it can be placed into a memory location using an unsigned `qword`. Remember when using hexadecimal number that the left most position of the number must be a digit and not a letter, so note the leading 0 as follows:

```
mask64 qword 0FFFFFFFF00000000h
```

Then an `and` instruction can be used,

```
and rax,mask64
```

which results in the following:

rax | 0123456700000000 |

Now if the new data to be put into the lower 32 bits was AABBCCDDh, it could be loaded into a 32-bit register such as `ebx`,

```
mov ebx,0AABBCCDDh
```

which would automatically clear out the upper bits of `rbx` as follows:

rbx | 00000000AABBCCDD |

And lastly, the data in `rbx` could be placed into the lower 32 bits of `rax` using an `or` instruction as follows:

```
or rax,rbx
```

which would result in the new data in the lower 32 bits while the original data in the upper 32 bits would remain undisturbed as shown below:

rax | 01234567AABBCCDD |

The completed code segment is as follows:

```
and rax,mask64
mov ebx,0AABBCCDDh
or rax,rbx
```

The result is that if a particular instruction does not exist to do precisely what needs to be done, it is usually not a problem because given the vast number of other instructions available, the appropriate task can be accomplished. If necessary, the resulting group of instructions can be placed into a macro using parameters as introduced in Chap. 7 and reviewed in Sect. 11.8. Further, this is left as an exercise at the end of the chapter.

11.5.3   Arithmetic

The use of 64-bit arithmetic is very similar to 32-bit arithmetic except much larger numbers can be used. Whereas there is very little difference with addition and subtraction, there are a few differences with multiplication and division.

Recall from Chap. 3 that when two 32-bit numbers are multiplied the result occupied 64 bits in the edx:eax register pair. A similar result occurs when two 64-bit numbers are multiplied where the results are placed in the 128 bits of the rdx:rax register pair. Consider the following code example:

```
mov rax,2147483647
mov rbx,2
imul rbx
```

The above number loaded into the rax number is the largest signed positive number that can be stored in 32 bits. If 32-bit multiplication were to be used the results would have extended into the edx register. However, when using 64-bit registers, the resulting product can be contained in the 64-bit rax register and only the sign-bit would be propagated into the rdx register. If the number were much larger than this, then it too would extend into the rdx register, but in this text, 64 bits should be more than sufficient.

Similar to 32-bit division where the edx:eax register pair contains the 64-bit dividend, 64-bit division needs to have the dividend initially in the 128-bit rdx:

rax register pair. Instead of using the cdq (convert double to quad) instruction prior to the 64-bit division, one must use the cqo (convert quad to oct, where oct refers to eight words) instruction. This extends the sign bit of rax into rdx prior to 64-bit division as illustrated in the following code segment:

```
mov rax, 7fffffffffffffffh
cqo
mov rbx,2
idiv rbx
```

A hexadecimal number is used to show that the largest possible positive number is being stored in the rax register where bit 63 is a 0. Similar to the previous 32-bit division, the quotient is stored in rax and the remainder is stored in rdx.

11.6 Control Structures

As mentioned at the beginning of this chapter, unfortunately high-level directives do not work in 64-bit mode. Fortunately, most of the ways that control structures can be created using comparisons and branches in 32-bit mode can be also be done in 64-bit mode. However, there are some potential areas that could cause problems when mixing 32-bit and 64-bit data. For example, consider the following code segment which loads a number into eax and then compares a number in rax register with the number 2. It then stores in rdx the address of msg3 indicating that it is equal or msg4 indicating that it is not equal for later output:

```
;  ****    Caution: possibly incorrectly implemented code  ****
          mov eax,2
          ; if rax == 2
if01:     cmp rax,2
          jne else01
then01:   lea rdx, msg3
          jmp endif01
else01:   lea rdx,msg4
endif01:  nop
```

As before, the condition is reversed using jne to branch to else01 if not equal and falls through to then01 if it is equal. Yes, it is probably not a good idea to initially load eax and then compare using rax, but assume for the time being that the data to be compared was originally in the eax register. The above code segment works okay in this particular instance, but what is a potential problem with the code segment? Instead, consider if eax contained a -2 and was compared to a -2 instead as shown below:

```
;  ****    Caution: incorrectly implemented code  ****
          mov eax,-2
          ; if rax == -2
if01:     cmp rax,2
          jne else01
then01:   lea rdx, msg3
          jmp endif01
else01:   lea rdx,msg4
endif01:  nop
```

Although the previous code segment worked, would the above code work? The answer is no because recall from Sect. 11.1 that when data is moved into the eax register or related registers, the contents of the upper 32 bits of rax is set to zeros. The result is that the negative number in eax is a positive number in rax. To correct this problem, the movsxd instruction should be inserted in the second line to extend the sign bit into the upper 32 bits as follows:

```
          mov eax,-2
          movsxd rax,eax
          ; if rax == -2
if01:     cmp rax,2
          jne else01
then01:   lea rdx, msg3
          jmp endif01
else01:   lea rdx,msg4
endif01:  nop
```

Although it was technically not needed in the initial code using positive numbers, it should probably be inserted there as well to ensure that if a negative number is input instead of assigned, the code would work correctly.

In another example, what if one wants to use the loop instruction with 64-bits? In the following segment the rcx register would be loaded with the appropriate number.

```
          mov rcx, 100000000h
for01:    nop
          ;body of loop
          loop for1
endfor01: nop
```

In the above case a hexadecimal number is being used to show that the number in rcx is larger than 32 bits. However, note that the loop will iterate over four billion times and it might be slow depending on the speed of the computer being used. Further, even larger numbers can be used with 64 bits in the above code segment and the loop could take a significant amount of time to execute.

As with preceding examples using an if statement and mixing 32-bit and 64-bit registers, care must be taken. Although one would not want to load a negative number into the `rcx` register using a `loop` instruction, a similar error could occur with other forms of loop control. Consider for example the following loop that starts with a negative number in `ecx`, adds one to it until it reaches zero, and the count of the number of iterations is kept in `rax`.

```
;  ****    Caution: incorrectly implemented code ****
          mov rax,0
          mov ecx, -3
          ; while ecx < 0
while01:  cmp rcx,0
          jge wend01
          inc rax
          inc ecx
          jmp while01
wend01:   nop
```

Although `ecx` is a negative number there are all zeros in the upper 32 bits of the `rcx` register. The result is that `rcx` is a positive number and the count of iterations would be zero. If the `movsxd` instruction is added, note that there is yet another problem with the above code segment. Notice that `ecx` is being incremented in the body of the loop instead of `rcx` which again causes the upper 32 bits to be zero and the loop only iterates once. The corrected code is as follows:

```
          mov rax,0
          mov ecx, -3
          movsxd rcx,ecx
          ; while ecx < 0
while01:  cmp rcx,0
          jge wend01
          inc rax
          inc rcx
          jmp while01
wend01:   nop
```

The simple solution to such problems is to avoid mixing 32-bit and 64-bit registers. However, if one must use both, be careful that the code works the way one intended by running sufficient tests.

11.7 Arrays

Indexing 64-bit arrays is similar to indexing 32-bit arrays. Instead of declaring the array with sdword, they are declared using sqword. The code is very similar except that 64-bit registers are used. A simple example that uses only a five-element array, sums the contents of the array in rax, uses rsi for the index, and uses the loop instruction is as follows:

```
        mov rax,0
        lea rsi,numarray
        mov rcx,5
for2:   add rax,[rsi]
        add rsi,8
        loop for2
endfor1: nop
```

As before, the rsi register needs to be initialized with the address of the array. Notice that it is similar to an array of 64-bit real8 numbers. Since eight-byte quad words are being used instead of four-byte double words, rsi is incremented by 8 instead of 4.

Likewise, an example using the rbx register in conjunction with the name of the array is as shown in the code segment below:

```
        mov rax,0
        mov rbx,0
        mov rcx,4
for2:   nop
        add rax,numarray[rbx]
        add rbx,8
        loop for2
endfor2: nop
```

Again, ebx should be incremented by 8 instead of 4. Both ways of addressing an array are similar to the 32-bit methods and either can be chosen based upon the task at hand or whichever is more convenient.

11.8 Procedures and Macros

As initially discussed in Chap. 7, procedures and macros are extremely helpful for taking common code and not having to rewrite it over and over again. It is suggested to review that chapter if necessary before proceeding with this section.

11.8.1 Calling 64-Bit Procedures

Having called the `printf` and `scanf` procedures, much has already been learned on how to use procedures. Simple procedures can be called using memory locations and various registers as done with 32-bit procedures, but then their use would be restricted to only those memory locations and registers. Instead, the same conventions that are used to call procedures like `printf` and `scanf` can be used which would allow for consistency in the passing of information via `rcx`, `rdx`, `r8`, and `r9` as necessary and a value could be returned via `rax`.

Recall that there is a complete program in Sect. 7.2 to implement the power function. A limitation to this program is that when restricted to just the 32 bits of the `eax` register, the largest signed number that could be calculated would be slightly over two billion and the largest non-signed number is slightly over four billion. When using 64-bits the largest signed number that can get calculated, as mentioned at the beginning of this chapter, is in excess of nine quintillion and the largest unsigned number is over eighteen quintillion.

Without rewriting the entire program, which is left as an exercise at the end of this chapter, the following only implements the calculation portion using only positive integers to illustrate the sending and returning of values. First, the calling program segment is shown below:

```
mov rcx,x
mov rdx,n
call power
mov answer,rax
```

Recall that values are passed in the registers `rcx`, `rdx`, `r8`, and `r9`, and that a value is returned in `rax`, so that x and n are passed via `rcx` and `rdx`, and answer can be returned via the `rax` register. The procedure is implemented as follows:

```
power      proc
           push rbx
           push rdx
           push r8
           mov r8,rdx
           mov rbx,1
           mov rax,1
           ; while rbx <= r8
while01:   cmp rbx,r8
           jg endw01
           imul rcx
           inc rbx
           jmp while01
endw01:    nop
           pop r8
           pop rdx
           pop rbx
           ret
power      endp
```

Notice that the value in rdx is copied to the r8 register in the procedure; why is this? The reason is that the product from the imul instruction is stored in the rdx: rax register pair, so that the exponent n passed in rdx would get destroyed the first time through the loop. As a result, the value is moved to r8 for comparison in the loop. Since rbx and r8 are destroyed in the implementation of the loop, and rdx is destroyed via the multiplication, they are pushed and popped off the stack.

11.8.2   Using a Macro to Call printf

The problem when using input and output is that there are a number of instructions that need to be written before and after the calling of printf and scanf. Further, if one is not careful, there could be cases where information that was left unintentionally in registers could be lost. Is there a way that this can be simplified? One way is to write a procedure that could contain all the necessary code. But the problem would be that a procedure would be written that would call another procedure and this could get a little confusing.

As an alternative, a macro could be written to contain all the required information that in turn would call the appropriate input or output procedure. As should be recalled from Chap. 7, the disadvantage of this would be that each time the macro is invoked a copy of all the code in the macro is inserted into the program. However, this would be no more code than what would have to have been written in the first place. As discussed previously, there are a number of alternatives than can be used when writing macros. To keep it somewhat simple here only the common case where a string is followed by an integer will be considered. For example, the following typical code segment,

```
lea rcx, msg1fmt
lea rdx, msg1
mov r8,num64
sub rsp, 40
CALL printf
add rsp, 40
```

could be placed into a macro as follows,

```
output64 macro
         lea rcx, msg1fmt
         lea rdx, msg1
         mov r8,num64
         sub rsp, 40
         CALL printf
         add rsp, 40
         endm
```

and could be invoked by just typing:

```
output64
```

Although this cleans up the main program considerably, it only allows the user to output the contents of num64 with msg1 according to the format in msg1fmt. To allow more versatility, parameters should be used. To again keep things simple and to make sure that exactly three parameters are used, the :REQ directive is used in the following macro definition:

```
output64 macro format:REQ, message:REQ, number:REQ

        lea rcx, format
        lea rdx, message
        mov r8,number

        sub rsp, 40
        CALL printf
        add rsp, 40

        endm
```

To invoke it would be as follows:

```
output64 msg1fmt,msg1,num64
```

Of course, when using parameters as above, other formats, messages, and integers could be used as arguments. Though this works well, sometimes users of procedures such as printf forget that registers can be altered. Further, macros tend to hide any other registers that are being altered. Although programmers should be extra careful when using procedures and macros to ensure that the data in registers is saved, it is sometimes helpful to have the macro save the registers. Though this takes up even more memory space each time they are invoked, the subsequent time saved in debugging might be worthwhile especially in the early stages of writing a program. Then later the saving and restoring of registers in the macro could be removed and the code optimized.

Of the 12 general purpose registers rax through rdx and r8 through r15, seven of them have their contents altered by the macro and subsequent procedure call. Obviously rcx, rdx, and r8 are altered by the macro, but also recall that rax and r9 through r11 are altered by printf as well. Only rbx and r12 through r15 are left untouched. Unfortunately, there is not a 64-bit equivalent of the 32-bit pushad and popad instructions that saves and restores all the registers on the stack. Instead the seven affected registers need to be saved and restored individually. This can be done either by using the stack, storing them in separate memory locations, or using an array. Using a different name for the macro can be helpful so that the programmer can chose between the one that saves registers and the one that does not as needed. Looking at the stack option, the macro definition for output64s where the s stands for save is as follows:

```
output64s macro format:REQ, message:REQ, number:REQ

            push rax
            push rcx
            push rdx
            push r8
            push r9
            push r10
            push r11

            lea rcx,format
            lea rdx,message
            mov r8,number
            sub rsp, 40
            CALL printf
            add rsp, 40

            pop r11
            pop r10
            pop r9
            pop r8
            pop rdx
            pop rcx
            pop rax

        endm
```

Yes, the appearance of seven push and seven pop instructions does look rather unwieldy and takes up a number of memory locations. Again, if one is careful to always return data from registers to memory locations, then using the non-saving macro would not cause a problem.

If one does not want to use the stack for saving the registers, then as mentioned previously, seven different memory locations each with the name of the saved register as part of their names could be created to save and restore the seven registers, Also, a seven element array maybe called saveregs could be used. Although neither of these two options would save any instructions and would in fact use just a little more memory, they are alternatives to using the stack and are left as exercises at the end of the chapter.

Also, instead of having two separate macros, one macro could be written using conditional assembly as discussed in Sect. 7.5 and this is left as an exercise. Further, a macro could also be written for scanf and this is also left as an exercise at the end of the chapter.

11.9   Complete Program: Reversing an Array

To incorporate a number of the items in this chapter, a simplified version of the program at the end of Sect. 8.2 to reverse an array is rewritten using 64-bit processing and shown below:

```
printf      PROTO
scanf       PROTO

            .data
msg1fmt     byte "%s",0
msg2fmt     byte 0Ah,"%s",0Ah,0Ah,0
msg3fmt     byte "   %lld", 0Ah,0Ah,0
in1fmt      byte "%lld",0
msg2        byte "Enter an integer: ",0
msg3        byte "Reversed",0
n           sqword 5
arry        sqword 5 dup(?)
            .code
main        proc

            mov rcx,n                ; initialize rcx to n
            mov rbx,0                ; initialize rbx to 0
for01:      nop
            push rcx                 ; save rcx
            lea rcx, msg1fmt
            lea rdx, msg2
            sub rsp, 40
            CALL printf
            add rsp, 40
            lea rcx, in1fmt
            lea rdx,arry[rbx]
            sub rsp,40
            call scanf
            add rsp,40
            pop rcx                  ; restore rcx
            add rbx,8                ; increment rbx by 8
            loop for01
endfor01: nop

            lea rcx, msg2fmt
            lea rdx, msg3
            sub rsp, 40
            CALL printf
            add rsp, 40
            mov rcx,n                ; initialize rcx to n
            sub rbx,8                ; subtract 8 from rbx

for02:      nop
            push rcx                 ; save rcx
            lea rcx, msg3fmt
            mov rdx, arry[rbx]
            sub rsp, 40
            CALL printf
```

```
              add rsp, 40
              pop rcx                          ; restore rcx
              sub rbx,8                        ; decrement rbx by 8
              loop for02
    endfor02: nop

              ret
    main      endp
              end
```

Notice that the value of rcx is pushed onto the stack at the beginning of each loop and popped off the stack at the end of each loop since rcx is used to communicate information to the printf and scanf procedures. Also, the simplified code only inputs a fixed number of items, but to input a variable number of items by inputting and checking that the value in n is non-negative is left as an exercise at the end of the chapter.

11.10 Summary

- Remember that moving data into the lower 32 bits of a 64-bit register causes the upper 32 bits to be cleared to zeros.
- The movsxd instruction copies the contents of a 32-bit register or memory location into a 64-bit register and then extends or propagates the sign into to the upper 32 bits of the 64-bit register.
- One cannot mix in an instruction using the upper 8 bits of the corresponding 16-bit register, such as ah in the ax register, with the lower 8 bits of the new numbered 64-bit registers such as r8b.
- Use %11x format to be able to output all the bits of a 64-bit word in hexadecimal.
- The PROTO statements do no need a parameter list.
- Both the printf and scanf statements use CALL statement instead of INVOKE.
- Use the rcx, rdx, r8 and r9 registers to send information to the printf statement.
- Remember that when invoking a macro all the code in the macro is inserted into the program.
- Remember to load the address of the input format into rcx and the address of the memory location to be input into rdx prior to calling scanf.
- When accessing the elements of an array of 64-bit integers, be sure to increment the register, rsi, rdi, or rbx, by 8 instead of 4.

11.11   Exercises (Items Marked with an * Have Solutions in Appendix D)

1. Given the following code segments, indicate the contents of the 64-bit register (show all 64 bits in hexadecimal).

```
*a. mov rax, 0FFFFFFFFFFFFFFFFh    b. mov rbx, 0
    mov eax, 0                        mov ebx, -2


*c. mov rcx, 0011002200330044h    d. mov rdx, 0FFFFFFFF01234567h
    mov cx, -1                        mov edx, 789ABCDEh
```

2. Implement the following C code segments in MASM assembly language as done in Sect. 11.3.

```
   a. #include <stdio.h>
      int main(){
          long long num1 =   5, num2 =   7;
          printf("\n%lld\n",num1);
          printf("%s\n"," is not = ");
          printf("%lld\n\n",num3);
          return 0;
      }


   b. #include <stdio.h>
      int main(){
          long long num1 =   1, num2 =   2, num3 = 3, num4 = 4;
          printf("\n%lld%s%lld",num1," < ",num2);
          printf("%s%lld%s"," < ",num3," < ");
          printf("%lld\n\n",num4);
          return 0;
      }
```

3. Write a macro to implement the code segment at the end of Sect. 11.5.2.
4. Rewrite the program from Sect. 7.2 to incorporate 64-bit processing and parameter passing as described in Sect. 11.8.1.
5. Rewrite the macro definition output64s in Sect. 11.8.2 to use each of the following and then invoke them in a program:

   a. Use memory locations saverax, savercx, etc., to save and restore the seven affected registers.
   b. Use a seven-element array called saveregs to save and restore the seven affected registers.

6. As an alternative to having two macros to output, one that saves registers and one that does not, write a single macro using conditional assembly as discussed in Sect. 7.5. A fourth parameter could be used and if the parameter is blank it does not save the registers, otherwise it does.

7. Write a macro called `input64` that incorporates a prompt via a parameter, inputs using `scanf`, and returns the value input via the `rax` register.

8. Write a macro using parameters to move data from a 32-bit memory location into the lower 32 bits of another 64-bit memory location without altering the upper 32 bits.

9. Modify the complete program in Sect. 11.9 to input the value of n and make sure that it is not a negative number as done in the original program in Sect. 8.2.

10. Modify the complete program in Sect. 11.9 to use `rsi` instead of `ebx`. Start by replacing the second instruction `mov ebx,0` with `lea rsi,arry`.

Selected Machine Language Instructions

12

12.1 Introduction

The purpose of this chapter is to help draw further connections between assembly language and computer organization. The advantage of using assembly language is that one can see computer organization from a software perspective. Further, by examining machine language one can see some of the principles discussed in a computer organization text. It is especially helpful to see these principles implemented in a real machine language.

As may have been learned from a computer organization text, there are many considerations that need to be taken into account and many different formats that can be used for machine language instructions. One of the first considerations is the size of the instruction. With a larger the instruction, more opcodes can be included, more registers can be referenced, and more memory locations can be addressed. Also, how a particular instruction is divided up indicates how many of each of the above can be included. For example, assume a 16-bit word is divided up as follows: bits 15–13 for the opcode, 12–11 for referencing registers, and 10–0 for addressing memory locations, as shown in Fig. 12.1.

Since there are 3 bits allocated for the opcode, there are 2^3 or 8 possible opcodes. Given 2 bits for the register, there are 2^2 or 4 possible registers, and given 11 bits allocated for addresses, there are 2^{11} or 2,048 possible addresses for memory locations.

Although there is a very formal procedure and elaborate mechanism for determining the machine code for Intel machine language, one can discover the format of many instructions by examining the machine code of particular instructions. What is interesting about this method is that one can examine the machine language of almost any given processor and see some of the instruction layouts merely by inspection.

© Springer Nature Switzerland AG 2020
J. T. Streib, *Guide to Assembly Language*, Undergraduate Topics
in Computer Science, https://doi.org/10.1007/978-3-030-35639-2_12

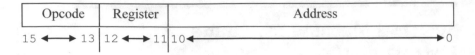

Opcode	Register	Address

15 ⟷ 13 | 12 ⟷ 11 | 10 ⟷ 0

Fig. 12.1 Hypothetical instruction

12.2   `inc` and `dec` Instructions

By turning on the assembly language listing option as discussed in Appendix A.4, the .lst file can be generated and the corresponding assembly language can be seen in the left columns of the listing. The complete program listings used in this chapter are shown in Sects. 12.9 and 12.10. Although the programs do not do anything relevant in terms of an algorithm, their sole purpose is to list out selected machine language instructions for comparison. Of course the machine language is given in hexadecimal, but it can always be converted to binary (see Appendix B) in order to see the corresponding bit patterns. Then the bit patterns can be carefully examined to help one understand the machine language.

For example, in the following section of code taken from the complete listing in Sect. 12.9, there are listed a number of similar instructions. Again, the code listed does not actually do anything useful, because the purpose is to understand the corresponding machine language. In this first example, only the single register `inc` instructions are shown for the sake of simplicity, where multiple register instructions, immediate data instructions, and instructions that address memory locations will be examined later:

Address	Machine	Assembly	Address	Machine	Assembly
00000000	40	inc eax	00000004	44	inc esp
00000001	41	inc ecx	00000005	45	inc ebp
00000002	42	inc edx	00000006	46	inc esi
00000003	43	inc ebx	00000007	47	inc edi

First note that the above `inc` instructions are only two hex digits long, or in other words these are 1-byte instructions, where each byte has its own sequential memory address to the left. In looking at the above code, it should be noticed that the last hexadecimal digit changes as the register changes, where the hexadecimal digits 0, 1, 2, 3, 4, 5, 6, and 7 correspond to the registers eax, ecx, edx, ebx, esp, ebp, esi, and edi, respectively. The equivalent numbers in binary would be 0000, 0001, 0010, 0011, 0100, 0101, 0110, and 0111, respectively. Note as discussed above, it took three binary digits (the three low-order bits of the second hex digit) to represent the eight registers, leaving five binary digits (four from the first hex digit and the one high-order bit from the second hex digit) to represent the opcode for `inc` as 01000. The format for `inc` 32-bit register instruction is as in Fig. 12.2.

inc reg | 01000XXX | ,where XXX is the register.

Fig. 12.2 Format for the inc instruction

Expanding on the above, the following is a listing of the dec reg instruction:

Address	Machine	Assembly	Address	Machine	Assembly
00000008	48	dec eax	0000000C	4C	dec esp
00000009	49	dec ecx	0000000D	4D	dec ebp
0000000A	4A	dec edx	0000000E	4E	dec esi
0000000B	4B	dec ebx	0000000F	4F	dec edi

Again, it should be noticed that each instruction is only 1 byte long as before. Yes, there is a hex 4 in the first four bits, but the second hex digit is not as obvious as the previous example. However, looking at the binary for these instructions, it becomes much more obvious:

Hex	Binary	Assembly	Hex	Binary	Assembly
48	01001000	dec eax	4C	01001100	dec esp
49	01001001	dec ecx	4D	01001101	dec ebp
4A	01001010	dec edx	4E	01001110	dec esi
4B	01001011	dec ebx	4F	01001111	dec edi

In examining the binary carefully, it should be noticed that the same bit pattern appears again in the right three bit positions representing the registers eax through edi. The only difference is that bit position 3 (fourth from the right) is a 1 instead of a 0. The result is that the only difference between the inc and dec instructions is this one bit, where a 0 tells the processor to increment the specified register by 1, whereas a 1 tells the processor to decrement the specified register by 1. The machine code for the dec 32-bit register instruction is as in Fig. 12.3.

For convenience, a summary of the machine code representation of the registers can be found below, where the first column shows the machine code and the second column shows the corresponding register:

Machine code	Register
000	eax
001	ecx
010	edx
011	ebx
100	esp
101	ebp
110	esi
111	edi

```
dec reg    │ 01001XXX │   ,where XXX is the register.
```

Fig. 12.3 Format for the dec instruction

12.3 mov Instruction

Before looking at how memory is addressed, it is helpful to first examine the mov
instructions that are used with registers to notice some similarities and differences
between them and the inc reg and dec reg instructions. First, the mov reg,
reg instructions will be examined, but instead of listing out all possible register
combinations, only some of the possibilities are shown in the interest of saving
space. Besides, the patterns should become obvious by examining only a select few
of these instructions:

Address	Machine	Assembly
00000010	8B C0	mov eax,eax
00000012	8B C1	mov eax,ecx
00000014	8B C2	mov eax,edx
00000016	8B C3	mov eax,ebx
00000018	8B C4	mov eax,esp
0000001A	8B C5	mov eax,ebp
0000001C	8B C6	mov eax,esi
0000001E	8B C7	mov eax,edi
00000020	8B C8	mov ecx,eax
00000022	8B C9	mov ecx,ecx
00000024	8B CA	mov ecx,edx
00000026	8B CB	mov ecx,ebx

The first thing to notice is that the address of each instruction is incremented by 2
each time and that the machine language is now 4 hex digits long, which is 16 bits
or 2 bytes long. The first byte in all the instructions is an 8B which one can
probably assume is part of the opcode of the instruction indicating a register-to-
register mov instruction. Although there appears to be somewhat of a pattern in the
second byte of the first eight instructions, it probably would not hurt to convert
these to binary to see the pattern in all of the instructions more clearly as in
Table 12.1.

Table 12.1 Binary of
second byte of the mov reg,
reg instruction

Hex	Binary (2nd byte)	Assembly
8B C0	11000000	mov eax,eax
8B C1	11000001	mov eax,ecx
8B C2	11000010	mov eax,edx
8B C3	11000011	mov eax,ebx
8B C4	11000100	mov eax,esp
8B C5	11000101	mov eax,ebp
8B C6	11000110	mov eax,esi
8B C7	11000111	mov eax,edi
8B C8	11001000	mov ecx,eax
8B C9	11001001	mov ecx,ecx
8B CA	11001010	mov ecx,edx
8B CB	11001011	mov ecx,ebx

The suspicions of the first set of instructions appear to be correct, where eax through edi are 000 through 111, respectively, just like the inc and dec instructions previously. Then looking at the last four instructions, the same pattern appears to begin again with eax through ebx with 000 through 011, respectively.

In examining bits 3 through 5 (the 4th through 6th bits from the right), it can be noticed that for the first eight instructions, the bits are set at 000 and for the second four instructions they are set at 001, which happens to correspond to the first registers in the operand, eax and ecx, respectively. So part of the reason why this mov reg,reg instruction is larger than the inc reg instruction is that it needs to have room to reference two registers instead of one. The result is that one should be able to surmise that the mov between two registers has the format shown in Fig. 12.4.

Having looked at a few of the single and double register instructions, what does an instruction with immediate data look like? Staying with the mov instruction is a convenient next step:

Address	Machine	Assembly
00000028	B8 00000001	mov eax,1
0000002D	B9 0000000A	mov ecx,10
00000032	BA FFFFFFFF	mov edx,-1
00000037	BB FFFFFFF6	mov ebx,-10

```
mov reg,reg   | 10001011 | 11XXXYYY |
```

where XXX is the destination register
and YYY is the source register

Fig. 12.4 Format for the mov reg,reg instruction

Note that the addresses of each instruction is incremented by 5 and that each instruction is 10 hexadecimal digits long, equating to 40 bits, indicating that each instruction is 5 bytes long. It should be noticed that the last four bytes of each instruction is the hexadecimal equivalent of the immediate data in the instruction, where it should be remembered that negative numbers are represented in two's complement notation (see Appendix B). Again it helps to convert the first byte to binary to determine the machine code as follows:

Hex	Binary	Register
B8	10111000	eax
B9	10111001	ecx
BA	10111010	edx
BB	10111011	ebx

As before, the last three binary digits 000, 001, 010, 011 are the same digits as in previous instructions representing the eax, ecx, edx, and ebx registers, respectively. The format then is as illustrated in Fig. 12.5.

As can be seen, the immediate data instructions are fairly straightforward, so how would memory addresses be represented in an instruction? Just as the first instruction in the .code segment starts at *relative* address or relative memory location 00000000, the first memory location declared in the .data segment will also start at relative memory location 00000000 as shown below:

Address	Machine	Assembly language
		.data
00000000	00000003	num1 sdword 3
00000004	00000005	num2 sdword 5
00000008	00000000	num3 sdword ?

A relative memory location is relative to the beginning of either the .data or the .code segment, because at the time of assembly it is not known where in memory the segments will be loaded. When the machine language is subsequently loaded into memory, the relative addresses are eventually changed into the *absolute* addresses or absolute memory locations within RAM, where the first memory location in RAM is absolute memory location 00000000. Using the memory locations declared above, consider the following mov instructions that use the eax register and address memory locations num1 and num2:

```
mov reg,imm    | 10111XXX | YYYYYYYY | YYYYYYYY | YYYYYYYY | YYYYYYYY |

where XXX is the register and YYY is the immediate data
```

Fig. 12.5 Format for the mov reg, imm instruction

Address	Machine	Assembly
0000003C	A1 00000004	mov eax,num2
00000041	A3 00000008	mov num3,eax

As with immediate data, note that these two instructions are both 5 bytes long. Unlike the immediate instructions, where the data in the rightmost four bytes was the actual number contained in the instruction, here it should be noticed that address of the memory locations num2 and num3 appears in the right four bytes. In other words, instead of the numbers 00000005 or 00000000 appearing in the instruction, the addresses of the memory location num2 and num3, 00000004 and 00000008, appear in the instructions, respectively. In converting the first byte to binary, notice that there is only one bit difference between the instructions:

Hex	Binary	Assembly
A1	10100001	mov eax,mem
A3	10100011	mov mem,eax

When moving from memory to the eax register, bit 1 (second from the right) is set to 0, and when moving from the eax register to memory, note that bit 1 is set to 1. The format of these instructions is as shown in Fig. 12.6.

But what about moving to and from memory into the other registers? Consider the following instructions using the other three general purposes registers:

Address	Machine	Assembly
00000046	8B 0D 00000004	mov ecx,num2
0000004C	8B 15 00000004	mov edx,num2
00000052	8B 1D 00000004	mov ebx,num2
00000058	89 0D 00000008	mov num3,ecx
0000005E	89 15 00000008	mov num3,edx
00000064	89 1D 00000008	mov mum3,ebx

The address part of the instruction in the rightmost four bytes looks okay. Also the mov reg,mem instructions all have an 8B in the first byte and all the mov mem,reg instructions have an 89 in the first byte. Again looking at the binary:

Hex	Binary	Assembly
8B	10001011	mov reg,mem
89	10001001	mov mem,reg

Note that some of the leftmost five bits are different from the eax instructions in Fig. 12.6, where instead bit 3 (fourth from the right) is a 1 instead of a 0 and bit 5

| mov eax,mem | 10100001 | YYYYYYYY | YYYYYYYY | YYYYYYYY | YYYYYYYY |

| mov mem,eax | 10100011 | YYYYYYYY | YYYYYYYY | YYYYYYYY | YYYYYYYY |

where the eax register is implied and YYY is the address

Fig. 12.6 Format for the mov eax,mem and mov mem,eax instructions

(sixth from the right) is a 0 instead of a 1. Further, it is opposite from the mov eax,mem and mov mem,eax instructions, where bit 1 (second from the right) is a 0 when transferring from memory to a register and a 1 when transferring from a register to memory.

The most noticeable difference is that these instructions are 1 byte longer than their eax counterparts, 6 bytes instead of 5. Recall from Chap. 1 when discussing registers, it was said that the eax instruction is usually the preferred register, because it tends to be shorter. Further, in many of the code examples in this text, the eax register tends to be used more often than any other register. As can be seen in the code segment above, the use of the other registers is indeed a little less efficient in terms of memory utilization.

The first byte above is indeed the opcode, but look carefully at the binary of the second byte below. Clearly the first two bits on the left are the same. Also, the last three bits are the same and do not contain the register bits as they have in the past. However, in examining the middle bits, specifically bits 3 through 5 (fourth through sixth from the right), they are different with each instruction. As with previous instructions, 001, 010, and 011 correspond to the registers ecx, edx, and ebx, respectively:

Hex	Binary	Register
0D	00 001 101	ecx
15	00 010 101	edx
1D	00 011 101	ebx

Since this instruction format is a little more complicated than all the other ones examined thus far, in order to analyze the bits of this second byte, it is helpful to break it down and look at the machine language format of this byte. Although there are many possible bit combinations, this text only looks at a few of them. The basic format of this byte is shown in Fig. 12.7.

As seen previously, the bits in the middle (bit positions 3 through 5) indicate the register and is abbreviated as reg. The two bits on the left (bit positions 6 and 7) indicate the mode of the instruction and is abbreviated as mod. The three bits on the right (bit positions 0 through 2) indicate the register and mode, abbreviated as r/m. With a 00 in the mod field and a 101 in the r/m field, this means that it is

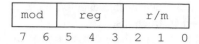

Fig. 12.7 Format of mod reg r/m

displacement only addressing mode or in other words direct addressing mode. Again, the meaning of the contents of this byte can be very complicated and will vary with other instructions that use different addressing schemes, but only a few of the simpler instructions are discussed here to serve as an introduction.

12.4 add and sub Instructions

Having looked at some of the inc, dec, and mov instructions, what about some of the arithmetic instructions? Instead of looking at all the registers as done in previous examples, only a few select registers will be examined, since the bit patterns of the registers have already been established. Consider the following register-to-register add and sub instructions:

Address	Machine	Assembly	Binary equivalent
0000006A	03C0	add eax,eax	00000011 11 000 000
0000006C	03C1	add eax,ecx	00000011 11 000 001
0000006E	03C2	add eax,edx	00000011 11 000 010
00000070	03C3	add eax,ebx	00000011 11 000 011
00000072	2BC8	sub ecx,eax	00101011 11 001 000
00000074	2BC9	sub ecx,ecx	00101011 11 001 001
00000076	2BCA	sub ecx,edx	00101011 11 001 010
00000078	3BCB	sub ecx,ebx	00101011 11 001 011

Note that instead of separating the binary equivalent of the opcodes on separate lines, it is now included off to the right for convenience. The first thing to notice is that the opcode for the add instruction and sub instruction differs by only 2 bits, where bit position 3 and 5 of the first byte (fourth and sixth from the right) are each a 1 instead of a 0 for the subtract instruction. Also notice that the rightmost six bits of the second byte appear to represent the registers, just like the register-to-register mov instruction earlier. However, given the previous information on mod, reg, and r/m sections in the mov instruction, it sheds some further light on the format of this and the previous mov reg,reg instruction. The reg section is indeed the first register that appears in the operand. However, the 11 in the leftmost two bits of the second byte is actually part of the mod section and indicates that the r/m section holds the code for the second register in the operand. This is true for all three of the reg, reg instructions examined in this chapter: the mov reg, reg, add reg, reg, and sub reg, reg instructions.

Given the reg mod r/m byte, there can be up to 256 bit combinations which allow for a large number of addressing modes. This is one of the reasons the Intel processor is known as a complex instruction set computer (CISC) as opposed to a computer with fewer instructions and addressing modes known as a reduced instruction set computer (RISC).

Looking at add and sub instructions referencing memory locations below, what similarities and differences can found between them and various previous instructions?

First, one should notice that the first byte is the same as the previous add and sub register-to-register instructions. Next, the last four bytes (32 bits) are the relative addresses of the memory location num2, just like the previous mov reg, mem instructions. Lastly, the mod reg r/m byte is different than the add reg, reg and sub reg, reg instructions, but they are the same as the previous mov reg, mem instructions because they are addressing memory in the same fashion.

Address	Machine	Assembly	Binary equivalent
0000007A	03 05 00000004	add eax, num2	00000011 00 000 101
00000080	03 0D 00000004	add ecx, num2	00000011 00 001 101
00000086	03 15 00000004	add edx, num2	00000011 00 010 101
0000008C	03 1D 00000004	add ebx, num2	00000011 00 011 101
00000092	2B 05 00000004	sub eax, num2	00101011 00 000 101
00000098	2B 0D 00000004	sub ecx, num2	00101011 00 001 101
0000009E	2B 15 00000004	sub edx, num2	00101011 00 010 101
000000A4	2B 1D 00000004	sub ebx, num2	00101011 00 011 101

12.5 mov offset and lea Instructions

Having looked at the moving of the contents of a memory location to a register, what is the difference between that type of instruction and a lea instruction or mov offset instruction. First consider the following mov and lea instructions:

Address	Machine	Assembly	Binary equivalent
000000AA	8B 35 00000004	mov esi, num2	10001011 00 110 101
000000B0	8B 3D 00000004	mov edi, num2	10001011 00 111 101
000000B6	8D 35 00000004	lea esi, num2	10001101 00 110 101
000000BC	8D 3D 00000004	lea edi, num2	10001101 00 111 101

The first two instructions are the same as previous mov instructions, where in this case they use the esi and edi registers and the middle bits of the mod reg r/m byte are 110 and 111, respectively. The two lea instructions have the same format in the second byte as the mov instructions. The only difference is in the first byte, where bit positions 1 and 2 (second and third from the right) are opposite of each other. As before, the result is that when the processor encounters the mov instructions, the "contents" of memory location num2 are loaded into the specified register and with the lea instructions the "address" of memory location num2 is loaded into the specified register. In this instance in the former case, the contents 5 is loaded and in the latter case the address 4 is loaded.

Remember from Chap. 8 that the mov offset and lea instructions effectively perform the same task, where they both load the address of the memory location into the specified register. The only difference is that the mov offset instruction is static and the lea instruction is dynamic, where in the former the address is determined at assembly time, and in the latter the address can be indexed by a register and is determined at run-time. In looking at the machine language for the mov offset instruction below, the address is in the last four bytes of the instruction as with many other instructions before. Further, its machine language equivalent is 1 byte shorter than its lea counterpart, where instead of the esi and edi registers being included in a mod reg r/m byte, they are in the rightmost three bits (bit positions 0 though 2) of the opcode byte as 110 and 111, respectively:

Address	Machine	Assembly	Binary equivalent
000000C2	BE 00000004	mov esi,offset num2	10111 110
000000C7	BF 00000004	mov edi,offset num2	10111 111

The significant difference, as discussed in Chap. 8, is that instead of the "contents" of the memory location being moved to the register, the "address" of the memory location is moved to the register. Although probably not readily apparent, the machine language for the opcode of the mov offset instruction should be familiar. In fact it is the same, 10111, as the mov reg,imm instruction discussed in Sect. 12.3. Compare the following instructions with the instructions above:

Address	Machine	Assembly	Binary equivalent
000000CC	BE 00000004	mov esi,4	10111 110
000000D1	BF 00000004	mov edi,4	10111 111

Note that the machine language of the mov reg,imm instructions looks the same as that of the mov reg,offset mem instructions. Does this mean that one should use the immediate instructions to try to load the address of a memory location? The answer is no, because if the contents of the register in both cases were to be output, there would be a difference between the two. Recall from Sect. 12.3 the discussion of relative and absolute addresses. Although the value in the immediate case is 4, the value in the offset case is not the relative address of num2 which is 4, but rather the absolute address of the memory location num2 which can vary depending on where the program is loaded in memory. For example, when running a test program on one computer, the value in the register was 00404008 (in hex) and when running the same program on another computer, the value in the register was 010F4008 (in hex).

Even if one could use the correct address of a particular variable, is this method of addressing memory a good idea? As might be suspected, the answer is no, because the location of the variable could change and cause potential logic or execution errors. Using immediate values to access memory instead of variable names or pointers essentially reduces an assembly language instruction back to that of a machine language instruction, thus eliminating the purpose of using an assembler in the first place.

12.6   jmp Instructions

As discussed in Chap. 4, the jmp instruction is known as an unconditional jump because it jumps regardless of the setting of the eflags register. Although the code is somewhat nonsensical, the machine language of the jmp instruction can be found in the following sample code segment:

Address	Machine	Assembly language instruction	
000000D6	EB 04		jmp around
000000D8	90	above:	nop
000000D9	90		nop
000000DA	EB FC		jmp above
000000DC	90	around:	nop

The opcode for the jmp instruction is EB, but what is interesting to note is that the machine code for the jmp around instruction does not contain the address of the around: nop instruction. Why is this and is it referring to memory location 04? The answer to the latter part of this question is no, because the jmp instruction is referring to a location that is relative to itself. However, if a 04 is added to the address of the memory location where the jmp around instruction is located, 000000D6, the new address is 000000DA. But looking at the above code segment, 000000DA is the address of the jmp above instruction and not the around: nop instruction. If the 04 is the address relative to jmp around instruction, why does the number seem incorrect? The answer is that the number is not incorrect because the number is relative to where the instruction pointer is pointing.

To those who have had or are currently taking a computer organization course, the following explanation should be somewhat familiar. As a program executes, the instruction pointer or instruction counter in the CPU points to the instruction that it is about to fetch and subsequently execute. After an instruction is fetched, the instruction pointer is then incremented to point to the next instruction that follows the current instruction. Then when the current instruction is decoded and executed, the instruction pointer is no longer pointing at the current instruction but rather to the next instruction in anticipation of fetching it. In the above case, the instruction pointer is not pointing to memory location 000000D6, but rather 000000D8, so that when 04 is added to 000000D8, the answer is 000000DC which is the address of the correct instruction. The value 000000DC is then placed into the instruction pointer so that when the next instruction is fetched, it is not to the above: nop instruction but rather the around: nop instruction.

However, what about the jmp above instruction? Shouldn't it be a jump backward and not a jump forward? The answer is yes, where the FC is not a positive number but rather a negative number (11111100 in binary) and it is in two's complement form. Using the techniques learned in Appendix B, 11111100 in binary is equal to –4 in decimal. Remembering that the instruction pointer is not pointing to the current instruction, jmp above, but rather the instruction after it at memory location 000000DC, subtracting a 04 results in the address 000000D8, which is the correct location and instruction.

Notice that only 1 byte is used to store the relative offset address and this allows for jumps of only +127 bytes or −128 bytes away. On older 16-bit machines, this sometimes posed a problem and on occasion a code segment needed to be rewritten to accommodate jumps in excess of the above limitations. Fortunately, with the newer 32-bit processors, this does not pose a problem because should the unconditional jump be more than the above limits, a 32-bit relative offset is generated.

12.7 Instruction Timings

As has been mentioned at various points throughout this text, some instructions are faster than others. It has been implied that the faster instructions should be used over their slower counterparts when necessary, and also when it does not interfere with the readability and maintainability of the program. Why is it that some instructions are faster than others? The reasons for this can have to do with many different factors including the size of the instruction, whether the instruction references registers as opposed to memory locations, the complexity of the operation, and how the processor is designed. When a processor is said to be rated at a speed 2.0 GHz, that means that the processor can execute at two billion cycles per second, where different instructions take different number of cycles to execute. For the discussion that follows, the instruction timings are based on a 32-bit Pentium processor.

Generally, instructions that do not reference memory tend to be faster than instructions that do reference memory. For example, an inc eax instruction takes only one clock cycle of the CPUs time, whereas an inc instruction that references memory such as inc number takes three clock cycles. The reason why registers are faster is that registers are internal to the CPU, whereas memory is external to the CPU and it takes time for data to be transferred from RAM to the CPU or from CPU to RAM.

Does this mean that memory should be avoided? No, because there are only four general purpose registers in the 32-bit Intel processor and it would be impractical to restrict a program to only four registers. What it does mean is that when in a critical section of the program where speed is important, a value might be left in a register in lieu of returning the value back to memory so that readability is sacrificed for efficiency.

In looking at a few other instructions, take the imul instruction for example. To multiply the contents of eax by the contents of another register such as the ecx register would take 10 clock cycles. Similarly, the idiv ecx instruction takes 46 clock cycles. However, if in each case the contents of the ecx register are a power of 2, an arithmetic shift instruction could be used instead. For example, if the contents of the ecx register in an imul ecx instruction were a 4, then a sal eax, 2 instruction could be used instead, which would take only three clock cycles which is over three times faster. Likewise, if the contents of ecx in an idiv ecx instruction were a 32, a sar eax, 5 instruction could be used which also takes only three cycles and would be 15 times faster. This is the reason why some programmers will use arithmetic shift instructions instead of multiplication and division instructions. Does this mean that arithmetic shifts should always be used over their arithmetic counterparts? No, not necessarily. If the code appears in a non-critical section of a program that is executed only once, then the increase in speed may not be worth the decrease in readability. However, if the arithmetic operation occurs in a time-sensitive section of a program, then the increase in execution speed far outweighs any loss of readability or maintainability.

12.8 Floating-Point and 64-Bit Instructions

Having examined 32-bit integer instructions, it is interesting to look at some of the similarities and differences in comparison with floating-point and 64-bit integer instructions. Because the instructions sets are so large, only a few of these latter instructions will be examined in this section.

12.8.1 Floating-Point Instructions

Just as there were differences in the machine language between various 32-bit integer instructions, there are also differences in the machine language of floating-point instructions. For example, assuming that the variables x, y, and z are declare as real4, consider the fld, fst, and fstp instructions as shown below:

Machine language	Assembly language	Binary of the second byte from the left
D9 05 00000000	fld x	000 00 101
D9 15 00000004	fst y	000 10 101
D9 1D 00000008	fstp z	000 11 101

Note that the instructions are six bytes long, where the last four bytes is the operand that contains address of the memory location. In the second byte from the left there are some differences and the binary equivalent is shown on the last column on the right. It is separated by spaces to help indicate where the differences are in the bit patterns. Notice that it is the middle set of bits that indicate whether the instruction is a fld, fst, or fstp instruction.

Similarly, differences can be found between the fadd and fsub instructions as shown below:

Machine language	Assembly language	Binary of the second byte from the left
D8 05 00000000	fadd x	00000101
D8 25 00000004	fsub y	00100101

Again, the operand is in the last four bytes and contains the address of the memory location. Notice the difference between the two instructions is in the second byte from the left. Note that in the binary, the third bit from the left is a 0 or 1 for the fadd or fsub, respectively. The result is that just like with 32-bit integer instructions, the differences between various operations such as adding or subtracting can be just a single binary digit.

12.8.2 64-Bit Instructions

The similarities between 32-bit and 64-bit integer instructions are quite noticeable. However, with more registers, the instructions need to be larger. Although it is a rather large list, consider the following partial list of register to register instructions

Machine language	Assembly language	Right 4 bits of first byte on the left	Binary of the last byte on the right
48 8B C0	mov rax,rax	1000	11 000 000
48 8B C3	mov rax,rbx	1000	11 000 011
48 8B D8	mov rbx,rax	1000	11 011 000
48 8B DB	mov rbx,rbx	1000	11 011 011
49 8B C0	mov rax,r8	1001	11 000 000
49 8B C7	mov rax,r15	1001	11 000 111
49 8B D8	mov rbx,r8	1001	11 011 000
49 8B DF	mov rbx,r15	1001	11 011 111
4C 8B C0	mov r8,rax	1100	11 000 000
4C 8B C3	mov r8,rbx	1100	11 000 011
4D 8B C0	mov r8,r8	1101	11 000 000
4D 8B C7	mov r8,r15	1101	11 000 111
4C 8B F8	mov r15,rax	1100	11 111 000
4C 8B FB	mov r15,rbx	1100	11 111 011
4D 8B F8	mov r15,r8	1101	11 111 000
4D 8B FF	mov r15,r15	1101	11 111 111

First, note that the second byte from the left in the 64-bit instructions is the same as the first byte on the left in the 32-bit instructions in Sect. 12.3. As before, notice that the binary representation of the last byte on the right has added spaces to help readability. Similar to their 32-bit counterparts, rax through rbx (rax, rcx, rdx, and rbx) have bit patterns 000 through 011 and that new numbered registers r8 through r15 varies from 000 to 111. Also, notice that rax and r8 have the same bit pattern; so how does the computer know which register is which? The answer lies in the first byte on the left, specifically the right-most four bits as shown above. Upon careful inspection, can the pattern be seen? First notice that when the two registers in the instruction are rax through rbx, the first and third bits from the right are both 0. Then notice that when the two registers are r8 through r15 the same two bits are 1. It follows that when the first register is rax through rbx the third bit from the right is 0 and when the second register is r8 through r15 the first bit from the right is a 1. Of course, when the types of registers are reversed, the two bits are reversed. It is these two bits in the first byte on the left that allows the same bit patterns in the last byte on the right to be used for different registers.

Continuing on to another example, if a 64-bit instruction is using an immediate operand that is 32 bits or less, then notice only 32 bits need to be allocated in the machine language instructions as shown below:

Machine language	Assembly language
48 C7 C0 00000001	mov rax,1
48 C7 C1 343EFCEA	mov rcx,876543210
48 C7 C2 FFFFFFFF	mov rdx,-1
48 C7 C3 CBC10316	mov rbx,-876543210

As before, notice above that the third byte from the left, that the value goes from C0 to C3 indicating the different registers. Further, in comparison the 64-bit instruction is seven bytes long as opposed to just five bytes long for the 32-bit instruction in Sect. 12.3.

What happens if the immediate value in the operand is larger than 32 bits? In the examples below notice that the instructions are now ten bytes long in order to accommodate the 64-bit values. Note that the right-most bits of the second byte on the left indicate the register used as shown below:

Machine language	Assembly language	Right 4 bits of 2nd byte on the left
48 B8 000000024CB016EA	mov rax,9876543210	1000
48 B9 018EBBB95EED0E13	mov rcx,112233445566778899	1001
48 BA FFFFFFFDB34FE916	mov rdx,-9876543210	1010
48 BB FE714446A112F1ED	mov rbx,-112233445566778899	1011

Turning to the addressing of memory, consider the instructions below:

Machine language	Assembly language	Right 4 bits of first byte on the left	Binary of the third byte from the left
48 8B 05 0000000C	mov rax,a	1000	00 000 101
48 8B 1D 00000014	mov rbx,b	1000	00 011 101
4C 8B 05 0000001C	mov r8,c	1100	00 000 101
4C 8B 3D 00000024	mov r15,d	1100	00 111 101

Again, the bit pattern for the third byte from the left appears in the right column with spaces to help with readability. Notice that the middle bits are 000 through 011 for rax through rbx and 000 through 111 for r8 through r15. As before, the right most four bits of the left-most byte are also shown above. Again, notice that the third bit from the right is set to 0 for rax through rbx and 1 for r8 through r15. Lastly, the four bytes on the right is the operand and indicate the address of the memory location being referenced.

Similar to their 32-bit counterparts, there is only a slight difference between the load and store 64-bit operations as can be seen below:

Machine language	Assembly language	Binary of the second byte on the left
48 8B 05 0000000C	mov rax,a	1000 1011
48 89 05 00000014	mov b,rax	1000 1001

The binary equivalent of the second byte from the left is shown above to the right, Notice that the second bit from the right is set to 1 for the load operation mov rax,a and it is set to 0 for the store operation mov b,rax. Again, the four bytes on the right are the operand that indicate the address of the memory location being referenced and this will be discussed further in the next section. Further, similar bit patterns can be found for other instructions such as add and sub, which is left as an exercise at the end of the chapter.

12.8.3 Memory Addressing

In both of the last two examples in the preceding section, was anything noticed that might have seemed inconsistent? Note that the addresses for the variables for the 64-bit integer instructions are only 32-bits long which is the same length as with 32-bit integer instructions. Even though the values that are stored in memory locations and registers are 64-bits, the addresses remain at 32-bits.

Although the operands are the same length between the two instruction sets, it should be noted that the way in which addressing of the memory locations occurs is different. Even though the difference cannot be seen in the assembly listings, in 32-bit (×86) mode the addressing scheme has the address of the memory location in operand of the instruction whereas the 64-bit (×64) mode the addressing scheme has an offset from the current instruction located in the operand of the instruction. This is true for both the 32-bit and 64-bit instructions when in 64-bit (×64) mode.

In looking at a 32-bit instruction in 32-bit (×86) mode, assume that the following variable dog is declared at the address 00000020 in memory as shown below:

Address	Machine language	Assembly language
00000020	00000005	dog sdword 5
00000040	8B 05 00000020	mov eax, dog

Notice the operand portion of the mov eax, dog instruction has the address of the memory location dog as 00000020. On the other hand, 64-bit instructions (or 32-bit instructions) in 64-bit (×64) mode access the memory location differently. Assume in this case that the variable cat is declared at memory location 00000060 in memory as shown below:

Address	Machine language	Assembly language
00000060	0000000000000007	cat sqword 7
00000070	48 8B 05 FFFFFFE9	mov rax, cat

Notice that operand of the machine language instruction does not contain the address 00000060, but rather FFFFFFE9 which is a −17 in base ten and is the offset or how far away the memory location cat is from the mov instruction. If the variable was located at a memory location greater than the address of the instruction, the offset in the operand would be positive.

To find out if FFFFFFE9 is the correct offset, take the address of the instruction 00000070 and add the length of the instruction (in this case 7) which results in the address of the next instruction 00000077. Then this number is added to the offset in the operand, FFFFFFE9, and the result is the address 00000060 of the memory location cat.

Again, unfortunately, this cannot be seen in an assembly language listing file where in 64-bit (×64) mode the address in the operand looks the same as in 32-bit (×86) mode. In order to see this one must run the debugger to look at the memory locations and this is left as an exercise at the end of the chapter.

12.9 Complete Program: 32-Bit Assembly Listing

To help readability, the following is a cleaned-up version of the assembly listing (.lst file) showing the machine language of the instructions discussed in Sects. 12.2 through 12.6. The source code for this program can be found at the website listed at the end of the Preface. The program should be run in 32-bit (x86) mode as discussed in Section A.2 and the directions for obtaining a listing are discussed in Section A.4.

```
                                      .686
                                      .model flat,c
                                      .stack 100h

                                      .data
00000000   00000003        num1       sdword 3
00000004   00000005        num2       sdword 5
00000008   00000000        num3       sdword ?
                                      .code
                           main       proc

00000000   40                         inc  eax
00000001   41                         inc  ecx
00000002   42                         inc  edx
00000003   43                         inc  ebx
00000004   44                         inc  esp
00000005   45                         inc  ebp
00000006   46                         inc  esi
00000007   47                         inc  edi

00000008   48                         dec  eax
00000009   49                         dec  ecx
0000000A   4A                         dec  edx
0000000B   4B                         dec  ebx
0000000C   4C                         dec  esp
0000000D   4D                         dec  ebp
0000000E   4E                         dec  esi
0000000F   4F                         dec  edi
00000010   8B C0                      mov  eax,eax
00000012   8B C1                      mov  eax,ecx
00000014   8B C2                      mov  eax,edx
00000016   8B C3                      mov  eax,ebx
00000018   8B C4                      mov  eax,esp
0000001A   8B C5                      mov  eax,ebp
0000001C   8B C6                      mov  eax,esi
0000001E   8B C7                      mov  eax,edi
00000020   8B C8                      mov  ecx,eax
00000022   8B C9                      mov  ecx,ecx
00000024   8B CA                      mov  ecx,edx
00000026   8B CB                      mov  ecx,ebx

00000028   B8 00000001                mov  eax,1
0000002D   B9 0000000A                mov  ecx,10
00000032   BA FFFFFFFF                mov  edx,-1
00000037   BB FFFFFFF6                mov  ebx,-10
```

```
0000003C   A1 00000004                         mov eax,num2
00000041   A3 00000008                         mov num3,eax

00000046   8B 0D 00000004                      mov ecx,num2
0000004C   8B 15 00000004                      mov edx,num2
00000052   8B 1D 00000004                      mov ebx,num2

00000058   89 0D 00000008                      mov num3,ecx
0000005E   89 15 00000008                      mov num3,edx
00000064   89 1D 00000008                      mov num3,ebx

0000006A   03 C0                               add eax,eax
0000006C   03 C1                               add eax,ecx
0000006E   03 C2                               add eax,edx
00000070   03 C3                               add eax,ebx
00000072   2B C8                               sub ecx,eax
00000074   2B C9                               sub ecx,ecx
00000076   2B CA                               sub ecx,edx
00000078   2B CB                               sub ecx,ebx

0000007A   03 05 00000004                      add eax,num2
00000080   03 0D 00000004                      add ecx,num2
00000086   03 15 00000004                      add edx,num2
0000008C   03 1D 00000004                      add ebx,num2
00000092   2B 05 00000004                      sub eax,num2
00000098   2B 0D 00000004                      sub ecx,num2
0000009E   2B 15 00000004                      sub edx,num2
000000A4   2B 1D 00000004                      sub ebx,num2

000000AA   8B 35 00000004                      mov esi,num2
000000B0   8B 3D 00000004                      mov edi,num2
000000B6   8D 35 00000004                      lea esi, num2
000000BC   8D 3D 00000004                      lea edi, num2

000000C2   BE 00000004                         mov esi, offset num2
000000C7   BF 00000004                         mov edi, offset num2

000000CC   BE 00000004                         mov esi,4
000000D1   BF 00000004                         mov edi,4

000000D6   EB 04                               jmp around
000000D8   90                  above:          nop
000000D9   90                                  nop
000000DA   EB FC                               jmp above
000000DC   90                  around:         nop

000000DD   C3                                  ret
                               main            endp
                                               end
```

12.10 Complete Program: Floating-Point and 64-Bit Assembly Listing

To help readability, the following is a cleaned-up version of the assembly listing (.lst file) showing the machine language of the instructions discussed in Sect. 12.8. The source code for this program can be found at the website listed at the end of the Preface. The program should be run in 64-bit (x64) mode as discussed in Section A.3 and the directions for obtaining a listing are discussed in Section A.4.

Also, note that the floating-point programs that incorporate I/O as in Chap. 10 are to be run in 32-bit mode. However, to examine just the machine language without I/O the floating-point instructions from Sect. 12.8.1 are included in this program for convenience.

```
                                           .data
00000000    40A00000                  x    real4    5.0
00000004    40000000                  y    real4    2.0
00000008    00000000                  z    real4    ?

0000000C    0000000000000001          a    sqword 1
00000014    0000000000000002          b    sqword 2
0000001C    0000000000000003          c    sqword 3
00000024    0000000000000004          d    sqword 4

                                           .code
                                      main proc

00000000    D9 05 00000000                 fld x
00000006    D9 15 00000004                 fst y
0000000C    D9 1D 00000008                 fstp z

00000012    D8 05 00000000                 fadd x
00000018    D8 25 00000004                 fsub y

0000001E    48 8B C0                       mov rax,rax
00000021    48 8B C3                       mov rax,rbx
00000024    48 8B D8                       mov rbx,rax
00000027    48 8B DB                       mov rbx,rbx

0000002A    49 8B C0                       mov rax,r8
0000002D    49 8B C7                       mov rax,r15
00000030    49 8B D8                       mov rbx,r8
00000033    49 8B DF                       mov rbx,r15

00000036    4C 8B C0                       mov r8,rax
00000039    4C 8B C3                       mov r8,rbx
0000003C    4D 8B C0                       mov r8,r8
0000003F    4D 8B C7                       mov r8,r15

00000042    4C 8B F8                       mov r15,rax
00000045    4C 8B FB                       mov r15,rbx
00000048    4D 8B F8                       mov r15,r8
0000004B    4D 8B FF                       mov r15,r15
```

```
0000004E   48 C7 C0 00000001                    mov rax,1
00000055   48 C7 C1 343EFCEA                    mov rcx,876543210
0000005C   48 C7 C2 FFFFFFFF                    mov rdx,-1
00000063   48 C7 C3 CBC10316                    mov rbx,-876543210


0000006A   48 B8 000000024CB016EA              mov rax,9876543210
00000074   48 B9 018EBBB95EED0E13              mov rcx, 112233445566778899
0000007E   48 BA FFFFFFFFDB34FE916             mov rdx,-9876543210
00000088   48 BB FE714446A112F1ED              mov rbx,-112233445566778899

00000092   48 8B 05 0000000C                   mov rax,a
00000099   48 8B 1D 00000014                   mov rbx,b
000000A0   4C 8B 05 0000001C                   mov r8,c
000000A7   4C 8B 3D 00000024                   mov r15,d

000000AE   48 8B 05 0000000C                   mov rax,a
000000B5   48 89 05 00000014                   mov b,rax

000000BC   C3                                  ret
                                        main    endp
                                                end
```

12.11   Summary

- The number of bits allocated for an instruction and how that instruction is divided up indicates the number of opcodes, the number of register references, and the number of memory locations that can be addressed.
- Much can be learned about the machine language of many assembly languages by mere inspection.
- Sometimes the difference between two operations can be the difference of the setting of only one bit.
- Some instructions such as `mov eax,mem` take up less memory than do `mov reg,mem` instructions.
- The Intel processor is known as a complex instruction set computer (CISC) as opposed to a reduced instruction set computer (RISC), due to the number of instructions and addressing modes.
- When dealing with powers of 2, using arithmetic shift instructions can be significantly faster than using `imul` and `idiv` instructions.
- Just because an instruction is faster does not mean that it needs to be used all the time. The decision must be based on the necessity for execution speed versus readability and maintainability.

- In ×86 mode the operand contains the address of the corresponding memory location whereas in ×64 mode the operand contains the offset of the corresponding memory location.

12.12 Exercises (Items Marked with an * Have Solutions in Appendix D)

*1. If there is an 8-bit instruction, where 2 bits are reserved for the opcodes and 0 bits for the registers, how many opcodes and registers are there, and how much memory can be addressed?

2. If there is a 16-bit instruction, where 4 bits are reserved for the opcodes and 1 bit for the registers, how many opcodes and registers are there, and how much memory can be addressed?

*3. If there is a 16-bit instruction, where 5 bits are reserved for the opcodes and 2 bits for the registers, how many opcodes and registers are there, and how much memory can be addressed?

4. If there is a 32-bit instruction, where 8 bits are reserved for the opcode and 4 bits for the registers, how many opcodes and registers are there, and how much memory can be addressed?

5. If there is a 32-bit instruction, where 10 bits are reserved for the opcode and 6 bits for the registers, how many opcodes and registers are there, and how much memory can be addressed?

6. Convert the following assembly language instructions to their machine language equivalents. List the answers in both hex and binary:

   *A. `add ecx,ebx`   B. `sub ecx,edx`
    C. `add esi,edi`   D. `sub edx,esi`

7. Write an assembly language program and generate the `.lst` file to determine the machine language format of the following 1-byte instructions. Write out the answers in both hex and binary:

   *A. `nop`   B. `cld`   C. `ret`   D. `std`

8. Write an assembly language program and generate the `.lst` file to determine the machine language format of the following 2-byte instructions. Write out the answers in both hex and binary:

   *A. `and eax,ebx`
    B. `or ebx,ecx`
    C. `xor eax,eax`
    D. `test ecx,edx`

9. Key in the following program and obtain the assembly listing (.lst) file (see Appendix A.4). Looking at the machine code for both instructions, indicate which bit or bits are different between the two instructions.

64-bit(x64) Mode

```
              .data
number    sqword 5
              .code
main      proc
              add rax,number
              sub rax,number
              ret
main      endp
              end
```

10. The instructions and data in the following similar programs are both 32-bit to allow them to be executed in both ×86 and ×64 modes. When assembling the programs, be sure to also create the assembly listing (.lst) files (See Appendices A.2, A.3, and A.4) so that one can refer to the machine code.

32-bit (x86) Mode

```
              .686
              .model flat,c
              .stack 100h
              .data
number    sdword 5
              .code
main      proc
              mov eax,number
              ret
main      endp
              end main
```

64-bit (x64) Mode

```
              .data
number    sdword 5
              .code
main      proc
              mov eax,number
              ret
main      endp
              end
```

For both programs in both modes, set a breakpoint on the first executable instruction by right clicking on the instruction, selecting *Breakpoint*, and clicking on *Insert Breakpoint*. Then in the *Debug* pull-down menu select *Step Into*. To turn on the registers, in the *Debug* pull-down menu, select *Windows*, and then select *Registers*. Do the same for memory but select *Memory* and then select *Memory 1*.

Looking first at the *Registers* window, note the address in the `eip` or `rip` instruction pointer register. Then find the memory location and the corresponding machine code for the instruction in the *Memory 1* window. If it is not in the window, type in the address from the `eip` or `rip` register in the `Address` box, or alternatively type in `&main`.

Although the first byte in ×86 mode or two bytes in ×64 mode of the instructions look okay, the operand portion appears backwards. This is because inside the computer the addresses in instructions and data in memory locations are stored with the least significant byte first. For example, the data `00012468` would be stored as `68240100`. This is known as *little endian order*. All one has to do to read the bytes in reverse order to determine the address in an operand or the data stored in a memory location.

In a ×86 mode, this represents the actual address of the memory location. (Note that this might be different every time the program is executed.) One can then find the memory location by typing in the address in the *Address* box and see the contents of memory, which will also be in little endian order. Alternatively, one could just type in the name of the memory location preceded by an ampersand as &*number*.

However, when running the program in ×64 mode, the address in the operand represents an offset. As discussed in the text, to find the location add the length of the current instruction (which would be 6 in this case) to the address of the current instruction. Then be sure to again reverse the bytes of the operand and add it also. Using the calculated address, the contents of the referenced memory location can then be seen, again in little endian order.

In both cases, write down how each instruction looks in memory and the address of the memory location, number. In the ×64 mode case, be sure to show you work on how the address was calculated.

Appendix A: Directions for MASM in Visual Studio 2019 Community Edition

Note that each of the complete programs in this text have been run using Visual Studio 2019 Community Edition. Although there are similarities in each of the following three sections, there are also difference and the directions are written separately to avoid confusion. The first is for C programs with inline assembly, the second for 32-bit integer and floating-point MASM programs, and the third is for 64-bit integer MASM programs. Also, the fourth section contains directions for obtaining an assembly listing for MASM programs (.lst file).

A.1 C Programs with Inline Assembly

- To create a new project, on the *Visual Studio 2019 Get Started* page, click *Create new project*.
- On the next *Create a new project* page, choose *Empty Project* (where it also says *C ++*, *Windows*, and *Console* underneath this selection), and click *Next*.
- On the *Configure your new project* page, in the *Project Name* box use the default *Project1* name or key in another name such as *TestInLine*. Then determine *Location* where the project should be stored, whether in the default folder given or key in another location such as *F:* for a jump drive. By default, the *Solution name* is the same as the *Project name*, then click the *Create* button.
- In the *Solution Explorer*, right click on the name of the application (default *Project1*), select *Properties*, then under *Linker*, select *System*, and verify that the *SubSystem* is *Console*. (If not select it from the list).
- Again, in the *Solution Explorer*, expand *Project1* (if not done so already), and right click on *Source Files*, hover on *Add*, and click *New Item*. Note that the default is *C ++ File (.cpp)*. At the bottom of the screen use the default name *Source* or use a different name and change the extension from *.cpp* to *.c* (as in *source.c*). In either case be sure to use a *.c* extension (because this indicates to use the C compiler instead of the C ++ compiler) and then click *Add*.

© Springer Nature Switzerland AG 2020
J. T. Streib, *Guide to Assembly Language*, Undergraduate Topics in Computer Science, https://doi.org/10.1007/978-3-030-35639-2

- One can now key in a program or copy and paste a complete program from the "Guide to Assembly Language" website. Then click on *BUILD* and *Build Solution*. If there are no syntax errors, then click on *DEBUG* and then *Start Without Debugging*.

A.2   32-Bit Integer and Floating-Point MASM Programs

- To create a new project, on the *Visual Studio 2019 Get Started* page, click *Create new project*.
- On the next *Create a new project* page, choose *Empty Project* (where it also says *C ++*, *Windows*, and *Console* underneath this selection), and click *Next*.
- On the *Configure your new project* page, in the *Project Name* box use the default *Project1* name or key in another name such as *Test32Bit* or *TestFloatingPoint*. Then determine *Location* where the project should be stored, whether in the default folder given or key in another location such as *F:* for a jump drive. By default, the *Solution name* is the same as the *Project name*, then click the *Create* button.
- Make sure in the ribbon that *x86* appears in the *Solution Platforms* box which is next to the *Solution Configurations* box that has the word *Debug* in it. If not, select it from the list. By hovering over the boxes, one can see the names of the boxes.
- Now in the *Solution Explorer* (which can appear on either the left or right side), right click the name of the application which appear in bold near the top (default *Project1*), then hover on *Build Dependencies* and then click *Build Customizations*. Then check the *masm* box and click *OK*.
- Again, in the *Solution Explorer*, right click on the name of the project (default *Project1*) and select *Properties*. Then expand *Linker* and then click on *Input*. In the *Additional Dependencies*, type or paste *msvcrt.lib;legacy_stdio_definitions. lib;* at the beginning of the list. Be careful not to delete any other entries, do not forget the semi-colons, and then click *OK*. Alternatively, or if there are problems when building a solution, the above can be added at the beginning of the program as follows:

```
includelib msvcrt.lib
includelib legacy_stdio_definitions.lib
```

- Then again in the *Solution Explorer*, right click on the name of the application (default *Project1*), select *Properties*, then under *Linker*, select *System*, and verify that the *SubSystem* is *Console*. (If not select it from the list). Also, under *Linker*, select *Advanced* and verify the *Entry Point* is blank (and does not say main).
- Now in the *Solution Explorer*, expand *Project1* (if not done so already), and right click on *Source Files*, hover on *Add*, and click *New Item*. Note that the default is *C ++ File (.cpp)*. At the bottom of the screen use the default name

source or use a different name and change the extension from *.cpp* to *.asm* (as in *source.asm*). In either case be sure to use a *.asm* extension (because this indicates to use the Microsoft Assembler, MASM, instead of the C ++ compiler) and then click *Add*.

- One can now key in a program or copy and paste a complete program from the "Guide to Assembly Language" website. Then click on *BUILD* and *Build Solution*. If there are no syntax errors, then click on *DEBUG* and then *Start Without Debugging*. (For information on using the Debugger, see problem 10 in Sect. 12.12.)

A.3   64-Bit Integer MASM Programs

- To create a new project, on the *Visual Studio 2019 Get Started* page, click *Create new project*.
- On the next *Create a new project* page, choose *Empty Project* (where it also says *C ++*, *Windows*, and *Console* underneath this selection), and click *Next*.
- On the *Configure your new project* page, in the *Project Name* box use the default *Project1* name or key in another name such as *Test64Bit*. Then determine *Location* where the project should be stored, whether in the default folder given or key in another location such as *F:\for* a jump drive. By default, the *Solution name* is the same as the *Project name*, then click the *Create* button.
- Select *x64* in the ribbon in the *Solution Platforms* box which is next to the *Solution Configurations* box that has the word *Debug* in it. By hovering over the boxes, one can see the names of the boxes.
- Now in the *Solution Explorer* (which can appear on either the left or right side), right click the name of the application which appear in bold near the top (default *Project1*), then hover on *Build Dependencies* and then click *Build Customizations*. Then check the *masm* box and click *OK*.
- Again, in the *Solution Explorer*, right click on the name of the project (default *Project1*) and select *Properties*. Then expand *Linker* and then click on *Input*. In the *Additional Dependencies*, type or paste *libcmt.lib;legacy_stdio_definitions. lib;* at the beginning of the list. Be careful not to delete any other entries, do not forget the semi-colons, and then click *OK*. Alternatively, or if there are problems when building a solution, the above can be added at the beginning of the program as follows:

```
includelib libcmt.lib
includelib legacy_stdio_definitions.lib
```

- Again, in the *Solution Explorer*, right click on the name of the project (default *Project1*) and select *Properties*. Then expand *Linker* and then click on *System*. In the *Enable Large Addresses*, select *No (/LARGEADDRESSAWARE:NO)*.

While in the *System* area, verify that the *SubSystem* is *Console*. (if not select it from the list). Then click *Apply* and then click *OK*.

- Then again in the *Solution Explorer*, right click on the name of the application (default *Project1*), select *Properties*, then under *Linker*, select *Advanced* and verify the *Entry Point* is blank (and does not say main).
- Now in the *Solution Explorer*, expand *Project1* (if not done so already), and right click on *Source Files*, hover on *Add*, and click *New Item*. Note that the default is *C ++ File (.cpp)*. At the bottom of the screen use the default name *source* or use a different name and change the extension from *.cpp* to *.asm* (as in *source.asm*). In either case be sure to use a *.asm* extension (because this indicates to use the Microsoft Assembler, MASM, instead of the C ++ compiler) and then click *Add*.
- One can now key in a program or copy and paste a complete program from the "Guide to Assembly Language" website. Then click on *BUILD* and *Build Solution*. If there are no syntax errors, then click on *DEBUG* and then *Start Without Debugging*. (For information on using the Debugger, see problem 10 in Sect. 12.12.)

A.4   MASM Assembly Listings (.1st File)

These directions are for obtaining an assembly listing (.1st file) for 32-bit integer, floating-point, and 64-bit integer MASM programs as created in Sects. A.2 and A.3.

- Right click on the name of the project in the *Solution Explorer*, click on *Properties*, and expand *Microsoft Macro Assembler*. Make sure that if assembling a 32-bit program, such as the one in Sect. 12.9, that the *Platform:* in the top part of the window says *Win32* and if assembling a 64-bit program, such as the one in Sect. 12.10, that the *Platform:* in the top part of the window says *x64*. Then click on *Listing File* and select *Yes(/Sa)* for *List All Available Information*, and type in *$(ProjectName).lst* for *Assembled Code Listing File*. Then click *Apply* and then *OK*.
- After building the program as discussed in the last bullet point in Sects. A.2 and A.3, the .1st file can be found by clicking *File*, then *Open*, then *File...*, and then clicking on the .1st file to open it.
- Be careful not to make changes to the .1st file, but only to the .asm file because the changes made to the .1st file will be ignored by the assembler.

Appendix B: Binary, Hexadecimal, Logic, Arithmetic, and Data Representation

The purpose of this appendix is to introduce the reader to binary and hexadecimal numbers (the latter often abbreviated as simply "hex"), how to convert back and forth between the two, and how to convert them to and from the decimal number system. This chapter also introduces logic, signed integers, and binary arithmetic. Further, it illustrates floating-point numbers and character representations. Although there are calculators which can perform some of these conversions, it is sometimes faster to just do the conversions by hand, which also helps one better understand number representation. If the reader already has knowledge of these concepts, this appendix can either be skipped or serve as a good review.

B.1 Decimal and Binary Numbers

The reader is obviously familiar with the decimal numbering system, otherwise known as the base 10 numbering system, which contains the ten decimal digits 0 through 9. In base 10, the number 2137 can be represented as shown below:

2	1	3	7

$$10^3 \quad 10^2 \quad 10^1 \quad 10^0$$

As should be known, 10^3 is equal to 1000, 10^2 is equal to 100, 10^1 is equal to 10, and 10^0 is equal to 1, where in the number 2137 there is a 2 in the one thousand's position, a 1 in the one hundred's position, a 3 in the ten's position, and a 7 in the one's position. If each number in each position was multiplied by the value of the position they are in, then the result would be 2 times 1000 equals 2000, 1 times 100 equals 100, 3 times 10 equals 30, and 7 times 1 equals 7. If the products of each of these are added together, the answer is 2137:

© Springer Nature Switzerland AG 2020
J. T. Streib, *Guide to Assembly Language*, Undergraduate Topics
in Computer Science, https://doi.org/10.1007/978-3-030-35639-2

$$
\begin{array}{rcl}
2 \ * \ 1{,}000 &=& 2{,}000 \\
1 \ * \ 100 &=& 100 \\
3 \ * \ 10 &=& 30 \\
7 \ * \ 1 &=& 7 \\
\hline
\text{sum} &=& 2{,}137
\end{array}
$$

Although this explanation of the base 10 numbering system should be fairly obvious, it is fundamental to any numbering system, regardless of what base is used. Computers use the binary numbering system, or in other words the base 2 numbering system. It is much easier to distinguish between just two digits, 0 and 1, in electronic circuits than it is to represent 10 different digits. A binary digit is known as a bit, where typically 8 bits make up a byte. For example, the number 10111_2 in the binary number system would be represented as follows:

1	0	1	1	1

$$2^4 \quad 2^3 \quad 2^2 \quad 2^1 \quad 2^0$$

Again, 2^4 equals 16, 2^3 equals 8, 2^2 equals 4, 2^1 equals 2, and 2^0 equals 1. Of course, one can go through the next step of multiplication as done previously with decimal numbers:

$$
\begin{array}{rcl}
1 \ * \ 16 &=& 16 \\
0 \ * \ 8 &=& 0 \\
1 \ * \ 4 &=& 4 \\
1 \ * \ 2 &=& 2 \\
1 \ * \ 1 &=& 1 \\
\hline
\text{sum} &=& 23
\end{array}
$$

However, since a placeholder is only a 1 or a 0, where 0 times anything is 0, one only needs to look at the places where there is a 1 and add up the value of the corresponding placeholder. The result is that there is a 1 in the sixteen's, four's, two's, and one's positions, which adds up to 23. In fact, it is the above method that makes it easy to convert binary numbers to decimal numbers. All one has to do is add up the placeholder positions of those containing a 1 and the result is the decimal equivalent. As another example, given the number 10010_2, what is the decimal equivalent? There are 1 s in the sixteen's and two's positions, so the decimal equivalent is 18. There are a number of exercises at the end of this appendix to allow the reader the opportunity of additional practice.

What about conversion of decimal numbers to binary numbers? There are two methods that can be used to accomplish this task. The first is in a sense a reverse of the method of converting binary to decimal. Instead, one just asks how large a particular power of two could go into a decimal number and then subtracts that power of two. The difference is then moved to the next position and a 1 placed in

Fig. B.1 Conversion of decimal to binary using subtraction method

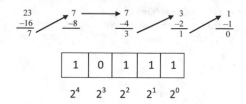

1	0	1	1	1

2^4 2^3 2^2 2^1 2^0

the current position, but if the difference is negative, a 0 is placed in the current position, and the original number is placed in the next column. Using the previous example of 23, where the largest power of two that can be subtracted from 23 is 16, a 1 is placed in the 16's position and after the subtraction a 7 remains. The process is repeated and since an 8 cannot be subtracted from 7 without the results being negative, a 0 is placed in the 8's position. However, a 4 can be subtracted from 7, so a 1 is placed in the 4's position and a 3 remains. Further, a 2 can be subtracted from a 3, so a 1 is placed in the 2's position and a 1 remains, which is placed in the 1's position so that the number is 10111_2. A visual representation of this method showing the subtraction and the corresponding binary digits in the appropriate positions is illustrated in Fig. B.1.

Although the above method works fairly well with smaller numbers, it can get rather cumbersome with larger numbers. Another method is repetitive division by 2, where one just continually divides by 2 and keeps track of the remainders. For example, 23 divided by 2 is 11 with a remainder of 1. This process continues with 11 divided by 2 is 5 with a remainder of 1, 5 divided by 2 is 2 with a remainder of 1, 2 divided by 2 is 1 with a remainder of 0, and 1 divided by 2 is 0 with a remainder of 1. Once the result is a 0, the division should stop and the remainders are written in reverse order as 10111_2, which is correct. An easy way to perform this is shown in Fig. B.2, where the division is repeated until there is a 0, and then the remainders are written from the bottom up, as 10111_2.

Fig. B.2 Conversion of decimal 23 to binary using division method

$$2 \overline{)\,23} \quad \frac{11}{} \quad r1 = 1011\,$$

$$2 \overline{)\,11} \quad \frac{5}{} \quad r1$$

$$2 \overline{)\,5} \quad \frac{2}{} \quad r1$$

$$2 \overline{)\,2} \quad \frac{1}{} \quad r0$$

$$2 \overline{)\,1} \quad \frac{0}{} \quad r1$$

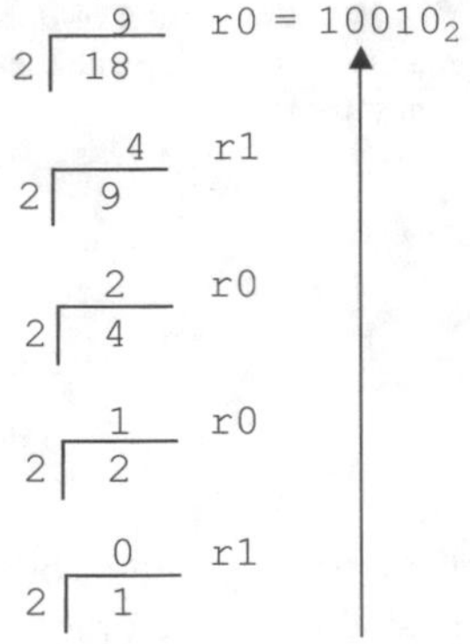

Fig. B.3 Conversion of decimal 18 to binary using division method

$$
\begin{array}{r}
9 \\
\hline
2 \lceil 18
\end{array}
\quad r0 = 10010_2
$$

$$
\begin{array}{r}
4 \quad r1 \\
\hline
2 \lceil 9
\end{array}
$$

$$
\begin{array}{r}
2 \quad r0 \\
\hline
2 \lceil 4
\end{array}
$$

$$
\begin{array}{r}
1 \quad r0 \\
\hline
2 \lceil 2
\end{array}
$$

$$
\begin{array}{r}
0 \quad r1 \\
\hline
2 \lceil 1
\end{array}
$$

As another example, what is the binary equivalent of the decimal number 18, which was converted from binary to decimal previously? Again, either method can be used, where the repetitive division method is illustrated in Fig. B.3.

Once a conversion has been made from one base to another, it can be checked for accuracy by converting the number back to its original base. Although this is not a guarantee that the original conversion was done properly, because a mistake might have been made in both conversions, it does provide a way to check one's work and avoid some possible mistakes.

B.2 Hexadecimal Numbers

Often times, binary numbers need to be stored in an 8-bit byte, a 16-bit word, a 32-bit double word or a 64-bit quad word, where a bit is a binary digit. So, a decimal number 2 would be stored in binary in an 8-bit byte as 00000010, in a 16-bit word as 0000000000000010_2, and so on, where the leading zeros will almost always be shown. As can be seen, this can become very prone to error, where one might accidently leave off a bit, especially when dealing with 32-bit double words or 64-bit quad words. In order to help alleviate this problem, assembly language programmers will often group 4 bits together to form what is known as a hexadecimal digit. Hexadecimal is often just shortened to the word "hex" and stands for the base 16 numbering system. In hex there are 16 digits, where the first 10 digits are the digits 0 through 9 from the decimal numbering system, and the last 6 digits are the letters A through F from the English alphabet. Table B.1 illustrates the numbers 0 through 15 in the decimal, binary, and hex numbering systems.

Conversions between binary and hex are very common, so it is important that the reader can readily convert back and forth between these first 16 numbers where Table B.1 should probably be memorized. The first 10 digits are fairly easy, because they are the same as decimal, but the second 6 letters of the alphabet can be a little awkward at first, but this becomes easier with practice. Once one is comfortable with the equivalencies, the conversion back and forth between hex

Table B.1 Decimal, binary, and hex numbering systems

Decimal	Binary	Hex	Decimal	Binary	Hex
0	0000	0	8	1000	8
1	0001	1	9	1001	9
2	0010	2	10	1010	A
3	0011	3	11	1011	B
4	0100	4	12	1100	C
5	0101	5	13	1101	D
6	0110	6	14	1110	E
7	0111	7	15	1111	F

numbers and binary numbers is fairly easy, where each group of four binary digits is represented by one hex digit and vice versa. The usefulness of hex can be seen in the following, where instead of representing a number in a combination of 16 different ones and zeros, the same number can easily be converted to hex, where it can be represented in just four hex digits:

16-bit Binary   16-bit Hex Equivalent
0000 0010 1100 0101   02C5

One can convert numbers directly from hex to decimal, by using the same techniques learned with binary, where each digit position is a power of 16. Looking at the above number 02C5, it can be represented as done previously and as shown below:

| 0 | 2 | C | 5 |

$$16^3 \quad 16^2 \quad 16^1 \quad 16^0$$

Again, 16^3 is 4096, 16^2 is 256, 16^1 is 16, and 16^0 is 1. Then looking only at the positions that do not contain a 0, then 2 times 256 is 512, C (which is 12) times 16 is 192, and 5 times 1 is 1, and adding 512, 192, and 5 equals 709. The same conversion process learned previously can be performed on the binary number, which should result in the same number, thus helping to confirm that the conversion between the binary and hex was performed properly. Again, this does not guarantee that the conversion was done properly but allows one to check one's work for simple errors. In another example, what is $10EA_{16}$ in decimal? Again, 1 times 4096 is 4096, E (which is 15) times 16 is 240, and A (which is 10) times 1 is 10, resulting in a total of 4346.

The conversion from decimal to hex is a little more difficult. For example, trying to decide how many times the number 4096 goes into a number can be a little challenging, but converting the above number 709 should provide a sufficient example. It is obvious that the number 4096 will not work but the number 256 does twice, so subtracting 512 from 709 leaves 197, so the first two hexadecimal digits are 02. The number 16 goes into 197, 12 times, which is the hexadecimal digit C,

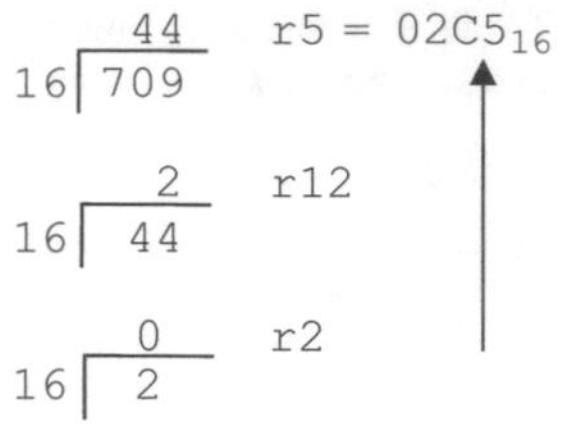

Fig. B.4 Conversion of decimal 709 to hexadecimal
using division method

$$
\begin{array}{r}
44 \\
16\overline{)709}
\end{array} \quad r5 = 02C5_{16}
$$

$$
\begin{array}{r}
2 \\
16\overline{)44}
\end{array} \quad r12
$$

$$
\begin{array}{r}
0 \\
16\overline{)2}
\end{array} \quad r2
$$

leaving the number 5, so the last two digits are C5, resulting in the number 02C5. The repetitive division method can be equally challenging, where 709 divided by 16 is 44 with a remainder of 5, 44 divided by 16 is 2 with a remainder of 12 (which is C in hex), and 2 divided by 16 is 0 with a remainder of 2, for an answer of $02C5_{16}$ as shown in Fig. B.4.

Note that the 12 is converted to C in hex and that a leading 0 is shown in order to show all 16 bits. Given the complexity of dividing by 16, it is sometimes easier to convert a number to binary and then convert the number to hexadecimal. It is also sometimes advisable for especially large numbers to use a calculator, but for the exercises at the end of this appendix, the conversions from decimal to hexadecimal and vice versa will be kept small, so the use of a calculator should not be necessary and is not recommended.

B.3   Overview of Logic

Prior to examining arithmetic, it might be helpful to first look at logic. Recall from high-level languages that a "not" operation causes a false to become a true and a true to become a false. With an "and" operation, both operands need to be true in order for the result to be true, and with an "or" operation, only one operand needs to be true for the result to be true. Whereas an "or" is often called an inclusive-or, another type of "or" operation is the exclusive-or, (often abbreviated as "xor"), where either of the operands can be true for the result to be true, but not both. A convenient way to remember the difference between the two is that the inclusive-or includes the case where both operands are true, and the exclusive-or excludes that case. Note that instead of trucs and falses, ones and zeros can be used instead, as shown in the truth table in Table B.2.

Table B.2   Truth table

x	y	not x	x and y	x or y	x xor y
0	0	1	0	0	0
0	1	1	0	1	1
1	0	0	0	1	1
1	1	0	1	1	0

In the following examples, only 8 bits will be used instead of 16 to 64 bits to make it simpler to understand. Given the following unsigned 8-bit memory location called flag, where the high-order bit on the left is bit position 7 and the low-order bit on the right is bit position 0,

flag | 01101010

what if bit position 2 (third from the right) needed to be set to 1? A *mask* would need to be created to change bit position 2 to a 1 and yet keep all the other bit positions unchanged. Given the previously introduced knowledge of logic, which logic operation and bit pattern should be used to set bit 2? If one thinks about the basic logic operations for a few minutes, one ought to be able to reason it out. Recall that with an "or" operation, either or both of the conditions must be true and with an "xor" operation either one or the other, but not both, condition must be true. Assuming that 1 stands for true and 0 stands for false, if bit position 2 is a 0, and one wants to make it a 1, then in looking at the truth table in Table B.2, either an "or" or an "xor" operation could be used.

However, what if bit position 2 were already a 1? Whether bit position 2 is a 1 or a 0, the task is to set it to a 1. Using an "xor" would cause the 1 to switch to a 0, which is not what is needed. However, using an "or" would cause the result to be a 1 regardless of whether the initial value was a 1 or a 0, which is the intended result. In fact as a general rule, anytime a bit needs to be set, regardless of the previous value, an "or" operation should be used.

What about the other bits? Although bit 2 can be set to a 1, how can it be that the other bits remain unchanged? In further examining the truth table, it should be noticed that a 0 "or" a 0 is a 0, and a 0 "or" a 1 is a 1. In other words, if all the other bit positions in the mask are set to 0, the result would be that those bit positions would remain unchanged. The resulting mask is 00000100 as shown below, where only bit 2 is set to 1 regardless of whether the original bit position is a 1 or a 0, and all the other bit positions remain unchanged:

```
        01101010 = Flag         01101110 = Flag
        00000100 = Mask         00000100 = Mask
or     ─────────────────  or   ─────────────────
        01101110 = Result       01101110 = Result
```

What if instead of setting bit 2 to 1, it needed to be tested whether bit 2 is set to 1? A simple comparison will not do because of the other bits in the byte which may or may not be set to 1. In other words, 00000100 does not equal 01101110, even though bit 2 is set to 1 in both cases. As one might have guessed, a mask is needed to filter out or clear the other bits so that only bit 2 is compared. Again, examining the truth table, it should be noticed that the "and" operation might be a good choice, where a 0 "and" either a 1 or a 0 results in 0, and a 1 "and" either a 0 or a 1 results

Table B.3   Logic operations

Operation	Logic
Set	Or
Clear	And
Test	And
Toggle	Xor

in either a 0 or a 1, respectively. After clearing all of the other bits, all that remains is the value of bit position 2, and all the other bit positions are set to 0:

and
```
        01101110 = Flag
        00000100 = Mask
      ─────────────────
        00000100 = Result
```
and
```
        01101010 = Flag
        00000100 = Mask
      ─────────────────
        00000000 = Result
```

What if one wanted to just reverse or toggle a single bit? At first thought, the "not" operation sounds good, but it must be noted that the not operation would complement all the bits in the byte and not just a single bit. As hinted at previously with the discussion of the inclusive-or, the exclusive-or ("xor") might be a good possibility. Again examining the truth table, a 0 "xor" 1 is a 1, and a 1 "xor" 1 is a 0, thus performing the toggling operation. However, what about the other bits? Well, a 0 "xor" 0 is a 0 and a 1 "xor" 0 is a 1, which would not alter the other bits. Looking at the two examples below, notice that in each case, bit 2 is toggled and the other bits remain the same:

xor
```
        01101010 = Flag
        00000100 = Mask
      ─────────────────
        01101110 = Result
```
xor
```
        01101110 = Flag
        00000100 = Mask
      ─────────────────
        01101010 = Result
```

Given the above, the result is that Table B.3 is a useful summary of which logical operator should be used for which type of operation needed. Although once in a while it seems that some other operation will do, as was indicated in the discussion of the inclusive-or, it is best to stick with the following table to help subsequent programmers who might need to update code and also avoid some difficult logic errors that can take quite a bit (no pun intended…) of time to debug.

B.4   Unsigned Numbers and Addition

Prior to examining signed numbers, it is helpful to first understand unsigned numbers and binary addition. Unsigned numbers are just the non-negative numbers, or in other words the number 0 and the positive numbers. For the sake of simplicity and space, again the following discussion concerning unsigned numbers and addition will be limited to using only 8 bits instead of 16 to 64 bits, but all the concepts can be readily expanded to 16, 32, and 64 bits. Given only 8 bits, what then is the largest unsigned number that could be represented? That number would be 11111111_2, FF_{16}, or 255_{10}. If necessary, use the techniques learned previously to verify that these three numbers are equal to each other.

Binary addition is similar to decimal addition except for the change in base. For example, when two decimal digits are added together such as $1 + 1$, the answer is obviously 2. However, when two binary digits are added together and the sum is greater than the largest digit available in binary, which is the digit 1, the solution is to carry a 1 to the next position. The result is similar to base 10 when adding $9 + 1$, where the result is 10. The same principle holds true in binary, where when a digit is not available, a carry of 1 occurs to the next position. Although this is not a problem when adding numbers such as in $0 + 1$, where the result is 1, but when adding $1 + 1$, the digit 2 is not available, so a 1 is carried into the next position, where $1 + 1$ is 10_2. The following shows the results of adding the four possible bit combinations in binary:

```
  0      0      1      1
 +0     +1     +0     +1
 ───    ───    ───    ───
  0      1      1     10
```

When more than one-digit numbers are being added together in the decimal numbering system, it is possible that a carry of 1 is generated, where the carry is then added to the next column. Although this is second nature to us, an example is shown below:

```
  11   ← Carries
  157
 +978
 ─────
 1035
```

When carrying into the next position, it is possible to have three digits to add together. This is true in binary as well, where the following shows the results of adding the eight possible bit combinations together in binary, where the top digit is the possible carry-in from the previous addition:

```
  0      0      0      0      1      1      1      1   ← Possible carries
  0      0      1      1      0      0      1      1
 +0     +1     +0     +1     +0     +1     +0     +1
 ───    ───    ───    ───    ───    ───    ───    ───
  0      1      1     10      1     10     10     11
```

As with decimal addition, the same occurs in binary, where two or more ones will also generate a carry of 1 into the next column as shown below:

```
  11 111 ← Carries
 00110111
+00110011
─────────
 01101010
```

Although at first binary addition may seem a little awkward, this is just because of one's familiarity with the decimal numbering system. However, with a little practice it becomes much easier and there are exercises at the end of the chapter to help one get used to binary addition.

What happens if one tries to add two numbers that end up with a sum that is too large for an 8-bit byte? For example, consider adding the decimal numbers 202 and 168, which result in the number 370? Remember from the beginning of this section that the largest unsigned positive number that can be stored in a byte is the number 255_{10}. In looking at the binary arithmetic for this example, where 202_{10} equals 11001010_2 and 168_{10} equals 10101000_2, the result is

```
 11001010
+10101000
─────────
101110010
```

With unsigned numbers, it is fairly obvious when a number does not fit in 8 bits, because there is a carry-out of the leftmost or most significant bit position. In this case what is known as the carry flag (CF) would be set to 1 in the central processing unit (CPU). However, as will be seen later, this method does not work when dealing with signed numbers and negative numbers.

B.5   Signed Numbers

Again for the sake of simplicity and space, the following discussion concerning signed numbers will be limited to using only 8 bits instead of 16 or more bits, but all the concepts can be readily expanded to 16, 32, and 64 bits. In decimal, negative numbers are commonly represented by the appearance of the minus sign to the left of the number. Unfortunately in a computer, everything is represented as either a 0 or a 1, which rules out the use of a minus sign. A simple solution would be to use one of the bits in a number to represent the sign of the number, where, for example, a 0 in the leftmost byte could represent a positive number, and a 1 could represent a negative number. Of course, this would limit the largest possible number to only 7 bits, but in exchange, the representation of negative numbers is gained. For example, 01111111_2 would represent a positive 127 and 11111111_2 would represent a negative 127, where the leftmost bit would represent the sign and would be called the sign bit. This method of representing negative numbers is called the signed magnitude method. However, it does have a disadvantage, which is that although the number 0 could be represented as 00000000_2, there also exists the possibility of 10000000_2, which is a negative zero. Another disadvantage is that it is more difficult for a computer to do arithmetic using the signed magnitude method, because beyond requiring circuitry to perform addition in the arithmetic logic unit (ALU) in the CPU, there also needs to be circuitry to perform subtraction. Thus although this method appears to be intuitively easy, it is not used in computer architectures.

Another method to represent negative numbers is the one's complement method, which makes it easier for the CPU to perform arithmetic. The reason for this is that only circuitry for addition is needed because subtraction can be done using the addition of negative numbers, which will be demonstrated shortly.

The way a negative number is represented using one's complement is that for each bit in a number, the complement is taken, similar to using the not instruction. For example, a positive 7 in base 10 is represented as 00000111 in binary. A negative 7 in base 10 is represented in base 2 by merely complementing each bit as 11111000_2. In order to determine whether a number is negative, one first looks at the sign bit. If it is a 0, indicating a positive number, the number is just converted to decimal. If the sign bit is 1, indicating a negative number, then the one's complement must be done first, then it is converted to decimal, and also remember to include a minus sign.

Although arithmetic is easier with one's complement, there still remains a problem with both a positive and a negative zero, where the complement of 00000000_2 is 11111111_2. Although this method has been used in computers in the past, it tends not to be used in more modern computer designs.

Two's complement is just a little more complicated than one's complement, but is easier to perform arithmetic and avoids the problem on both a positive and a negative zero. As with the previous two mechanisms, positive numbers are represented in the same fashion, and the leftmost bit is used as a sign bit. If it is a 0, then the number is positive, otherwise if it is a 1, then the number is negative.

In order to convert a positive number to a negative number, first take the one's complement and then merely add a 1 to the resulting number. For example, a positive 7 is represented as 00000111_2. To convert it to a negative 7, first perform the one's complement of 11111000_2 and then add 1 to the one's complement, thus creating the two's complement: 11111001_2. Although slightly more complicated, it makes arithmetic easier as will be seen shortly and also avoids the problem of both a negative and a positive zero. For example, a 0 is represented as a 00000000_2. The one's complement is 11111111_2, and when a 1 is added to this number to obtain the two's complement, the result is 00000000_2. Although when adding 1, there is a 1 carried out of the leftmost bit position which would cause the carry flag to be set, it should be noted that this does not indicate overflow since this is a signed number as will be explained in the next section. The result is the carry-out discarded and 00000000_2 is a self-complementing number.

What this does is free up one bit combination, 10000000_2, which represents -128 and means that there is one more negative number than there are positive numbers. If one converts 10000000_2 to a positive number, first by taking the one's

Table B.4 Three ways of representing positive and negative numbers

Sign-magnitude		One's-complement		Two's-complement	
Base 2	Base 10	Base 2	Base 10	Base 2	Base 10
01111111	+127	01111111	+127	01111111	+127
00000000	+0	00000000	+0	00000000	0
10000000	−0	11111111	−0	11111111	−1
10000001	−1	11111110	−1	11111110	−2
11111110	−126	10000001	−126	10000001	−127
11111111	−127	10000000	−127	10000000	−128

complement 01111111_2 and then adding 1 to it, it becomes 10000000_2, which makes −128 also a self-complementing number.

Because of the ease of performing arithmetic and the lack of both a positive and a negative zero, this method is the most common method used in today's modern computers, including the Intel processor. Table B.4 shows the range of numbers that are possible in each of the three ways of representing positive and negative numbers.

To calculate the largest positive number that can be stored in n bits, where n equals 8 in this example, note that in all three cases the largest positive number is $2^{n-1} - 1$, which equals $2^7 - 1$, or $128 - 1$, or 127. The largest negative number in sign magnitude or one's complement is $-2^{n-1} - 1$, or −127. But in the case of two's complement as mentioned above, note that the largest negative number is -2^{n-1}, or −128.

B.6   Addition and Subtraction of Signed Numbers

In Sect. B.4, it was seen that if two numbers were added together that were too large for a byte, a carry-out of the leftmost bit was generated and the carry flag was set to 1. However, what about the following case when adding the signed numbers 127 plus 127? When adding these two numbers together, the answer is 254, which is less than 255, so it should not be a problem, should it? It would not be if unsigned numbers were used, because as mentioned previously the largest number that can be stored in an unsigned 8-bit number is 255, or 11111111 in binary. But the question asked here is what would happen if the signed numbers 127 plus 127 were added together. In this case, the largest number that can be stored as a signed 8-bit number is 127, and clearly 254 is larger than 127.

To help clarify this further, it helps to carefully examine the binary equivalent of these numbers when they are added together:

```
  01111111
+01111111
-----------
011111110
```

If the two numbers 127 are considered to be unsigned, then the result of 11111110 is equal to 254 and there is no carry-out of the leftmost bit, so there is no overflow. However, if the numbers are considered to be signed numbers, then it is now the case that the answer of 11111110 is no longer a positive number, but rather a negative number due to the 1 in the sign bit. Using two's complement and converting the above number 11111110 to determine its decimal equivalent, the result is that the answer for adding a 127 plus a 127 is a −2, which is clearly incorrect. How can the sum of two positive numbers end up being a negative number? The answer is that they cannot and this is a case where overflow has occurred. Although as humans we can see that something has gone wrong here, there is a simpler way for the computer to determine an overflow condition. Whether or not there is a carry-out from the leftmost bit position, if the carry into the leftmost bit position is equal to the carry-out of the leftmost bit position, then no overflow has occurred. But if one looks at the above situation, the carry-into the last position is a 1, and the carry-out is a 0, thus indicating that overflow has occurred in this situation, and the overflow flag (OF) in the CPU would be set to 1.

Although this might seem a little difficult, it really is not, because instead of the system trying to keep track of what sign the numbers are and then trying to determine under what circumstances overflow might have occurred, it is much simpler to check these two carry bits. In fact it is much easier than even performing any sort of comparison, and only a simple logic operation can be used. So the question should be which logic operation can be used in this situation? If one takes a few minutes to think about it, the answer is fairly simple. If the carry-in and the carry-out are the same, such as both 0 or both 1, there is no overflow, so the carry flag should be set to 0. If the carry-in and carry-out are different, such as 0 and 1, or 1 and 0, respectively, then there is overflow, so the carry flag should be 1. The results are in the form of the truth table in Table B.5.

Given the previous overview of logic in Sect. B.3, it should be apparent that the above operation is the exclusive-or operation, where the result is a 1 if either of the operands are 1 but not when both operands are either a 1 or a 0. For those who have had or are currently taking a computer organization and architecture course, it should be noted that the computer circuitry in the arithmetic logic unit (ALU) could use a simple exclusive-or gate that uses as input both the carry-in and the carry-out

Table B.5 Overflow

Carry-in	Carry-out	Overflow flag
0	0	0
0	1	1
1	0	1
1	1	0

and the output of the gate fed to the overflow flag that can then be subsequently tested by programmers.

With respect to subtraction, the advantage of using one's complement and two's complement representation of negative numbers over sign magnitude representation of negative numbers is that instead of subtracting the subtrahend from the minuend, subtraction can easily be performed by just negating the subtrahend and then adding it to the minuend.

Besides the absence of a positive and a negative zero, to illustrate the other advantage of using two's complement over one's complement when performing subtraction, it helps to first see how subtraction is performed in one's complement. In order to perform subtraction using one's complement, only the complement of the subtrahend needs to be done and then add, but the problem with this is that the answer is sometimes off by 1 less than it should. In these cases, there is a carry-out of the leftmost bit position and this is added to the answer to obtain the correct answer. For example, $7 - 5$ would be the same as saying $7 + (-5)$ as shown below. But notice that the answer is 1 instead of 2. So in the next line, the carry-out of the leftmost bit position 1 is added to correct the problem:

```
    00000111
+   11111010
   100000001
+ └────────→ 1
    00000010
```

The advantage of two's complement is that 1 never needs to be added and thus the logic circuitry in the ALU is simpler. In order to perform the above subtraction of $7 - 5$, only the equivalent of $7 + (-5)$ needs to be performed by taking the two's complement of the subtrahend and then adding:

```
    00000111
+   11111011

    00000010
```

Unlike using unsigned numbers, it is not readily apparent whether or not overflow has occurred. Although it is not shown, looking at and walking through the addition above, there appears to have been carry-out of the leftmost bit position and the carry flag is set to 1. However, given the previous discussion concerning signed numbers, would this be considered an overflow condition? It would not be, because the carry-into the leftmost bit is the same as the carry-out of the leftmost bit. Looking at a simpler and more obvious example, consider adding $(-1) + (-1)$, where the answer is obviously -2 in base 10. Looking at the addition below, it looks as though when the two numbers are added together, there is a carry-out into the next bit position:

```
  11111111
+ 11111111
```
___
```
111111110
```

Again, the difference here is that overflow is not determined by whether or not there has been a carry-out of the leftmost bit position, but rather overflow is determined again by examining the carry-in into the leftmost bit position and the carry-out of the leftmost bit position. The two numbers are the same and again there has been no overflow.

B.7 Floating-Point Numbers

Similar to how integers can be represented as powers of ten, so too can floating-point numbers. Consider the base-10 number 103.375. As discussed in Sect. B.1, looking first at the whole number part it can be represented as follows:

$$1 * 100 + 0 * 10 + 3 * 1$$

Or using exponents as

$$1 \times 10^2 + 0 * 10^1 + 3 * 10^0$$

The fractional part would also be represented as powers of 10, but instead of whole numbers they would be fractions as follows:

$$3 * 1/10 + 7 * 1/100 + 5 * 1/1000$$

In order to represent the fraction, the exponents would be negative as follows:

$$3 * 10^{-1} + 7 * 10^{-2} + 5 * 10^{-3}$$

So, the complete number would be represented as:

$$1 \times 10^2 + 0 * 10^1 + 3 * 10^0 + 3 * 10^{-1} + 7 * 10^{-2} + 5 * 10^{-3}$$

But how could this be represented in binary? As before, the whole part is converted to binary using the procedures from Sect. B.1, where 103 would be represented as follows:

$$1 * 64 + 1 * 32 + 0 * 16 + 0 * 8 + 1 * 4 + 1 * 2 + 1 * 1$$

Or using exponents,

$$1 * 2^6 + 1 * 2^5 + 0 * 2^4 + 0 * 2^3 + 1 * 2^2 + 1 * 2^1 + 1 * 2^0$$

Before continuing on with the fractional part, it helps to look at the generic case. Just as a whole part of a binary number is represented as powers of 2, so too can the fractional part. For example, each position to the right of the decimal point can be represented as follows where the question marks represent either a 1 or a 0.

$$? * 1/2 + ? * 1/4 + ? * 1/8 + ? * 1/16 + ? * 1/32 \ldots$$

Or represented as powers of 2 using negative exponents:

$$? * 2^{-1} + ? * 2^{-2} + ? * 2^{-3} + ? * 2^{-4} + ? * 2^{-5} \ldots$$

Further, just as there are two methods to convert the whole part of a decimal number to binary, there are two ways to convert the fractional part. The first way is to determine the largest fraction that can be subtracted from the fractional part. To help with the method, the above representations can be expressed as follows:

$$? * 0.5 + ? * 0.25 + ? * 0.125 + ? * 0.0625 + ? * 0.03125 \ldots$$

For example, using the fractional part of the above number 0.375, a 0.5 can't be subtracted from it, so the first position to the right of the decimal point would be a 0. However, a 0.25 could be subtracted leaving 0.125, so the second position would be a 1. Lastly, a 0.125 could be subtracted leaving 0 indicating the process is complete and there would be a 1 in the third position. The following can help illustrate the process,

```
0.375  ──→ 0.375        0.125
- 0.5       - 0.25      -0.125
           ───────      ──────
            0.125   ╱    0.0
```

and the result would be:

$$0 * 2^{-1} + 1 * 2^{-2} + 1 * 2^{-3}$$

So, the representation of 0.375 in decimal would be 0.011 in binary. The advantage of this method is that it works well with numbers that happen to be small numbers that are fractional powers of two. However, the disadvantage is that with numbers that have a large number of binary digits in the fractional part requires one to know or remember the fractional powers of two which can be more difficult than remembering the whole number powers of two.

An alternative method is to use division, although it is different than the method for whole numbers mentioned in Sect. B.1. For example, given the fractional part of the previous number, 0.375, one would need to recognize that it is the equivalent of 3/8. Then using the binary equivalent of both the numerator and denominator, 11/1000, the corresponding division in binary is performed as follows:

```
            .0 1 1
  1000 | 1 1.0 0 0
       - 1 0 0 0
         1 0 0 0
       - 1 0 0 0
               0
```

The problem with this method is that one needs to recognize what fraction is being represented. However, if beginning with a fraction instead of the decimal representation, this method might be easier.

A difficulty with either method that should be mentioned is that just as there are some fractions that cannot be finitely represented in base 10 such as 1/3 there are some fractions that cannot be represented in base 2. One such example is 1/10, or in other words 0.1, which in base 2 would start off as follows:

$$0.00011001100011\ldots$$

The problem with using either conversion method in cases like these is that one would never reach a state where the remainder is zero and it would be difficult to determine if and when the conversion is complete.

An even larger problem is with applications in the financial world. Given that ten cents is one tenth of a dollar, the binary value would need to be rounded and successive rounding would cause errors leading to inaccurate results. The solution to this problem is to use what is known as Binary Coded Decimal (*BCD*) or what is sometimes referred to as just Decimal. Essentially each base-10 digit is converted to a 4-digit binary number.

The disadvantage of BCD is that each of the ten decimal digits 0 through 9 are stored using the bit patterns 0000 through 1001, but the remaining bit patterns 1010 through 1111 are unused in each of the 4-bit groups. The result is that BCD numbers tend to take up more memory and use special arithmetic hardware and instructions. This is the method used in many calculators and the COBOL programming language, which is useful with currency applications. A complete discussion of BCD is beyond the scope of this text and further information can be found in a text such as *Introduction to Assembly Language Programming* by Dandamudi [2].

Continuing, in the early days of computing floating-point numbers were represented using different formats. To help create a common representation, the IEEE (Institute for Electrical and Electronics Engineers) created Standard 754 in 1985, updated it in 2008, and made revisions in 2019 [1]. The three formats are Single, Double, and Extended precision using 32, 64, and 80 bits and are represented in MASM as REAL4, REAL8, and REAL10, respectively.

Using more bits in the exponent allows for larger numbers and more bits in the fractional part allows for more precision. However, the tradeoff is using more memory, especially with arrays. Since the concepts for each of the formats is similar, single precision will be discussed here and the format is as follows:

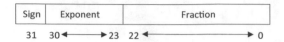

As with integers the sign bit indicates the sign of the number: 0 for positive and 1 for negative. The fractional part is the entire number represented as a fraction, with the leftmost 1 not shown. Since all numbers except for 0.0 will have at least one digit that is a 1, there is no need to store it in this format. For example, the binary number 0.011 would be left justified as 0.1 and to indicate that a shift has occurred the exponent portion of the number would be the equivalent of 2^{-2}. How this is actually represented in binary will be discussed shortly. Although this might seem acceptable for fractions, what of whole numbers? The same thing is done except in the opposite direction. For example, the binary number 110.101 would be represented in the fraction part as 0.10101 and the exponent would be the equivalent of 2^2.

But notice that in addition to whether the entire number is negative as indicated by the sign bit, the exponent can also be positive or negative. Does there need to be yet another sign bit? The answer is no, because the exponent can be what is called *normalized* so that a sign bit for the exponent is not necessary. Note that since there are 8 bits for the exponent, it could represent the numbers -128 to 127. However, some of the bit combinations in the IEEE standard are reserved for specific numbers or conditions and the result is that the range of possible exponent values are from -126 to 127 instead. So, what if the number 127 was added to each of these possible numbers? Then range would be from 1 to 254, thus there is no need for a negative number. To denormalize an exponent the number 127 is merely subtracted. Of the special bit combination, if the sign is 0, the exponent is 0, and the fraction is 0, then it represents the number 0.0.

Recall that 0.375 is 0.011 in binary and would be represented as $0.1 * 2^{-2}$. To represent the exponent of -2 the number 127 would be added, thus making the normalized exponent 125 and would be represented as the 8-bit binary number 01111101. So, the entire number would be represented with spaces inserted to help readability as:

0 01111101 10000000000000000000000

What of whole numbers, such as 23? It would be represented as 10111 in binary. Since all numbers are represented in the fractional part, it would need to be shifted to the right 4 positions which would $0.0111 * 2^4$. To convert the exponent, 127 is added to 4 which results in 131 and would be 10000011 in binary. The complete number would be represented as:

0 10000011 01110000000000000000000

Returning the original number presented at the beginning of the section, 103.375, with the binary equivalent of:

1100111.011

The number would need to be shifted to the right 6 positions which would $0.100111011 * 2^6$. To convert the exponent, 127 is added to 6 which results in 133 and would be 10000101 in binary. The complete number would be represented as:

$$0\ 10000101\ 10011101100000000000000$$

Lastly, what of a negative number such as -48.5? It would be represented as 110000.1 in binary. The sign bit would set to 1 and the number would be shifted to the right 5 positions which would result in $0.10001 * 2^5$. To convert the exponent 127 would be added which would be 10000100 in binary. The results would be as follows:

$$1\ 10000100\ 10001000000000000000000$$

Note that additional exercises can be found in Sect. B.11.

B.8 Characters

Although a computer uses binary to perform various logic and arithmetic operations, all the input and output are performed using character data. For simple letters and strings, the data that is input stays in character format, is processed as such, and then in turn is output as character data. However, when it comes to numbers that need to be processed using arithmetic, the character representation of the numbers needs to first be converted to base 2 so that the arithmetic logic unit (ALU) portion of the CPU can perform the arithmetic, and if the numbers need to be output, they will then need to be converted back to characters so that they can be displayed. This is one of the reasons why assembly language input/output can be difficult, because in addition to special routines necessary to communicate with the device in question, specialized operating system functions must be called or unique routines need to be written to perform the conversions. This is also one of the reasons why it is helpful to have the ability to use the input/output facilities of the C programming language as discussed in Chap. 2. However, even character data needs to be stored in ones and zeros and various codes have been developed to represent the character data. On mainframe computers, many times an 8-bit format called EBCDIC (Extended Binary Coded Decimal Interchange Code) is used. The Java programming language uses Unicode, which is a 16-bit code that can incorporate many of the symbols from languages other than English. However, many microcomputers and some interface devices use an 8-bit code called ASCII (American Standard Code for Information Interchange).

The hexadecimal representations of these characters can be found in the table in the next section. It is interesting to note that not only are the character representations of the digits in ascending order but also all of the upper and lowercase letters are in ascending order, which makes it possible to sort character data, because the letter A has a lower value than the letter B, and so on. It is also interesting to note that the upper and lowercase representations of the alphabetic letters differ by only 1 bit, thus making is easy to convert between the two using simple logic operations, as described in Chap. 6. To see which bit, convert the hex codes in the table to binary using the techniques described in Sect. B.2.

B.9   Hex/ASCII Table

Hex	Character	Hex	Character	Hex	Character	Hex	Character
00	null	20	space	40	@	60	`
01	☺	21	!	41	A	61	a
02	☻	22	"	42	B	62	b
03	♥	23	#	43	C	63	c
04	♦	24	$	44	D	64	d
05	♣	25	%	45	E	65	e
06	♠	26	&	46	F	66	f
07		27	'	47	G	67	g
08	♀	28	(	48	H	68	h
09		29	)	49	I	69	i
0A	line feed	2A	*	4A	J	6A	j
0B	♂	2B	+	4B	K	6B	k
0C	♀	2C	,	4C	L	6C	l
0D	return	2D	–	4D	M	6D	m
0E	♫	2E	.	4E	N	6E	n
0F	☼	2F	/	4F	O	6F	o
10	►	30	0	50	P	70	p
11	◄	31	1	51	Q	71	q
12	↕	32	2	52	R	72	r
13	‼	33	3	53	S	73	s
14	¶	34	4	54	T	74	t
15	§	35	5	55	U	75	u
16	▬	36	6	56	V	76	v
17	↨	37	7	57	W	77	w
18	↑	38	8	58	X	78	x
19	↓	39	9	59	Y	79	y
1A	→	3A	:	5A	Z	7A	z
1B	←	3B	;	5B	[	7B	{
1C	∟	3C	<	5C	\	7C	|
1D	↔	4D	=	5D	]	7D	}
1E	▲	4E	>	5E	^	7E	~
1F	▼	5F	?	5F	_	7F	⌂

Hex	Character	Hex	Character	Hex	Character	Hex	Character
80	Ç	A0	á	C0	└	E0	α
81	ü	A1	í	C1	┴	E1	ß
82	é	A2	ó	C2	┬	E2	Γ
83	â	A3	ú	C3	├	E3	π
84	ä	A4	ñ	C4	─	E4	Σ
85	à	A5	Ñ	C5	┼	E5	σ
86	å	A6	ª	C6	╞	E6	µ
87	ç	A7	º	C7	╟	E7	τ
88	ê	A8	¿	C8	╚	E8	Φ
89	ë	A9	⌐	C9	╔	E9	Θ
8A	è	AA	¬	CA	╩	EA	Ω
8B	ï	AB	½	CB	╦	EB	δ
8C	î	AC	¼	CC	╠	EC	∞
8D	ì	AD	¡	CD	═	ED	φ
8E	Ä	AE	«	CE	╬	EE	ε
8F	Å	AF	»	CF	╧	EF	∩
90	É	B0	░	D0	╨	F0	≡
91	æ	B1	▒	D1	╤	F1	±
92	Æ	B2	▓	D2	╥	F2	≥
93	ô	B3	│	D3	╙	F3	≤
94	ö	B4	┤	D4	╘	F4	⌠
95	ò	B5	╡	D5	╒	F5	⌡
96	û	B6	╢	D6	╓	F6	÷
97	ù	B7	╖	D7	╫	F7	≈
98	ÿ	B8	╕	D8	╪	F8	°
99	Ö	B9	╣	D9	┘	F9	∙
9A	Ü	BA	║	DA	┌	FA	·
9B	¢	BB	╗	DB	█	FB	√
9C	£	BC	╝	DC	▄	FC	ⁿ
9D	¥	BD	╜	DD	▌	FD	²
9E	₧	BE	╛	DE	▐	FE	■
9F	ƒ	BF	┐	DF	▀	FF	

B.10 Summary

- All numbering systems use the powers of their respective bases.
- It is helpful to memorize the first 15 numbers of binary and hexadecimal to help with conversions between the two.
- When using unsigned numbers, the carry flag indicates overflow.
- Use "or," "and," and "xor," to set, test or clear, and toggle a bit, respectively.
- There are three methods to represent negative numbers: signed magnitude, one's complement, and two's complement. The first two have the problem of both a positive and a negative zero, whereas the latter has an extra negative number.
- The two's complement method is the most common method to represent signed numbers and it is the method used in the Intel processor.

- Overflow occurs during addition with two's complement numbers when the carry-into the leftmost bit position is different than the carry-out of the leftmost bit position.
- Binary Coded Decimal (BCD) represents each decimal digit as 4 binary digits.
- 32-bit floating-point numbers are represented using the IEEE standard with one bit for the sign, 8 bits for the exponent, and 23 bits for the fraction.

B.11   Exercises (Items Marked with an ∗ Have Solutions in Appendix D)

1. Convert the following "unsigned" binary numbers to their decimal equivalent:

    *A. 00011111
    B. 01011110
    *C. 01111110
    D. 10101011
    E. 10101100

2. Convert the following "unsigned" decimal numbers to their binary equivalent:

    *A. 27
    B. 82
    *C. 110
    D. 245
    E. 127

3. Convert the following "signed" binary numbers to the decimal equivalent:

    *A. 01010111
    B. 11111110
    *C. 10101111
    D. 01110111
    E. 11001010

4. Convert the following "signed" decimal numbers to binary (use only 8 bits):

    *A. 54
    B. 127
    *C. −23
    D. −125
    E. −201

5. Convert the following "unsigned" decimal numbers to hexadecimal (use only 8 bits):

    *A. 73
    B. 162
    *C. 200
    D. 255
    E. 142

6. Convert the following "unsigned" hexadecimal numbers to decimal:

    *A. 2A
    B. 7E
    *C. AB
    D. EF
    E. 8C

7. Convert the following "signed" decimal numbers to hexadecimal (use only 8 bits):

    *A. 18
    B. 100
    *C. -79
    D. -112
    E. -247

8. Convert the following "signed" hexadecimal numbers to decimal:

    *A. 34
    B. 7A
    *C. 85
    D. E0
    E. F7

9. Convert the following binary numbers to hexadecimal, where signed or unsigned is irrelevant:

    *A. 01011100
    B. 10111111
    *C. 01111101
    D. 10001001
    E. 11000010

10. Convert the following hexadecimal numbers to binary, where signed or unsigned is irrelevant:

   *A. 12
   B. 6D
   *C. A1
   D. FE
   E. DA

11. Using the ASCII table, convert the following ASCII characters to their binary equivalent:

   *A. "9"
   B. "B"
   *C. "q"
   D. "*"
   E. "?"

12. Using the ASCII table, convert the following binary numbers to their ASCII equivalent:

   *A. 01000000
   B. 01111001
   *C. 01010001
   D. 01101000
   E. 00100001

13. Add the following "signed" binary numbers. Indicate whether or not overflow has occurred:

   *A. 00001001 + 00010111
   B. 11101010 + 11110111
   *C. 00101111 + 11111000
   D. 01101111 + 01110000
   E. 01111111 + 00000001

14. Given the following "signed" binary numbers, perform the subtraction by taking the two's complement of the subtrahend and then adding. Indicate whether or not overflow has occurred:

   *A. 10001000 - 00000001
   B. 01111011 - 01110010
   *C. 01011111 - 10111100
   D. 10000001 - 01011101
   E. 01111111 - 00010111

15. Convert the following base-10 numbers to binary. Do not put them in IEEE format.

   *a. 33.125
   b. 0.0625
   c. 127.25
   d. -128.75

16. Convert the following base-10 numbers to IEEE format using 32 bits. Show the results in binary.

   *a. 65.5
   b. 0.1875
   c. 256.0
   d. 255.25

17. Convert the following base-10 numbers to IEEE format using 32 bits. Show the results in hexadecimal.

   *a. 1.0
   b. 63.0
   c. -2.0
   d. 15.5

18 Convert the following hex numbers that are in 32-bit IEEE format to their equivalent in base-10. The process is the reverse of converting base-10 to IEEE format.

   *a. 42030000h
   b. 42808000h
   c. C0000000h
   d. 3E000000h

Appendix C: Selected Assembly Language Instructions

This appendix is useful for quick reference. It does not contain a complete listing of all instructions but rather only those used in this text. For further descriptions of the following instructions, use the index to find the page number in the text for more complete descriptions and examples of each of the following instructions. For a more complete list of instructions, see Appendix D of *Introduction to Assembly Language Programming* by Dandamudi, Springer, 2005 [2].

Abbreviations used	Selected flag abbreviations
reg = register	C = Carry flag
mem = memory	O = Overflow flag
imm – immediate	Z = Zero flag
xx = placeholder	S = Sign flag

Instruction	Operands	Status flags affected in **eflags** register
add	reg,reg reg,imm reg,mem mem,reg mem,imm	C, O, Z, S are modified
	Description:	Adds the contents of the source (second) operand to the destination (first) operand.
and	reg,reg reg,imm reg,mem mem,reg mem,imm	C and O set to 0 Z and S are modified
	Description:	Logical bit-wise and of the source (second) operand on the destination (first) operand.

© Springer Nature Switzerland AG 2020
J. T. Streib, *Guide to Assembly Language*, Undergraduate Topics
in Computer Science, https://doi.org/10.1007/978-3-030-35639-2

call	label	none are affected

Description: The address of the next instruction after the `call` instruction is saved on the stack and control is transferred to the location `label`.

cdq	none	none are affected

Description: Converts double to quad. Converts the 32-bit integer in the `eax` register to a 64-bit integer in the `edx:eax` register pair, where the sign bit of `eax` is propagated into the `edx` register.

Cqo	none	none are affected

Description: Converts quad to oct. Converts the 64-bit integer in the `rax` register to a 128-bit integer in the `rdx:rax` register pair, where the sign bit of `rax` is propagated into the `rdx` register.

cld	none	none

Description: Clears the direction flag to 0.

cmp	reg,reg	C,O,Z,S are modified
	reg,imm	
	reg,mem	
	mem,reg	
	mem,imm	

Description: An implied subtraction of the second from the first operand, where neither operand is altered and the flags set accordingly.

cmpsb	none	C,O,Z,S are modified

Description: Compares a string of bytes pointed at by the `esi` and `edi` registers and sets the flags accordingly. If the direction flag is cleared using `cld`, the `esi` and `edi` registers are incremented, otherwise if the direction flag is set using `std`, the `esi` and `edi` registers are decremented. The instruction is often used with the `rep` prefix.

dec	reg	O,Z,S are modified
	mem	C is not affected

Description: The operand is decremented by 1.

div   reg   C,O,Z,S are undefined
                 mem

                 Description: See the `idiv` instruction.

fadd   mem   none are affected
                 none

                 Description: Floating-point add. Add mem to ST(0) in the floating-point
                                  register stack. Without operand, add ST(0) to ST(1), pop ST(0),
                                  and sum moves up to ST(0).

fcomi   none   C,Z,P(Parity) are modified
                              O,S,A(Auxiliary) are set to 0

                 Description: Floating-point compare. Compares ST(0) with ST(i), both in the
                                  floating-point register stack, and sets the carry, parity, and zero
                                  flags.

fcomip   none   C,Z,P(Parity) are modified
                              O,S,A(Auxiliary)are set to 0

                 Description: Floating-point compare and pop. Compares ST(0) with ST(i),
                                  both in the floating-point register stack, sets the carry, parity, and
                                  zero flags, and pops the values from the floating-point stack.

fdiv   mem   none are affected
                 none

                 Description: Floating-point divide. Divides mem by ST(0) in the floating-point
                                  register stack. Without operand, divides ST(1) by ST(0) in the
                                  floating-point register stack, pops ST(0), and quotient moves up
                                  to ST(0).

fiadd   mem   none are affected

                 Description: Floating-point integer add. Converts mem to floating-point and
                                  adds to ST(0) in the floating-point register stack.

fild   mem   none are affected

                 Description: Floating-point integer load. Converts integer mem to floating-
                                  point and loads (pushes) it onto ST(0) in the floating-point
                                  register stack.

fistp   mem   none are affected

                 Description: Floating-point integer store and pop. Pop ST(0) from floating-
                                  point register stack, convert to integer (rounded), and store in
                                  mem.

fisttp   mem   none are affected

          Description: Floating-point integer store, truncate, and pop. Pop ST(0) from floating-point register stack, convert to integer (truncated), and store in mem.

fld   mem   none are affected

          Description: Floating-point load. Loads, or in other words pushes, mem onto the floating-point register stack, ST(0).

fmul   mem   none are affected
          none

          Description: Floating-point multiply. Multiplies ST(0) on floating-point register stack by mem. Without operand multiply ST(1) by ST(0), pop ST(0), and product moves up to ST(0).

fst   mem   none are affected

          Description: Floating-point store. Store the top element of the floating-point register stack ST(0) into mem. This instruction does not pop the value, but rather peeks at it and the value remains at the top of the stack ST(0).

fstp   mem   none are affected

          Description: Floating-point store and pop. Pop and store the top element ST(0) in the floating-point register stack into mem.

fsub   mem   none are affected
          none

          Description: Floating-point subtract. Subtract mem from ST(0) in the floating-point register stack. Without operand, subtract ST(0) from ST(1), pop ST(0), and difference moves up to ST(0).

idiv   reg   C,O,Z,S are undefined
          mem

          Description: The dividend in the eax register is divided by the divisor in the operand. The quotient is placed in the eax register and the remainder is placed in the edx register. The div instruc- tion is for unsigned division, whereas the idiv instruction is used for signed division. Prior to using the idiv instruction, be sure to use the cdq instruction with 32-bit integers and cdo with 64-bit integers. With 64-bits, rax and rdx are used instead.

| **imul** | reg | C,O are modified |
| | mem | Z,S are undefined |

Description: The multiplicand in the eax register is multiplied by the multiplier in the operand. The product is placed in the edx:eax register pair, where the high-order bits are in edx and the low-order bits are in eax. The mul instruction is for unsigned multiplication, whereas the imul instruction is used for signed multiplication. With 64-bits, rax and rdx are used instead.

| **inc** | reg | O,Z,S are modified |
| | mem | C is not affected |

Description: The operand is incremented by 1.

| **jecxz** | label | none are affected |

Description: Control is transferred to the location label when the ecx register is equal to 0.

| **jmp** | label | none are affected |

Description: Control is unconditionally transferred to the location label.

| **jxx** | label | none are affected |

Description: Control is conditionally transferred to the location label, depending on the particular instruction and the corresponding flag. See the list below:

Instruction:	**Description:**
je/jne	jump equal/jump not equal
jg/jng	jump greater than/jump not greater than
jge/jnge	jump greater than or equal/jump not greater than or equal
jl/jnl	jump less than/jump not less than
jle/jnle	jump less than or equal/ jump not less than or equal
ja/jna	jump above/jump not above
jae/jnae	jump above or equal/jump not above or equal
jb/jnb	jump below/jump not below
jbe/jnbe	jump below or equal/jump not below or equal

	`jz/jnz`	jump zero/jump not zero
	`jc/jnc`	jump carry/jump not carry
	`jp/jnp`	jump parity (even)/jump not parity
	`js/jns`	jump sign (negative)/jump not sign
	`jo/jno`	jump overflow/jump not overflow

lea   `reg,mem`   `none are affected`

Description: The address of the source (second) operand is copied into the destination (first) operand.

lodsb   `none`   `none are affected`

Description: Load the `al` register from a string of bytes from where the `esi` register is pointing. If the direction flag is cleared using `cld`, the `esi` register is incremented, otherwise if the direction flag is set using `std`, the `esi` register is decremented.

loop   `label`   `none are affected`

Description: The contents of the `ecx` register are decremented, and if it is not zero, control is transferred to the location `label`, otherwise control falls through to the next instruction after the `loop` instruction.

mov   `reg,reg`   `C,O,Z,S are modified`
             `reg,imm`
             `reg,mem`
             `mem,reg`
             `mem,imm`

Description: The contents of the source (second) operand are copied to the destination (first) operand.

movsb   `none`   `none are affected`

Description: Copies a string of bytes from where the `esi` register is pointing to where the `edi` register is pointing. If the direction flag is cleared using `cld`, the `esi` and `edi` registers are incremented, otherwise if the direction flag is set using `std`, the `esi` and `edi` registers are decremented. The instruction is often used with the `rep` prefix.

movsxd   reg,reg   none are affected
                reg,mem

Description: Move with sign-extend double. Copies a 32-bit integer from
                the source register on the right to a 64-bit destination on the
                left and extends the sign-bit from bit 31 through to bit 63.

mul   reg   C,O are modified
                mem   Z,S are undefined

Description: See the `imul` instruction.

neg   reg   C,O,Z,S are modified
                mem

Description: Negates the operand, or in other words take the two's comple-
                ment of the operand.

nop   none   none are affected

Description: No operation.

not   reg   none are affected
                mem

Description: Performs a logical not (one's complement) operation on the
                operand.

or   reg,reg   C and O set to 0
                reg,imm   Z and S are modified
                reg,mem
                mem,reg
                mem,imm

Description: Logical bit-wise inclusive or of the source (second) operand
                on the destination (first) operand.

pop   reg   none are affected
                mem

Description: Pops a value from the stack into the operand.

popad   none   none are affected

Description: Pops the registers on the stack into the `edi`, `esi`, `ebp`, `esp`,
                `ebx`, `edx`, `ecx`, and `eax` registers.

push	reg	none are affected
	mem	
	imm	

Description: Pushes the operand onto the stack.

| **pushad** | none | none are affected |

Description: Pushes the eax, ecx, edx, ebx, esp, ebp, esi, and edi registers onto the stack.

rep	none	Z is modified
repe		C, O, and S are not affected
repne		

Description: Can be used as a prefix with instructions like cmpsb, lodsb, movsb, scasb, and stosb. The rep prefix decrements the ecx register and repeats until it is 0. The repe and repne both decrement ecx and repeat until it is 0, but repe will repeat while equal and stop if the result of a comparison is not equal and the repne will repeat while not equal and stop when the result of a comparison is equal.

| **ret** | none | none are affected |

Description: Control is transferred to the location immediately following the corresponding call instruction.

rol	reg,cl	C and O are modified
ror	reg,imm	Z and S are not affected
	mem,cl	
	mem,imm	

Description: The contents of the destination (first) operand are rotated to the left using the rol instruction or to the right using the ror instruction by the number of bits indicated in the second operand. When rotated to the left, the leftmost bit is moved into the rightmost bit position and when rotated to the right, the rightmost bit is moved into the leftmost position. On an 8086/8088 processor, imm can only be a 1.

sal	reg,cl	C, O, Z, and S are modified
sar	reg,imm	
	mem,cl	
	mem,imm	

Description: The contents of the destination (first) operand are shifted to the left using the `sal` instruction or to the right using the `sar` instruction by the number of bits indicated in the second operand. When shifted to the left, the leftmost bit is moved into the carry flag and the rightmost bit position is filled with a 0. When shifted to the right, the rightmost bit is moved into the carry flag and the leftmost bit position is copied into both the next position to the right and onto itself to maintain the sign bit. On an 8086/8088 processor, `imm` can only be a 1.

scasb   none   `C,O,Z,S are modified`

Description: Scans a string of bytes pointed at by the `edi` register for the character in the `al` register and when found sets the flags accordingly. If the direction flag is cleared using `cld`, the `edi` register is incremented, otherwise if the direction flag is set using `std`, the `edi` register is decremented. The instruction is often used with the `rep` prefix.

shl   `reg,cl`   `C, O, Z, and S are modified`
shr   `reg,imm`
             `mem,cl`
             `mem,imm`

Description: The contents of the destination (first) operand are shifted to the left using the `shl` instruction or to the right using the `shr` instruction by the number of bits indicated in the second operand. When shifted to the left, the leftmost bit is moved into the carry flag and the rightmost bit position is filled with a 0. When shifted to the right, the rightmost bit is moved into the carry flag and the leftmost bit position is filled with a 0. On an 8086/8088 processor, `imm` can only be a 1.

std   none   none

Description: Sets the direction flag to 1.

stosb   none   `none are modified`

Description: Stores the contents of the `al` register in a string of bytes pointed at by the `edi` register. If the direction flag is cleared using `cld`, the `edi` register is incremented, otherwise if the direction flag is set using `std`, the `edi` register is decremented. The instruction can be used with the `rep` prefix.

sub   reg, reg   C, O, Z, S are modified
                 reg, imm
                 reg, mem
                 mem, reg
                 mem, imm

         Description: Subtracts the contents of the source (second) operand from
                           the destination (first) operand.

test   reg, reg   C and O set to 0
                 reg, imm   Z and S are modified
                 reg, mem
                 mem, reg
                 mem, imm

         Description: Logical bit-wise and between the source (second) operand to
                           the destination (first) operand, where the destination (first)
                           operand is not altered and only the flags are altered.

xchg   reg, reg   none are modified
                 reg, mem
                 mem, reg

         Description: The contents of the source (second) operand are exchanged
                           with the destination (first) operand.

xor   reg, reg   C and O set to 0
                 reg, imm   Z and S are modified
                 reg, mem
                 mem, reg
                 mem, imm

         Description: Logical bit-wise exclusive or of the source (second) operand
                           on the destination (first) operand.

Appendix D: Answers to Selected Exercises

Chapter 1

1.A.   Correct
1.C.   Correct
1.F.   Incorrect, cannot include a decimal point.

2.A.   `initial byte ?`
2.C.   `x byte 'P'`
      `x byte 'Q'`
2.E.   `count sdword 0`

3.A.   Incorrect, `move` should be `mov`
3.C.   Correct
3.E.   Incorrect, cannot move a memory location into an immediate value
3.H.   Correct

4.A.   `mov i,1`
4.C.   Direct translation :
```
mov c,2
mov eax,c
mov b,eax
mov eax,b
mov a,eax
```

5.A.   `mov a,'B'`
5.C.   Direct translation :
```
mov d,'E'
mov al,d
mov e,al
```
5.E.   Direct translation :
```
mov a,'2'
mov b,'?'
mov a,b
```

© Springer Nature Switzerland AG 2020
J. T. Streib, *Guide to Assembly Language*, Undergraduate Topics
in Computer Science, https://doi.org/10.1007/978-3-030-35639-2

Chapter 2

1.A.   Correct
1.C.   Incorrect, delete the ADDR prior to number

3.   xb=b1byb=b2
        blank line
        blank line
        z=3

Chapter 3

1.A.   Incorrect, delete the , 1
1.C.   Incorrect, cannot add memory to memory
1.E.   Incorrect, cannot subtract from an immediate value

2.A.
```
mov  eax,3
imul number
mov  product,eax
```
2.C.
```
mov  eax,number
mov  ebx,2
cdq
idiv ebx
mov  answer,eax
```
3.A.
```
mov  eax,x
imul y
mov  ecx,eax
mov  eax,z
mov  ebx,2
imul ebx
add  ecx,eax
mov  x,ecx
```
3.C.
```
mov  eax,num3
imul num4
mov  ebx,eax
mov  eax,num1
cdq
idiv num2
sub  eax,ebx
mov  total,eax
```

4.A.
```
dec  i
```
4.C.
```
mov  eax,x
add  eax,y
neg  eax
mov  z,eax
```

Chapter 4

1.A.   Incorrect, change = to ==

1.C.   Although syntactically correct, it might not be what was intended logically

```
3.A.    if01:      cmp w,1
                    jne endif01
                    cmp x,2
                    jne endif01
        then01:    dec y
        endif01:   nop
3.C.    if02:      cmp w,1
                    je and02 :
                    cmp x,2
                    jne endif02
        and02:     cmp y,3
                    jne endif02
        then02:    inc z
        endif02:   nop
```

Chapter 5

1.A.   Incorrect, .for and .endfor do not exist in MASM
1.C.   Correct

3.A   Three times

```
5.A     mov edx,eax
        mov eax,0
        .while(edx >= ebx)
        sub edx, ebx
        inc eax
        .endw
```

Chapter 6

1.A.   Correct
1.C.   Incorrect: rotate is not an instruction, use rol or ror.
1.E.   Correct

```
2.B.    mov eax,amount
        add eax,number
        sal eax,2        ; multiply by 2
        mov result,eax
```

Chapter 7

1.A.   Incorrect: it should be `ret`, not `return`.
1.C.   Incorrect : there shouldn't be a decimal point prior to the `if` directive.
1.E.   Correct

Chapter 8

1.A.   Correct
1.C.   Correct
1.E.   Correct

2.A.   5
2.C.   200
2.E.   200

3.A.   `mov num+0,1`
3.C.   ```
mov eax,num[ebx]
mov num+4[ebx],eax   ; or better yet: mov num[ebx+4]
```

4.A.    5
4.B.    20
4.E.    3

## Chapter 9

1.A.    Incorrect, it should be `movsb`
1.C.    Correct
1.E.    Incorrect, it should be `rep stosb`

2.A.    ecx = 2, esi=undefined, edi = 103, al = "c"
2.C.    ecx = 1, esi=104, edi = 109, al = undefined

## Chapter10

1.A.    8

2.A.    ```
fld x
fld y
fsub
fld z
fadd
fstp answer
```

Chapter 11

1.A.   0000000000000000h

1.C.   001100220033FFFFh

Chapter 12

1. $2^2 = 4$ opcodes, $2^0 = 1$ register, $2^6 = 64$ memory locations
3. $2^5 = 32$ opcodes, $2^2 = 4$ registers, $2^9 = 512$ memory locations
6.   03CB and 0000001111001011
7.   90 and 10010000
8.   23C3 and 0010001111000011

Appendix B

1.A. 31_{10}
1.C. 126_{10}

2.A. 00011011_2
2.C. 01101110_2

3.A. 87_{10}
3.C. -81_{10}

4.A. 00110110_2
4.C. 11101001_2

5.A. 49_{16}
5.C. $C8_{16}$

6.A. 42_{10}
6.C. 171_{10}

7.A. 12_{16}
7.C. $B1_{16}$

8.A. 52_{10}
8.C. -123_{10}

9.A. $5C_{16}$
9.C. $7D_{16}$

10.A. 00010010_2
10.C. 10100001_2

11.A. 00111001_2
11.C. 01110001_2

12.A.   ''@''
12.C.   ''Q''

13.A. 00100000_2 No Overflow
13.C. 00100111_2 No Overflow

14.A. 10000111_2 No Overflow
14.C. 10100011_2 Yes Overflow

15.A 100001.001_2

16.A $0\ 10000101\ 00000110000000000000000_2$

17.A   3F800000h

18.A   32.75

Glossary

The descriptions of terms in this glossary should not be used in lieu of the complete descriptions in the text. Rather they serve as a quick review and reminder of the basic meaning of various terms that are first introduced in *italics* in the text. Should a more complete description be needed, the index can guide the reader to the appropriate pages where the terms are discussed in more detail.

Absolute   When a memory location's address is referenced from location 0 in RAM, then it is known as an absolute address.

Aliasing   Referencing the same memory location using two different names. In general, this should be avoided.

Assembler   A program that converts an assembly language program into a machine language program.

Assembly language   A low-level language that uses mnemonics and is converted to machine language by an assembler.

Bankers rounding   Floating-point numbers ending in 0.5 are rounded to the nearest even number to avoid the accumulation of rounding errors.

BCD   Binary Coded Decimal.

Bit bucket   A term used to describe where bits go when the shifted off the end of a register or a memory location.

Bit-wise   Whenever there are operations on individual bits within a register or memory locations, these are known as bit-wise operations, such as when using logic, shift, or rotate instructions.

Conditional assembly   A technique in a macro during assembly where one set of instructions can be generated under one set of circumstances and yet an entirely different set of instructions can be generated under other circumstances.

CPU   Central Processing Unit.

Directive   A command that tells the assembler what to do, as opposed to the CPU.

Dynamic   When a value is calculated during execution time as opposed to assembly time, it is known as dynamic.

FIFO   First In Last Out as with a stack.

Instruction   A command that tells the CPU what to do as opposed to the assembler.

© Springer Nature Switzerland AG 2020
J. T. Streib, *Guide to Assembly Language*, Undergraduate Topics
in Computer Science, https://doi.org/10.1007/978-3-030-35639-2

Immediate   An immediate value is a piece of data that is part of an instruction instead of being in a memory location or a register.

LIFO   Last In First Out as with a queue.

Little endian order   This means that the least-significant byte of an operand, or a word, double word, or quad word appears first in memory, followed by the next least-significant byte, and so on.

Load   A load operation is the copying of the contents of a memory location or immediate value into a register.

Machine language   The native language of a processor coded in ones and zeros.

Macro   A macro is a previously defined set of instructions that when invoked will cause the previously defined instructions to be inserted into the assembly language program.

Macro definition   The original copy of the macro as it was written. It does not take up any memory until it is invoked and expanded in the program.

Macro expansion   The code from the macro definition is inserted and expanded in the program at the point where the macro is invoked.

Macro invocation   Similar to calling a procedure except that instead of branching to and returning from a procedure, the macro definition is inserted into the assembly program at the point that the macro is invoked.

Mask   A bit pattern in a register, a memory location, or an immediate data that when used in logical operations will filter out all other bits that do not need to be tested or altered.

Mnemonics   Abbreviations used in an assembly language to represent various instructions.

Operator   Similar to a directive, it tells the assembler what to do with respect to an individual instruction.

Queue   A data structure often implemented as an array that allows data to be put in only on one end and removed only from the other end. The putting of information into a queue is known as an enqueue operation and the removing is known as a dequeue operation. The data first enqueued into a queue is the first data that is dequeued from the queue. This first-in first-out principle makes the queue a FIFO data structure.

RAM   Random Access Memory.

Register   A short-term memory location located in the CPU that is used for a variety of operations including arithmetic, logic, counting, indexing an array, and transferring data between memory locations.

Relative   When a memory location's address is referenced from some point in RAM other than memory location 0, then it is known as a relative memory address.

Stack   A data structure often implemented as an array that allows data to be only put in and taken out on one end. The placing of data on the stack is known as a push operation and the removing of data from the stack is known as a pop operation. The data last pushed onto the stack is the data first popped off the stack, where this last-in first-out principle makes the stack a LIFO data structure.

Static   When a value is calculated at assembly time prior to execution, then it is known as static.

Store   A store operation is the copying of the contents of a register or an immediate value into a memory location.

References

1. 754-2019—IEEE standard for floating-point arithmetic. https://standards.ieee.org/standard/754-2019.html
2. Dandamudi SP (2005) Introduction to assembly language, 2nd edn. Springer
3. Streib JT, Soma T (2017) Guide to data structures. Springer

Index

A

Absolute address, 274
add, 29, 30, 282, 334
Addition, 314
Addition instructions, 31
ADDR operator, 18–20
Aliasing, 160
American Standard Code for Information
    Interchange (ASCII), 311, 312
and, 323
And operator (&&), 62
Arithmetic instructions, 29–46
Arithmetic shift, 105–108
.asm, 291–292
Array of strings, 204–206
Arrays, 159–162
    64-bit arrays, 258–260
    floating-point arrays, 232–233
Assembler, 1
Assembly language, 1–2

B

Bankers rounding, 220
Binary Coded Decimal (BCD), 309
Binary numbers, 293–296
Bit, 294
Bit-bucket, 102
Bit manipulation
    set, 96, 300
    test, 96, 300
    toggle, 96, 300
Bit-wise, 99
Branch instructions, 47, 51, 61, 66, 76
break (C instruction), 58
byte directive, 5, 11

C

call, 123, 324
Carry flag, 102

Case structure, 58–59
cbw, 35
cdq, 35, 324
Central Processing Unit (CPU), 3, 7
Characters, 311
cld, 198, 324
cmp, 51–53, 324
cmpsb, 198, 204–208, 324
.code directive, 3
Comments, 4–6
Comparisons, 49
Conditional assembly, 138–141
Conditional assembly directives, 138
    else, 139
    endif, 139
    EQ, GE, GT, LT, LE, NE, 138
    if, 138, 142–144
    ifb, 138–141
    ifdif, 139
    ifdifi, 138, 142–143
    ifidn, 138
    ifidni, 138, 142–144
    ifnb, 138
Conditional jump, 51, 57, 66
C programming language
    break, 58
    for, 78
    if, 48–50
    printf, 18–24
    scanf, 25
    switch, 58–59
    while, 73
cqo, 251
cwd, 35

D

.data directive, 3
dec, 37, 264–265, 324
Decimal numbers, 296–298

© Springer Nature Switzerland AG 2020
J. T. Streib, *Guide to Assembly Language*, Undergraduate Topics
in Computer Science, https://doi.org/10.1007/978-3-030-35639-2

De Morgan's rules, 71
Direction flag, 49, 198
.686 directive, 3
Directives. *See individual listings*
div, 34, 324
Division instructions, 32, 34
Do-while loops, 76
dup operator, 161
dword directive, 5
Dynamic, 169

E
eflags register, 9, 49, 66–67
.else directive, 53
.elseif directive, 54
.endif directives, 54
endm directive, 132
endp directive, 4, 125
.endw directive, 74
EOD loop, 82
Errors, 13
Exclusive or, 96, 99, 298–300
Execution errors, 138

F
fadd, 213
fcomi, 226–227
fcomip, 226–228, 230
fdiv, 215
fiadd, 221
fild, 219
First In First Out (FIFO), 175
fistp, 219–221
fisttp, 221
Fixed iteration loop, 78–81
Flags, 50
fld, 211
Floating-point instructions, 210–221
Floating-point I/O, 221–226
Floating-point numbers, 307–311
fmul, 214
For loop, 78
fst, 212
fstp, 212
fsub, 214
fsubr, 214

H
Hello world program, 17
Hexadecimal numbers, 296–298
High-level languages, 6

I
idiv, 34, 326
IEEE standard, 309–310
.if directive, 51–52
If statements, 59, 64
Immediate data, 6–7
imul, 32, 327
inc, 37–38, 265–267, 327
Inclusive or, 119, 298–300, 329
Inline assembly, 13–14, 225–226
Input, 23–24
    64-bit input, 246
Instructions. *See individual listings*
Instruction timings, 275–276
Integers, 19–20
INVOKE directive, 18–21
Iteration structures, 73–90, 229–230

J
ja, 60, 327
jae, 60, 327
jb, 60, 327
jbe, 60, 327
jc, 67, 328
je, 51, 327
jecxz, 79, 327
jg, 51, 327
jge, 51, 327
jl, 51, 327
jle, 51, 327
jmp, 53, 54, 274–275, 327
jna, 60, 327
jnae, 60, 327
jnb, 60, 327
jnbe, 60, 327
jnc, 67, 328
jne, 51, 327
jng, 51, 327
jnge, 51, 327
jnl, 51, 327
jnle, 51, 327
jno, 67, 328
jnp, 67, 328
jns, 67, 328
jnz, 66, 328
jo, 66, 328
jp, 66, 328
js, 66, 328
Jump instructions, 51, 60, 66, 327–328
jz, 66, 328

L

Label field, 4
Last In First Out (LIFO), 111
lea, 272–273, 328
Lengthof operator, 174–175
Little endian order, 286
Load operation, 10
lodsb, 191, 194–195, 328
Logic, 298–300
Logical shifts, 100–104
Logic errors, 125
Logic instructions, 96–100
loop, 79–80, 328
Loop instructions, 78–87
Low-level languages, 2
.lst file, 52, 292

M

Machine language, 2, 266
macro directive, 132
Macros, 132–135, 138
    64-bit, 256–258
    definition, 134
    expansion, 134
    invocation, 133
    parameters, 135–136
Masks, 96, 299
Mnemonics, 2
model directive, 3
mov, 6–7, 14–16, 266–271, 328
movsb, 192–193, 328
movsxd, 239
mul, 32, 329
Multiplication instructions, 32–36

N

neg, 38, 39, 328
Nested if statements, 54–58
Nested loops, 85–87
nop, 52, 329
Normalization, 310
not, 97, 329
Not operator (!), 60
Number systems, 293–296

O

offset operator, 168–169, 272–274
One's complement, 303–304
Opcode field, 4
Operand field, 4
Operator precedence, 39–41
Operators. *See individual listings*
Or, 97–100
Or operator (‖), 61

Output, 19–21
    64-bit output, 241–245
Overflow flag, 50, 305–306

P

Parity flag, 50
pop, 111–112, 329
popad, 131, 329
Postfix, 215–219
Post-test loops, 76–78
Precedence, 41–44
Pre-test loops, 73–76
printf (C instruction), 20–24
proc directive, 3, 124
Procedures, 123–127
PROTO directive, 20–23
push, 111–113, 330
pushad, 130–131, 330

Q

Queues, 175–179

R

Random Access Memory (RAM), 7
Registers, 7–8
    eax, 8–11
    ebp, 9
    ebx, 8, 164–165
    ecx, 8–9, 78–81
    edi, 9, 168–173, 190–194
    edx, 8–9, 33–35
    eflags, 9, 49, 66
    eip, 9
    esi, 9, 168–173, 190–191, 195
    esp, 9
    r8–r15, 241
    rax, 239
    rbx, 238
    rcx, 238
    rdx, 238
rep, 193, 330
repe, 193, 330
.repeat directive, 78–80
.repeat–.untilcxz directives, 78–81
Repeat– until instructions, 76–77
repne, 194, 330
ret, 4, 124–129, 330
rol, 109–110, 330
ror, 109, 330
Rotate instructions, 108–110, 330

S

sal, 105–107, 331
sar, 105–108, 331

scanf (C instruction), 21–24
scasb, 191, 194–196, 331
sdword directive, 11
Search (sequential), 166
Selection sort, 180–183
Selection structures, 47–70
   floating-point, 226–229
Sentinel-controlled loop, 83
Sequential search, 166
Shift instructions, 100–104, 331
shl, 102–103, 331
shr, 102, 104, 331
Sign bit, 305
Signed numbers, 304–307
Sign flag, 50
Sign magnitude, 304
SIGN? operator, 50
sizeof operator, 173–175
Sort (selection), 180–185
sqword directive, 242
Stacks, 95–121
   .stack directive, 3, 111
Static, 169
std, 192, 331
Store operation, 7
stosb, 194–196, 331
Strings, 191–193
sub, 31, 271–272, 332
Subprograms, 123
Subtraction instructions, 31
Swap, 114

switch (C instruction), 58–59
sword directive, 5
Syntax errors, 13

T
test, 104–105, 332
Two's compliment, 303

U
Unary operations, 36–39
Unconditional jump, 54
Unsigned numbers, 300–302
.untilcxz directive, 78–80, 82
.until directive, 76–77

V
Variables, 1–6

W
.while directive, 74–75
While loops, 73–74
word directive, 5

X
xchg, 113–115, 332
xor, 96, 99, 332

Z
Zero flag, 50
ZERO? operator, 50

Printed in the United States
By Bookmasters